FRANK 'CHOTA' CAREY

FRANK 'CHOTA' CAREY

The Story of Group Captain
Frank Carey CBE DFC** AFC DFM

Norman Franks

GRUB STREET · LONDON

Published by
Grub Street
4 Rainham Close
London
SW11 6SS

British Library Cataloguing in Publication Data
Franks, Norman L.R.
  Frank 'Chota' Carey: the epic story of G/C Carey CBE, DFC
  and 2 bars, AFC, DFM, US Silver Star
  1. Carey, Frank 2. Fighter pilots – Great Britain – Biography
  3. World War, 1939-1945 – Aerial operations, British
  940.5'44941'092

ISBN 1 904943 38 1

Typeset by Pearl Graphics, Hemel Hempstead
Printed and bound by MPG, Bodmin, Cornwall

Contents

Acknowledgements

Although wanting to write Frank Carey's story for many years, and having collected items of interest about him during this time, I could not have progressed as far as I have done since Frank's sad passing without help. Foremost with this assistance is Marigold Carey, Frank's wife when he died, and Frank's daughter Jane. Marigold and Jane were exceptionally helpful in digging out all sorts of things from Frank's archives, including not only his jottings over many years, but also his photographs, many of which appear in this book. Thank you ladies.

On the day I met Jane, I met Ted Evans too, who had been his official RAF chauffeur in Australia at the time Frank was Air Advisor to the UK High Commissioner in Melbourne and Canberra. Their association turned to a lasting friendship, that continued up to Frank's death. Ted has a fund of stories and recollections about 'the Group Captain' which he was pleased to share with me. Thank you Ted.

Other recollections and anecdotes have come from many people who served with him in the RAF; sadly, some have now passed on too. In no particular order they are: D H 'Nobby' Clarke DFC AFC, F W T 'Bill' Davis, Air Commodores C D 'Kit' North-Lewis DSO DFC, James Coward AFC and Mrs Cynthia Coward; Gordon Conway DFC, Eric Batchelor, Jack Storey DFC, Alan 'Kit' Kitley, Viv Jacobs, Frank Wilding DFC, R E 'Bob' Windle, Guy Underwood, R 'Dick' Brown, and Kenneth B Cresswell. There was also a thoughtful letter from Lord Carrington.

My thanks also extend to my friend Andy Saunders, collector of all things RAF and in particular about 43 Squadron and RAF Tangmere, who made a number of pictures and information available to me. Also Min Larkin of the Halton Apprentices Association for delving into their archives.

Introduction

Unlike some of the other biographies of airmen that I have written, I had met my subject. The first encounter was more than 17 years ago after he had agreed to help me with one of my trilogy of books on the Burma air war.

After some initial correspondence I asked if I could visit his flat in Bognor Regis and interview him properly. He was reluctant at first but finally agreed, so long as he could ask two of his friends to be present, who in any event would also be able to help me with my project. I was more than happy, especially when he told me the two friends would be Eric Batchelor, who had been with 135 and 17 Squadrons in Burma, and Ken Hemingway, 17 and 67 Squadrons. Ken was also the author of the 1944 publication *Wings over Burma*. I already had a copy of that splendid book on my shelves (complete with its original dust-jacket!), so knew I was about to have a 'signed' copy in my book collection.

That was in July 1988, a week in which I also met Bill Davis, who had flown with 136 Squadron in Burma, and also knew Frank. Then Robin Hedderwick, who had been in Burma too, with 607 Squadron, as well as being one of Frank's instructors at Amarda Road, was visiting England from his home in Umtali. He came to my home so it turned out to be an interesting few days.

The July meeting with Frank and company went well and I later had separate interviews with Eric Batchelor and Ken Hemingway before the year was out, and also met Frank again in December. I think it was about then that I mentioned to Frank that I wouldn't mind writing his biography. Well that didn't produce anything other than the comment that he didn't think so, as he had not done anything special to warrant one!

That was the problem really, he was just too modest and anxious not to be seen to be 'shooting a line'. He was after all, from the old school, a pre-war airman and of course an NCO-pilot, and these men looked at things differently to other mortals. During a lull in that meeting, Frank left the room and his wife Kate, who had heard all this before, said to me quietly that "We'll sort something out..." I didn't think much of the remark until after the visit, and assumed she meant either she'd work on him or, at worst, she would give me the OK after he died.

At the time, Frank was 76 years old and looking hale and hearty, so if the latter was indeed the case I had sometime to wait – which was fine by me; he deserved a long life. Not long after that, Kate died, so any thought of a biography now, seemingly, was at an end.

Over the next few years I was in touch with Frank on occasion, and in May 1992, whilst staying with another former Burma (136 Squadron) pilot – Ian Adamson – at his home in Majorca, Frank arrived for a few days too. So I and my wife were able to spend our last five days in his company. I managed a few questions and although too much of a gentleman to shut me up completely, Frank was far more interested in talking about our host's approaching weekend barbecue, which were always a feature of life at Ian's *La Paloma Blanca*.

The last time I met Frank was at one of those signing sessions that producers of aviation prints organise. I knew he would be there, and he turned up with Pat Hancock, who had been the secretary of the Battle of Britain Pilot's Association. We talked about our stay in Majorca but had little idea it would be the last time I would see him.

When his death was announced it was, like so many obituaries one reads when one of these great men pass, a great sadness more than a shock. In recent years many RAF airmen who survived the world's conflicts had departed – and left the world a poorer place. They were special men. A breed apart. Frank had fought gallantly in the Battle of France, the Battle of Britain, and then during the retreat into Burma. By then he was not the youngster many of his contemporaries were, but his experience sustained him and he was able then to impart that same experience to the next generation of fighter pilots who were to continue the fight against the Japanese.

By the time of his death, Frank had married again. Once a reasonable time had passed by I plucked up the courage to telephone his third wife. When I explained who I was and what I hoped to do, she was all for it. I soon made the trip to see her, and I have to say Marigold Carey and I got along fine. She then told me that Frank's surviving daughter Jane, who lives in Australia, would be coming back to England to attend a ceremony to inter his ashes on what would have been his 93rd birthday, and that she was keen to meet me.

What follows here is my version of the story of Frank Carey. Whether he would have totally hated it or just shrugged his shoulders to the inevitable I don't know. But I hope that he would not totally disapprove, and that you, dear reader, will agree that his story had to be told. Whether I have done him due justice only his friends will be able to judge. Whether the book has any merit, only you can decide.

Norman Franks
Bexhill on Sea, East Sussex

Preface

'I spotted my Waterloo! About 3,000 feet above me was a Dornier 17 – all alone. It looked too good to be true, so I stalked it carefully from underneath, checking very warily for enemy fighters as it looked such perfect bait.

'All this time I was steadily climbing up to it, and finally, as I was getting close enough to get into a firing position, it suddenly turned round. At first I thought the crew had seen me, but apparently they must have been on a photographic reconnaissance, because, after the turn, it flew straight again but in the opposite direction. Being able to wait no longer I plunged in from astern and below, not more than 100 yards range. The effect of my burst of fire was electric because this large twin-engined aircraft did practically a perfect half-roll.

'It was an extraordinary thing to do. They were very fast – a lot faster than a Hurricane in a dive – so I followed it down, almost vertically. I imagine the pilot had been hit but before it crashed, the rear gunner fired back and hit me well and truly. It gave me such a shock that I noticed I was still pressing the gun button although my sights were nowhere near the Dornier.

'First of all my Hurricane was on fire, so I pulled it up into a near vertical stall, deciding I should get out. Levelling out I just caught sight of the Dornier going vertically into the ground. Checking my instruments I could see my oil pressure had disappeared and smoke was pouring back from the engine. I had been hit just below the knee by a bullet that subsequently passed between my legs and into the parachute pack. Nevertheless I decided I must bale out, so reduced speed and unhooked myself. I slid back the hood and stood up but was hit by a 100 mph slipstream and was thrown back, my parachute pack getting caught in the hood. I was also having trouble getting my good leg over the side of the cockpit. The aircraft went down into a vertical dive making it difficult to get out at all. Eventually I managed to get back into my seat – the fire having gone out – selected a nice large field and was able to make a reasonable crash landing, despite not having had time to strap myself back in again. After the bumping and scraping of the belly-landing had subsided, I could only hear the sound of the horn blaring, warning me that I had not lowered my wheels as my speed dropped off. It was with no small measure of vindictive pleasure that I pushed open the throttle to silence it!'

Front Line, south of Louvain, Belgium, 14 May 1940.

Chapter One

The Brat

Most biographers begin with their subject's date and place of birth. Not wanting to be out of step, I shall too. Frank Reginald Carey was born in the south London suburb of Brixton, on 7 May 1912, No.24 Geneva Road, a turning off Cold Harbour Road. It was not the Brixton one finds today being a well known community of many West Indian and Asian families. In 1912 its many large Victorian and Edwardian buildings held middle-class citizens, many with servants 'below stairs', who chose to live near to their work places in London while not being that far from the Surrey countryside.

His father was Alfred John Carey, born in Godstone, Surrey, in March 1885, so was aged 27 when Frank was born, and his mother was 22-year-old Elsie Mabel Carey (née Whatson) born in Balham, south London, in October 1889. Frank was the first of three sons, the second being Hugh John, born in 1914, followed by Roy Gerald in 1916.

For anyone not over-familiar with south London, Brixton itself is situated just to the east of the famed Clapham Common (SW4), north of Streatham (SW16), west of Herne Hill (SW24) and south of Kennington (SW9, home today of the renowned Oval cricket ground).

I make the point of indicating its exact location because during World War Two the press – always keen to pigeon-hole people – made much of Frank Carey being *The Cockney Fighter Ace*. I never asked him about that; there were other far more important things to discuss. However, to be a true cockney I believe one has to be born within the sound of Bow Bells. It would have to be a very quiet day and with a goodly north-east breeze for anyone in Brixton to hear the bells from that distance!

In any event, far from being brought up in south London, Alfred and Elsie moved from there to Blackheath (SE10), south of Greenwich (where Hugh was born), and soon afterwards to Shepherd's Bush (W12), north of the Thames, right next to the Royal Borough of

Kensington and Chelsea.

By this time, of course, the Great War of 1914-18 had begun, but Frank's only recollection of that conflict was that as a little lad he sometimes had to sleep under a table that was strapped over the top of his bed. The purpose being that it would shield him from the falling shrapnel of the exploding shells that anti-aircraft guns fired into the night sky from time to time, during German airship raids (Zeppelins etc). Frank later thought that this danger was far greater than anything falling bombs might inflict.

During the Great War, Frank's mother became ill with tuberculosis, a disease prevalent and widespread at the time. This demanded another move of home, this time much further south, to the Sussex countryside at Lindfield, just north of Haywards Heath (Roy was born here), where the country air would hopefully improve her condition. Sadly it did not and she died on 26 November 1924, aged 35. She is buried in Walstead Cemetery, Lindfield.

Frank's father had been a trainee engineer and later a chauffeur, so having now to leave London with a sickly wife, was set up in business by his father with an iron mongers shop which had a small attached light building section. Frank gave his address as High Street, Lindfield, the family living in accommodation above the shop. In company with many other such small businesses in the late 1920s, things did not work out well and Alfred Carey finally became bankrupt.

Frank's education had become a trifle disjointed but he had settled down since moving to Lindfield, and after a couple years at the village school he progressed to Belvedere School in Haywards Heath but only with the generous help of a relative who paid for his and his brother Hugh's schooling there. It was while at Belvedere that his interest first turned to flight and flying. It came about due to an earlier pupil at the school joining the Royal Air Force and having become a fighter pilot. His regular appearance flying over the school in an Armstrong-Whitworth Siskin, gave everyone great delight with aerobatic displays. In Frank's case these thrilling treats became the perfect inspiration for his own future career. He was determined to become a fighter pilot himself.

There was also another reason for young Frank to leave home. His father had remarried and his step-mother had brought her two sons into the family – Michael Robin (Bob) and Peter. Frank did not get on with his father's new wife so his plans for a career away from home took on a new urgency.

However, the parlous state of the family's finances added to the miserable educational attainments he had so far achieved, completely removed any chance of him being anywhere near acceptable to the RAF without some further serious preparation. The only method that seemed open to him was by way of the recently launched plan established by 'Father of the RAF', Lord Trenchard, the Halton Apprenticeship Scheme.

Although the RAF had been considerably reduced in size at the end of the Great War, there was still a need for a steady supply of trained airmen, especially as so many skilled mechanics had returned to civilian jobs in 1919. Young men and boys were therefore encouraged to join the RAF as apprentices to learn the various trades which meant a three-year commitment to training. Frank knew too that there was every possibility of eventually requesting pilot training. His apprentice training was to start at Halton Park – situated between Aylesbury and Tring, Buckinghamshire – although in the early days there was a shortage of accommodation. Up to a third of early entrants were housed at RAF Cranwell, and it was not until the end of 1926 that Halton became totally self reliant.

The first thing though was his standard of education. To overcome that hurdle extra schooling was necessary. In this he was lucky for his old headmaster at Lindfield village school agreed to coach him on Saturday mornings and some evenings to help him catch up to the required entrance examination standard.

In the autumn of 1926 Frank sat the entrance examination at Burlington Gardens, West London and just managed – as Frank said – to scrape through. Looking at Frank's record at Halton, scrape might not be the best descriptive word.

Describing himself as an easy-going country boy, Halton proved to be a great shock to the system. Rigid and stern discipline with many extra physical punishments for any slackness instantly being meted out often by former army NCOs and PT instructors, who were given a fairly free use of hand and a length of electric flex, certainly showed Frank a different world. Yet he was now a Halton Brat – something which he was justly proud of.

For the first two years Frank was subjected to all sorts of punishments, until he saw the light and began to buckle down to work. He admitted to being in almost permanent trouble which resulted in many extra fatigues and full-pack drills, but at least this had the virtue of keeping him very fit and lean. He also became good at games. Realisation that he might yet fail spurred him on. He could not have borne that. In the third and final year he really began to put his back into his work.

I spoke to 'Min' Larkin, of the RAF Halton Apprentice Association who said that in the mid-1920s it was extremely competitive to get into Halton (the civilian job market was bad so all sorts of young men were applying), and that Frank's entry qualifications would today be the equivalent of five GCE results at 'O' level. He had entered aged 15 years, four months, been given the RAF serial number 561516, his trade noted as metal rigger (which became rigger-airframes later) and at the end of his three year course – 16th Entry – he came out 227th from 419 entrants. Min Larkin also informed me that Frank had been assessed as a "...good average apprentice, slightly above in some areas." He qualified as AC1 with an average of 65% – what today might be the equivalent of a degree.

His educational standard was marked at 59.9%, including mathematics, science, engineering/drawing, mechanics and english. Marks for general service came out at 57.6% while his final practical technical board was 73.4%, thus producing his 65% average.

It was also noted that he could not have shown any obvious signs of command as he did not reach any NCO rank, not that he was alone in this. Frank recorded that despite his keenness, Halton was to prove a tougher nut than he had imagined and that any thought of flying was very obviously a long way off.

In 1930, with three years under his belt Frank became a fully blown mechanic and was posted to 43 Squadron RAF, based at RAF Station Tangmere, near Chichester, Hampshire. He found the difference between life as a mechanic in a wonderful squadron and his three years as a 'Brat' so great that it was difficult at first to take it all in.

His new squadron had been famous as a fighter unit in The Great War between 1916-1918. Equipped initially with Sopwith $1\frac{1}{2}$ Strutters, two-seater fighter-reconnaissance machines, it had later gone over to single-seat scouts, the famed Sopwith Camel. Late in the war it had been one of only two squadrons on the Western Front to equip and fly the Sopwith Snipe fighter.

The Squadron had been at Tangmere since the end of 1926 and Frank found to his delight that it was equipped with the same aeroplanes that had inspired his first desire to join the RAF – the Siskin. For the next three years Frank worked hard and obviously kept a 'clean sheet'. He was then posted back to Halton for a further twelve months in order to acquire a higher technical grade. Upon completion of this year of further training, he was posted to RAF Worthy Down near Winchester, and to 7 Squadron which had twin-engined Vickers Virginia bombers – huge biplane jobs, more reminiscent of World War One – which had been in service since 1924.

Working in the station workshops Frank enjoyed the additional experience of dismantling the Napier Lion XI engines, stripping them down and then putting them back together again following a complete overhaul.

By this time he had put in several applications to become a pilot and six months after going to Worthy Down, in 1935, his dreams were realised and he was selected for pilot training. He was sent to No.6 Flying Training School (FTS) at Netheravon, Wiltshire. Frank himself recalled this period:

'The flying course was a real joy and I was pleased to see that at last I was able to achieve something to be proud of. I left Netheravon with an "Above Average" overall pass with pleasing remarks about my achievements in flying standards.'

Sadly his first flying log book, in which his early flights would have been faithfully recorded was later lost, so we know little of his pilot training, but his year's course passed very quickly in his eyes and he at last gained his pilot's 'wings'. Again luck was with him, for when his first posting arrived it was back to 43 Squadron, still at Tangmere, as a sergeant pilot. In 1936 the Squadron was now flying Hawker Fury biplane open cockpit fighters, sleek silver-doped aircraft, upon the top wing of each, and the fuselage sides, was the black and white chequered identification marking of 43.[1] His commanding officer was Squadron Leader R E Bain.

Frank Carey had arrived. No one could have guessed that this little man was at the beginning of a startlingly successful career as a fighter pilot. His dream come true. Another dream of sorts had also been realised. He had also met his first wife, Kathleen Ivy Steele, known to everyone as Kay. She lived on Larkwhistle Farm, Easton, near Winchester, one of five children. She was 22 and they were married at Winchester Registry Office on 1 July 1936, Kay setting up home in Arundel.

---

[1] Although in the period of black and white photography these markings appeared black and white, a close look at some photographs show that while the black squares were indeed black the 'white' squares, in the early days, were actually unpainted. They were left blank, allowing the silver dope to act as the division between squares.

Chapter Two

Fighter Pilot

Sergeant Frank Carey, having achieved his goal at last, arrived at RAF Tangmere on 30 August 1936 to join, what many have described the Royal Air Force as being in the 1930s, the 'greatest flying club in the world'. With him came two other NCO pilots, Sergeants H J L Hallowes and A C Shawyer. Flight Lieutenant R I G MacDougall – the A Flight commander – was in temporary command of the squadron, while Flight Lieutenant J W C More commanded B Flight. The new CO would not be long in arriving, Squadron Leader R E Bain.

The new boys were allowed a day to get themselves settled in, also being sent off to various buildings in order to draw parachutes, flying gear, and to meet the other members of the squadron. Next day, 1 September, they were up in the air learning.

It appears that even at this early stage Carey, because of his 5 foot, 3 inch frame was given the name 'Chota' – one of many words absorbed from the RAF's time in India and the north-west frontier – which meant 'Little One'. Shawyer became 'Lofty' and Jim Hallowes was 'Uncle', which was his call sign. 'Dicky' Bain was not of large stature either, but nobody seems to have nicknamed him the same as Frank.

Despite some quite severe discipline, there was a fair amount of freedom of action in the air, and this period especially will be remembered as halcyon by those who were part of it. Advances in aircraft design had been slow, so that the biplane concept was still very much in vogue 15-20 years after the end of World War One. The new monoplanes were still on the drawing boards and would soon become a reality, but in 1936, the Hawker Fury, along with the Bristol Bulldog and the Gloster Gauntlet were state-of-the-art day fighters, while the Hawker Demon and Audax were the RAF's two-seat biplane day bombers.

Forty-Three Squadron, in company with 1 Squadron, were the almost permanent resident squadrons at RAF Tangmere and had been since the beginning of 1927. The regime was one of training, training and training. Although few people wanted to admit it, it did seem that another war with Germany was seemingly inevitable and the British government were finally accepting that the time for expansion of Britain's military forces had come. A nominal roll of pilots in 43 Squadron at the end of 1936 may be appropriate here, the main change being that Hank More had left and Freddie Rosier had replaced him:

S/Ldr R E Bain CO	A/P/O J W C Simpson
F/Lt R I G MacDougall OC A Flt	A/P/O J L Sullivan
P/O A M Bentley Adj	A/P/O A W Pennington-Legh
P/O F E Rosier OC B Flt	A/P/O R L Lorimer
P/O C B Hull	Sgt F R Carey
P/O A R L Griffiths	Sgt H J L Hallowes
P/O T J Fitton	Sgt A C Shawyer

Looking at this list today one can pick out several of these pilots who were to make names for themselves in the coming years. For example, Ralph MacDougall had been with 43 Squadron since 1931 and had been acting CO for a period. He would command other fighter squadrons and in the mid-war years take charge of airfields on Malta and in the Middle East as a wing commander.

Freddie Rosier had been with 43 since May 1936. During the Second World War he would fight in France and the Battle of Britain, later distinguishing himself in North Africa (DSO). He would retire from the service as an air vice-marshal GCB CBE DSO.

The wonderful Caesar Barraud Hull, from Southern Rhodesia, had joined 43 Squadron in August 1936. He was to command A Flight later and be Frank's flight commander. In May 1940 Hull was sent as a flight commander to 263 Squadron and with Gladiator fighters fought against the Germans in Norway before returning to 43 for the Battle of Britain.

John Simpson had arrived at Tangmere in October 1936. He would have a successful Battle of Britain and later command 245 Squadron. With the DFC and Bar he later had a number of staff appointments, rising in rank to Group Captain.

Alan Pennington-Legh, together with a handsome handlebar moustache, came to 43 in October 1936. He held command posts in 1939-41 and in 1942 led a Blenheim squadron in the Western Desert. He took his unit to Ceylon in 1942 but was to die with it in 1943 as a wing commander, in Burma, where Frank had met up with him again in early 1942.

After service with 43 Squadron, Robert 'Lorry' Lorrimer went to 1 Squadron and saw much action in France following the start of the

German invasion on 10 May 1940. Unfortunately he was to die in action just three days later.

Jim 'Darkie' (as well as 'Uncle') Hallowes was a Londoner, and just three weeks older than Frank, and like him had been a Halton Brat (1929-31). After a period as a metal rigger he too had applied for pilot training. As already recorded, he joined 43 Squadron on the last day of August 1936 along with Frank. He would have a distinguished fighting war – DFC, DFM and Bar – and would retire from the service with the rank of wing commander in 1956.

Time spent with 43 Squadron reflected similar experiences in every other RAF fighter squadron in Britain during this period. Pilots came and went, training continued and life was generally good and far from unpleasant. After all these young men were all volunteers and being paid to do what they liked best – to fly.

In January 1937 two further pilots arrived. Pilot Officer D I C Eyres posted in from 3 Squadron and Pilot Officer Cyril L F Colmore, in from 6 FTS, Netheravon. In early February MacDougall left to go to the Royal Aircraft Establishment at Farnborough, having been with the squadron for six years. The following month Alfred Bentley was posted away and Des Eyres became squadron adjutant. By the beginning of April, Caesar Hull was OC A Flight and the sergeant's mess had increased by three; sergeant pilots F G Berry, M H Baxter and A W A Messan coming in.

Frederick George Berry – known as 'Curly' on 43 – had been born in Ceylon where his father had been a PT instructor with the Royal Regiment of Fusiliers. Coming to England to join the RAF, Berry too had been a Halton Apprentice (1929-31). Another successful Brat to gain his pilot's brevet he had arrived on 43 in February. Just before the war began he would go to 1 Squadron, win the DFM, but die in the Battle of Britain.

In January 1937, the two Tangmere squadrons, 1 and 43, flew up to Sutton Bridge for the annual practice camp for Fighter Command units. There they would all compete for the highly prestigious Sassoon Trophy (the Sir Philip Sassoon Flight Attack Challenge Trophy) competed for annually. Squadron Leader Harry Broadhurst, OC 19 Squadron, and his pilots won the competition – Broadhurst himself had won the Brooke-Popham Air Firing Trophy for three consecutive years – but Frank had been in the 43 Squadron team, when led by MacDougall, along with Jim Hallowes.[2]

---

[2] Sir Philip Sassoon was the Under-Secretary of State for Air. Air Chief Marshal Sir Robert Brooke-Popham was AOC-in-C, Air Defence Great Britain.

June 26, 1937 saw the last of the famous Hendon Air Displays. A month before the display, Caesar Hull had come out first in the squadron's own eliminating contest for individual aerobatics. At Hendon Hull came out first again. Frank also did well at the Hendon Pageant. One competition was that of precision landing. The task was to land over a wire and touch down as near as possible to a given point. It was a close thing but Frank came second, even after several protests by 43 Squadron. In the end they had to admit defeat but resolutely refused to concur commenting: '...that in a world of perfection of judgement he would not have been [second but first].' Thus we see for the first time that Frank's piloting skill had already begun to show and be recognised, if not by the judges at least by his squadron comrades.

The year of 1937 heralded another milestone in Frank Carey's life, with the birth of his first daughter, Anne Geraldine, on 2 July. Frank was now 25.

Des Eyres left 43 to go to 54 Squadron in December, John Simpson taking over the job of adjutant. Early in the new year, Pilot Officers M K Carswell and J I Kilmartin arrived from 6 FTS while Flight Lieutenant A C P Carver came in from No.1 RAF Depot.

Malcolm Carswell was a New Zealander and was to have an exciting and dangerous time with 43 Squadron. John Ignatius 'Iggy' Kilmartin was another to move to 1 Squadron and have a distinguished fighting career with them in France, but came back to 43 in September 1940. He would end the war as wing commander OBE DFC and retire from the service in 1958.

One of 43 Squadron's hard working ground crew who arrived in 1938 was Kenneth Cresswell, assigned to B Flight. Frank, being a sergeant pilot, would naturally be in closer contact with the squadron's airmen, and of course, it was not so long since he was one himself. Ken Cresswell remembers him well and in addition recalls some of the incidents that happened on the squadron during these immediate pre-war years:

> 'Frank Carey was short, pleasant-faced, and soon became a friend to all ranks in the Flight; he was held in high esteem throughout the squadron and newly commissioned officers and other ranks were soon made to feel at home.
>
> 'He enjoyed his Wednesday afternoons off, as we all did our own particular sport in this free time. I remember Frank for his tennis and cross-country running, although the latter was a bit of a scrounge. Frank and his "oppos" would run with us "erks" to Goodwood but then send us back to camp whilst they went on a little farther – to a pub! It didn't take

us long to fathom that one out. But it was all taken in good fun and comradeship.

'These sporting activities on Wednesday afternoons were compulsory in peacetime and led to competitions in all aspects. Generally the finals of these competitions were held on the station on Empire Air Day.

'The same rivalry was carried over to the daily routines on training, especially when it came to "Quick re-arm and refuel". With the arrival of Hurricanes this operation was revised. Stop watches were kept fully wound up and flight sergeants were seen gnashing their teeth and stamping their feet if they found their Flight was a "shower".

'All the while, pilots and ground crews combined their skills to achieve a satisfactory squadron routine, and became "guinea pigs" for training the masses of airmen who were to become aircrew and ground crew. In time, results would show the value of this training.

'One of the highlights of life in 43 was the Squadron Dinner, held at a hotel in Goodwood. A and B Flights, workshops, RT, and admin staff, all transported, in the main, by pilots in their private cars. The food was good, a change from the Tangmere cook-house, and the drinks flowed freely. Entertainment was provided by various individuals, but all joined in singing our song – *Men of Sussex* – which generally lasted all the way home!

'I once rode home with Flying Officer Rosier in his Triumph car, to the barrack block where front doors were opened up for us. In we went and he started driving up the concrete staircase to the first floor. We managed to get as far as a half landing where the engine stopped. The car doors could not be opened because of the narrow staircase. Some of the workshop fitters, and Frank, reversed us down to floor level by various means and I wished them all a cheery good morning.

'Three days later I appeared on a charge for being late back from leave, and found myself up before Flying Officer Rosier. After both of us had a good laugh about the car incident, he became serious and awarded me an extra two ground duties!'

On 4 April 1938 the squadron lost Sergeant Baxter while training. He crashed at Racton in a Fury – K2074 – and was killed. A month later and Pilot Officer G P Christie arrived from 2 FTS, Brize Norton. George Christie was a Canadian, but it seems he soon left for 145 Squadron.

In late May 1938, Flight Lieutenant Carver, Flying Officer Hull,

Pilot Officer Pennington-Legh and Sergeant Carey flew to Roborough. It was Empire Air Day and they were to perform a flight aerobatic display of three machines. Pennington-Legh was the spare pilot.

For some time now there had been a third squadron at Tangmere, although it did not interfere with the time-honoured rivalry between 1 and 43. 217 Squadron was a general reconnaissance (GR) unit, equipped with twin-engined Avro Ansons. Apart from the type and designation, it was a Coastal Command outfit so the fighter types generally looked down on them. They also thought the Coastal people rather got in the way of their rivalry.

However, one notable pilot was posted in to 43 from 217 in June 1938, this being Flying Officer P W Townsend. Although born in Rangoon, Burma, Peter Townsend had been brought up in Devon and had joined the RAF in 1933. A graduate of RAF Cranwell he had initially been posted to 1 Squadron but in early 1936 had gone over-seas, to 36 Squadron based at Singapore, flying Vildebeest torpedo-carrying biplanes. In 1937 he returned to England, going initially to 217 – as an observer/navigator! However, after some protesting he managed a posting to his old squadron's earnest rivals. Group Captain Keith Park MC DFC was just ending his term as station commander at Tangmere, and Townsend believed this former WW1 fighter pilot had helped with his request to get back to single-seaters.

Before June was out, 43 Squadron had taken part in two more events, both being sponsored by the *Daily Mail*. First came the Civil Air Display at Gatwick, with a dress rehearsal on the 23rd, then the actual display on the 25th. Squadron Leader Bain was the leader in the Squadron Air Drill competition, and Flight Lieutenant Carver led the aerobatic flight along with Caesar Hull and Frank Carey.

It was not a good day weather-wise, 43 feeling distinctly second-rate, its pilots believing the formation was ragged, and 'pure hell' – especially for the two extreme wing men. However, reports next day in the press were full of praise, not just by the journalists, but by pilots from several countries who had watched the proceedings. The three aerobatic Fury pilots were also highly praised individually, with Hull finishing with a solo aerobatic display of some merit.

Sadly, the day at Gatwick was to prove the swan-song of the aerobatic Fury days. With the diplomatic scene in Europe obviously not going well, the days of silver-winged biplanes wowing crowds had become a thing of the past. Preparations for war seemed even more urgent.

Early in August the squadron went to No.2 Armament Training Station at RAF Aldergrove, Northern Ireland, for the annual air firing exercises. 43 Squadron's results were the best for some years. The nearby town of Antrim became a magnet due to its number of welcome hostelries, and the proprietor of a local shop which hired bicycles did a roaring trade during 43's stay in the province.

It seems too that at this stage a certain Sergeant Carey was pronouncing quite verbally his theories, and self-possessed fearlessness, of snakes. Just how this arose is unclear, Frank not ever having set foot in a country where snakes would have provided such experience for him. However, some of his brother pilots saw fit to acquire locally a number of eels, which they duly placed in his bed one night, much to his subsequent horror, when some hours and many beers later he bid his – quietly chortling – comrades good-night! Nobody ever heard much about snakes from Frank after that. Ken Cresswell adds to his earlier recollections by relating some events at this juncture:

'The camp was a new experience for many "erks" in many ways. The Furies of A and B Flights were to fly over to Aldergrove, the remainder of the squadron was to proceed by train and boat to Belfast. Both Flights flew over in two stages, in order to refuel. Meanwhile, ground crews and staff boarded a special train in London for Heysham [south of Morecambe, Lancashire]. The meal provided was pretty good with Guinness supplied to everyone.

'The day was Wednesday after the August bank holiday and the weather was pretty grim. On arrival at Heysham, complete with kit bags, we upset a load of Irish people by pushing through them and onto the boat. First on were accommodated in the hold, the rest of us had to stand on deck in the rain. It was also dark, and the Irish were in a funny mood as they had been waiting for the boat which should have left the day before – cancelled because of the stormy weather. However, by the time we reached Belfast we were all happy! Upon reaching Aldergrove all our brass buttons and hat badges were green, and we were allowed little rest till the "kites" flew in. B Flight was delayed en-route by fog for the night, so arrived a day late.

'Then the camp began. When the weather permitted around Lough Neagh, flying took place and consisted, in the main, of air-to-air drogue firing. The squadron leader shot off one blade of his propeller – interrupter gear malfunction – but landed safely. During the camp the Air Minister, Sir Kingsley Wood, flew over and was quite interested in what was going on. I was attending the petrol bowser when he asked how things were going. When I told him OK, he said: "Keep up the good work." It was funny really, for I had been "milking" the bowser into a bucket, for petrol to clean the engine cowlings!

'At the end of the camp all the "erks" went into Crumlin for supper. Six meals; two eggs, fried bread, bacon – 2/6d the lot! [12½ p although not comparable with today's prices.] All ranks were warned to wear civilian clothes when venturing out at any time due to the political situation [IRA].'

Shortly after the squadron's return from Aldergrove, Flight Lieutenant Carver left to join 85 Squadron. The annual summer leave period began in mid-August, but it was soon to be cut short.

It was now the time of Munich and everyone was on alert. Air raid shelters were being constructed around the aerodrome with slit trenches near the dispersal points. The silver-doped aircraft were over-painted and camouflaged a greeny-brown (battle paint) and the fins lost their white arrow-heads with 43's fighting-cock emblems. It was a tense time. Summer leave was in full swing but before time was up, telegrams were sent out to recall everyone. Even worse was the order that the Fury must also be a night as well as a day fighter. Frank commented later that: '...in the night-fighter role, even we felt we were rather badly placed. For a start the Fury had no navigation lights, no signalling lights (vital as it was the only way to request permission to land from the flare path) and no illumination at all in the cockpit. Neither were the instruments fitted with luminous dials. With the short stub exhaust pipes, even dusk flying could produce some blinding light when throttling back.'

To try and overcome some of these deficiencies the squadron managed to obtain some downward signalling lamps which were fitted to the biplanes, while the lack of cockpit lighting was overcome, to a degree, by fixing a hand torch to the top port longeron so that the airspeed indicator and altimeter could at least be read – just! Frank concluded:

'Had this ever been used, with the very restricted early wartime flare-path layout, the effect would have been quite dramatic, to say the least!'

However, Chamberlain came back from Germany with his 'peace in our time' piece of paper and the moment passed into history. Nevertheless, it did at least galvanise everyone into becoming more prepared. Next time there might not be a let-off.

One early result was that new types of aircraft began to appear. The Fury could not hope to catch any of the German medium bombers that might be encountered – day or night. Hence, in late November the first two Hawker Hurricanes were delivered – L1725 and L1757 from the factory at Brooklands. Others were then collected:

2 December: L1726, L1728
3 December: L1729, L1730
6 December: L1723, L1732
7 December: L1783
8 December: L1731, L1734
10 December: L1735, L1744
13 December: L1738
15 December: L1739
30 December: L1736

On the 30th two Furies were flown out to Brize Norton and to Shawbury, K3731 and K8256. In the new year of 1939 the rest were flown to the RAF storage depot at Kemble. Two new pilots arrived during this period, Pilot Officer C A Woods-Scawen on 19 December, and Pilot Officer S LeRougetel, on attachment from RAFVR Coventry for advance flying training. The squadron also received a Fairey Battle (single-engined bomber) to help convert to the new type. The pilots could now start to get used to lowering wheels (undercarriage) and flaps, and using radios, things the Fury never had. There was also the enclosed cockpit to contend with, with its sliding hood. There were brakes and oxygen too. Frank had amassed something like 600 hours on the Fury but was glad to get his hands on the new Hurricane, remarking that he: '...felt that the Hurricane would be quite a lot more useful in a fight than its predecessor.' One interesting aside that Frank once mentioned to me was the aircraft radio:

'Radio – R/T – was very knew to us, and in the beginning we didn't relish using it, after all, we had managed quite well without it for some time. In fact, in the early days anyone who did use it was regarded as a bit of a sissy.'

The squadron's first Hurricane casualty came on 22 April, Flying Officer C A Rotherham being killed. He hit a tree on a night approach and his machine exploded in flames (L1738).

Empire Air Day, held on 20 May 1939, was the last occasion when the British public was to see their air force in peacetime. At Tangmere, 1 and 43 Squadrons did their stuff in their new Hurricanes. They were all green and brown now, with black and white undersides. Long gone were the silver dope and squadron colour markings of the biplane era. It was all business now.

Mobilization came on 5 August, causing John Simpson, still adjutant, a great deal of work, recalling those men on leave, as well as sending out letters to reservists. The Air Exercises held during the month, flown in conjunction with the French air force, were short and sweet. 1,300 bombers 'attacked' England and RAF Tangmere's fighters claimed interception and – of course – a large number 'shot down'.

War was just around the corner now. Everyone was naturally apprehensive and felt as prepared as they could be. The squadron's nominal role on the eve of war is recorded as follows:

S/Ldr R E Bain	Commanding Officer
F/Lt C B Hull	OC A Flight
F/O A W Pennington-Legh	Armament Officer
P/O M K Carswell	
P/O C A Woods-Scawen	
P/O W C Wilkinson	
P/O J I Kilmartin	i/c secret and confidential publications
Sgt F R Carey	
Sgt H J Steeley	
Sgt T A H Gough RAFVR	
Sgt W H Whitfield RAFVR	
Sgt A W Woolley	
Sgt P J Wright	
F/Lt P W Townsend	OC B Flight
F/O J L Sullivan	Air Navigation Officer
F/O J W C Simpson	Adjutant
F/O P Folkes	Parachute Officer
P/O G P Christie	Gas Officer
P/O P E G Carter	
Sgt J Arbuthnott	
Sgt P G Ottewill	
Sgt H J L Hallowes	
Sgt C A H Ayling	
Sgt R Plenderleith RAFVR	
Sgt R V Burton RAFVR	

As can be seen the first RAF Volunteer Reserve pilots had arrived, although a couple of them moved on quite quickly. In fact, looking at this list, very few would still be with the squadron by the time the Battle of Britain began. Postings to other units and some accidents quickly changed the face of 43 Squadron.

Chapter Three

War

There was a moment or two of silence as Neville Chamberlain, the Prime Minister, said on the radio that a state of war now existed between Britain and Germany. For two days now, since Hitler had invaded Poland on 1 September, the tension had been almost unbearable. Not having heeded the Allied warning to get out of Poland, Hitler had effectively thrown down the gauntlet to Britain and France.

After those moments of silence, there were two reactions from the pilots of 43 Squadron. Stunned realisation that everything had now changed, and euphoria – possibly a little false – with perhaps a cheer of bravado. Caesar Hull, it is recorded, was jumping from one foot to the other in the officer's mess, saying, 'Wizard, Wizard!'

Frank took it in his stride. Despite being a married man with a young daughter, he was also a professional airman. All his recent training had been leading inexorably to this point. He was very experienced now. Without reference to his now lost log book it is difficult to know how many flying hours he had, but it must have been over 700.

Almost immediately, on 8 September, 43's sister squadron at Tangmere, No.1, flew out to France as part of the Advanced Air Striking Force (AASF), much to the chagrin of 'The Fighting Cocks' who were left behind.

On this same day 43 Squadron experienced a short period as balloon-busters. Iggy Kilmartin was sent off to shoot down a British barrage balloon that had broken free from its mooring at Portsmouth (raised to thwart any sort of low level attack by a hostile aircraft) and was drifting north. He found it and despatched it near Farnborough, using 1,200 rounds to do so.

Before the month was out other balloons had to be shot down. Obviously there was a problem keeping these gasbags firmly secured. On the 17th Peter Townsend destroyed one near Itchenor while Flying Officer Sullivan shot down another ten miles out to sea. Three days later Pilot Officer Wilkinson blasted two with 1,000 rounds. The first near Hamble, the second over the Isle of Wight. The final one was shot down by Darkie Hallowes two miles off Littlehampton early on the morning of the 23rd.

Squadron Leader Bain left on promotion to wing commander and was sent out to France. His replacement was Squadron Leader C G Lott, in from 11 Group Fighter Command HQ, Group Intelligence. Naturally at this stage, squadron commanders were being selected not only for their ability to command, but in order of rank and seniority. George Lott was aged exactly 33, had joined the RAF as an apprentice and by 1927 had learnt to fly and was with 19 Squadron as an NCO. Commissioned in 1933 he had seen service in Iraq with 41 Squadron before going to 11 Group in 1935.

The squadron then lost Pennington-Legh who left for 248 Squadron on the last day of October. Early in November Sullivan and Kilmartin were posted out to 242 and 1 Squadrons respectively. Sullivan was later killed in the French campaign as a flight lieutenant – oddly enough on the same day as Frank would be shot down – 14 May.

Still frustrated over not going to France in September, 43 appeared to move further from any possible fighting on a new Western Front, by being sent to RAF Acklington (13 Group), 20 miles north of Newcastle on Tyne on 18 November.

However, there was some sense to this. Since Fighter Command had come into existence in 1936, it had been assumed that any threat by Germany to attack Britain by air would come from Germany direct, its bombers heading in from across the North Sea. With the apparent size of the French Air Force, and that country's mighty Maginot Line fortifications, it was thought inconceivable that any threat would come from anywhere near southern England. Added to this, with hostile bombers coming across the North Sea the range involved would preclude them having any escorting fighters.

Thus over recent years Fighter Command squadrons had been practising interceptions and attacks upon single or at least small formations of unescorted bombers, whose range in any event would be limited after such a flight. By late 1938 it was estimated that German Heinkel He111 bombers could not penetrate the English mainland further than about Nottingham, while the Dornier Do17's range would only allow penetration to Sheffield, Leicester and London. The Junkers Ju86 had the best range, just about reaching Manchester, but these bombers were never used in the main bomber role against Britain. The Ju88s had better range but were designated as dive-bombers. It therefore made sense for 43 Squadron, and others, to be located facing the North Sea, over which German raiders were most likely to be expected.

In any event the winter of 1939-40 was severe, especially for the RAF squadrons posted to France, not that Frank and his comrades felt the benefits of remaining in England. Acklington was still a cold spot – just a mile in from the sea – and it was little more than a hutted camp that had served as a peacetime summer practise camp. 111 Squadron were already there which made living accommodation tight. Added to this there were no hangars and no runway. A base pressed into service by necessity. 111 Squadron left shortly afterwards, only to be replaced by 152 Squadron. Dick Brown was one of 43 Squadron's ground crew and recalls this period with the squadron:

> 'I was posted to 43 Squadron during the winter of 1939-40 as a Fitter IIE, to RAF Acklington on the north-east coast. It was about 35 miles from my home-town of Jarrow, County Durham, so I thought it was a good posting but it did not turn out as I expected. The weather was very bad and we had to wear gumboots, and leather jerkins and mittens to keep warm.
>
> 'We had a splendid lot of pilots on the squadron and were kept busy with scrambles after enemy aircraft attacking shipping off the coast. The airfield had to be cleared of snow for take-offs and landings, but there were successes for the pilots, downing He111s and Do17s.'

Hurricane L1725 was lost on 15 December, Sergeant Arbuthnott having to bale out after losing control during a spin in cloud. However, the first action was not long in coming and the squadron's first operational sortie since WW1 was flown on the 21st. Shortly after 3 pm the squadron was scrambled to intercept nine hostile aircraft apparently laying mines not far from the coast off Alnwick. However, it turned out to be a formation of seven RAF Hampdens of 49 Squadron returning from a patrol over the North Sea, which becoming short of fuel, were making for Acklington. One of the Hampdens, in trying to get into the airfield, crashed into and destroyed the church at Broomhill, just a mile from the airfield. Two of the crew were killed.

Obviously everyone was jumpy about raiders coming in and fighter controllers scrambled fighters to be on the safe side. On this same day, 602 Squadron were sent off to intercept more 'enemy aircraft' and they shot down two RAF Hampdens from 44 Squadron over the North Sea. Fishing boats rescued all but one of the eight men who came down in the sea.

Christmas and the New Year came and went but eighteen days into 1940, Sergeants Steeley and E C Mullinger collided at 800 feet over Broomhill village while engaged in a practise dogfight. Both men were killed. There followed a spate of minor accidents prompting George Lott to issue a stern warning that these would no longer be tolerated. Later that same day, the irrepressible Caesar Hull appeared to be making an approach to the runway with flaps down but wheels still up. As the Hurricane seemed about to belly-in, Hull gunned the engine and flew past an assembled group – including the CO – giving a vigorous 'Agincourt salute' as he went by, and no doubt grinning broadly beneath his oxygen mask.

Before January was out, 43 Squadron had again been operational. On the 29th, Hull and Red Section were sent out to investigate a 'bogey' and engaged a Heinkel 111 ten miles south-south-east of Hartlepool at 09.45. It was one of nine Heinkels of 6/KG26 that had flown over and split up near the English coast. Seeing the approaching Hurricanes, the German pilot quickly lifted up into low cloud. Hull and Frank Carey opened fire, with Pilot Officer H L North in close attendance, but without result, although Hull's ground crew later found a bullet hole in his machine (L1728).

More fun the next day, but this time it brought success. Again it was KG26 that had sent out no fewer than 26 Heinkels that had split up for individual searches off the coast. Hull (L1849) and Frank (L1728) were on patrol ten miles east of Coquet Island, off Amble, some time after noon and got the call. These snoopers, the squadron had found, generally came over when the cloud base was around 1,000 feet, looking for shipping. If they saw approaching fighters it was just too easy to lift up and be out of sight in seconds.

The pilots had discussed this and decided that whenever possible they would approach the German machine right on the deck, where hopefully the German crew would find it difficult to spot them. The bomber they attacked (they spotted two) was a He111 H-2 of the 4th Staffel (coded 1H+KM), piloted by Feldwebel Helmut Höfer. Following their attacks the bomber went into the sea, all four crewmen being lost. Hull later wrote in his combat report:

> Sighted two E.A., flying south, apparently attacking a small fishing vessel.
>
> I attacked one using beam to astern [attacks] six times. Number Two synchronised his attacks with me. E.A. seen to dive into sea and break up. No sign of other E.A., after this combat.

Frank later recalled seeing the huge tail-fin of the Heinkel lying flat on the water with its swastika in clear relief. He flew over using his cine-camera to record it but as so often happened in the early days, the camera failed to work.

There was another busy day on 3 February. KG26 were again out over the North Sea, some 24 Heinkels being flown out this date, plus two Ju88s from KG30. British radar plots came thick and fast, and John Simpson and Flying Officer J D Edmunds found two bombers and attacked one. This sped off trailing smoke and later apparently came down, its crew seemingly being picked up by a ship. It seems possible however, that this crew came from a lost Ju88, hit by AA fire, and that their Heinkel got back although badly damaged, force landing at its base.

Within minutes of this action, Peter Townsend. Flying Officer Folkes and Sergeant Hallowes engaged another Heinkel off Whitby. Badly damaged, its pilot decided not to trust his luck over the sea and instead, headed for England, where he crash-landed. The pilot and one crew man survived, the other two died. It was the first hostile aircraft to come down on English soil, landing at Sneaton Farm, near Whitby.[3] Then Hull, Carswell and North fought another which they could only claim as damaged.

Frank was part of Yellow Section (in L1726) scrambled at 11.15 to intercept raiders bombing ships fifteen miles east of Tynemouth. His companion was Sergeant Peter Ottewill (L1849). Frank opened the attack and after both fighters had expended their ammunition, the Heinkel, with engines out of action, glided onto the sea and sank. Survivors were later rescued, including the pilot, Oberfeldwebel Fritz Wiemer, although one crew man had died and another did so later from his injuries.

For these recent actions Frank was awarded the Distinguished Flying Medal, the first decoration given to a pilot of 43 Squadron in the present war. The announcement came on 21 February, as an Immediate award, that is to say it was in response to specific actions, rather than non-Immediate awards that were processed following a period of operations. The announcement came in the *London Gazette* dated 1 March 1940.

Apart from the official citation (see Appendix B), the AOC 13 Group, added the following to the recommendation: *I fully endorse the Squadron Commander's remarks concerning Sergeant Carey. This NCO has proved himself a skilful and courageous pilot in two successful actions against enemy aircraft and as a splendid example to his fellow pilots. I strongly recommend him for the award of the DFM.*

Dick Brown recalls the event:

'After Carey was awarded his DFM, Peter Townsend gathered some motor transport to take the whole of the

---

[3] The first enemy aircraft to come down on 'British' soil was another He111, brought down by 602 Squadron on the Lammermuir Hills, near Haddington, east of Edinburgh, Scotland, on 28 October 1939.

squadron to a hotel in Thurso for a good night out – which we all enjoyed.

'I found Frank a very modest man. He would refer to the ground crew as pilot supporters, not mechanics or riggers etc. He always said that he would not be able to fly the aircraft without good supporters.

'I met him after the war at 43 Squadron Association dinners. He was a remarkable pilot and would say to us that luck was with him.'

The last air action whilst 43 were operating from Acklington came on the 22nd, with Peter Townsend, Christie and Sergeant Ayling, patrolling off Farne Island. They saw white contrails above and began a steep climb. Christie's engine began to overheat and he had to drop back, but Townsend and Ayling continued on. For a few moments they lost the raider in cloud at 19,000 feet but quickly found it again. Townsend got beneath the bomber's tail – it was yet another He111, this time from 3/KG26 – and shot it down into the sea. There were no survivors.

Now came another move, this time even further north, to Wick, in Scotland. On 26 February Squadron Leader Lott and nine of his pilots flew there in order to help boost the protection of the British Home Fleet at its base at Scapa Flow. Wick was almost as far as one could go northwards. The next place to the north was John o'Groats, then out to sea to the Orkney Islands. There were two other Hurricane squadrons there also, plus a Coastal Command squadron. Squadron personnel were billeted in the local town but the bad news was that Wick was teetotal! The weather was even more atrocious than Acklington, with mud an added attraction. Dick Brown remembers:

'We were billeted in the town but there was nowhere to go in Wick, the town was dead. Duty crews had to contend with tents on the airfield. I remember at Wick, Flight Lieutenant Hull and Frank Carey used a Miles Magister as a "muck about" aircraft, practising combat skills and generally having fun.'

March came. Patrols were flown when possible, then just as dusk fell on the 16th, a formation of enemy aircraft made an attack on ships in Scapa Flow, dropping some 100 bombs on both naval vessels and land, which resulted in the first civilian death of the war. At 19.55 Squadron Leader Lott, Caesar Hull, Carey and Ottewill had gone off on patrol and were vectored towards the raiders but due mainly to the fading light, failed to make any contact. They faired better on the 28th.

Enemy aircraft were out looking for shipping around the Orkneys and Shetlands. With 43 Squadron having only just moved up to Wick two days earlier – joined by 605 Squadron – these Germans fliers were coming into their 'parlour'.

A patrol of 605 Squadron was already in the air as George Lott led A Flight to intercept a hostile aircraft 15 miles out from Wick. Sergeant Ottewill was the first to spot the bomber and he immediately opened fire. Caesar Hull, Frank and Sergeant Gough also lined up and opened fire in turn, the Heinkel clearly disabled. Again the German pilot could see little future in heading out to sea, so turned towards land, his fuselage on fire.

Unaware of 43's presence, pilots of 605 Squadron arrived on the scene and spotted the Heinkel. There was another exchange of fire and the bomber, now well and truly ablaze, fell into the sea. For once it was not a KG26 aircraft, but a machine from Korpsführung-skette.Flieger/Korps X. Oberleutnant Horst Gollmann and his crew did not survive.

Frank Carey's initial stay with 43 Squadron was shortly coming to an end, although he would fly with it again later in the year. Thus far he and the squadron had been involved in several combats and shared some success. Everything that had been instilled into their training had seemed to work. All this time, the thinking at Fighter Command was that RAF section leaders should put their aircraft into specific formations in order to carry out regulated attacks. These practised 'Fighter Command Attacks' had been drilled into fighter pilots for some time now.

Fighter Command were still assuming that any raiders coming to Britain would be either in small formations or just aircraft on their own. Therefore the attacking fighter pilots would have time to spread out into an echelon and one by one make an attacking pass on the target. Without fighter escort, the bomber crew would have to rely on cloud or their defensive gunfire to protect themselves. It was a wonderful theory and with recent actions over the North Sea or off the east coast of Scotland, one which appeared to fit the bill. However, two events were about to change the status quo and make RAF thinking out-moded. Firstly the Phoney War was about to end with the beginning of the Battle for France, and the RAF were about to meet German fighters in numbers, not only in France but by the summer, over England.

On 31 March Frank was promoted to flight sergeant, but before he could put up the 'crown' over his sergeant's stripes, his commission came through, dated 1 April. It was an auspicious date – the RAF's 22nd birthday. Then he was off. On 2 April he was posted to another

Hurricane squadron, No.3, based at RAF Kenley, south of London, in leafy Surrey. Frank had a week with his family, with time to kit himself out as 'an officer and a gentleman', then he went to locate his new unit, at RAF Manston.

Meantime, 43 Squadron had bagged yet another Heinkel, late on the evening of 8 April. Led by Peter Townsend, four Hurricanes – Townsend, Edmunds, Arbuthnott and Hallowes – intercepted six Heinkels and accounted for two. One went into the sea, its crew lost, while the other force-landed on Wick aerodrome.

Hallowes, after firing into the latter, over the Pentland Firth, had his guns fall silent due to a fractured pneumatic line. Heading down through the clouds he lined up to land at Wick. It was dark now but the flare-path was lit. No sooner was he down than he noticed a Heinkel following him. The German pilot had circled, and in the gloom thought he was landing at a seaplane base near Scapa and made a wonderful belly landing. A dinghy was thrown out before they realised they were on a runway. Almost at once Hallowes was confronted by the Intelligence Officer who said he had just shot down an RAF Hudson! Hallowes took him over to the crashed Heinkel to disprove the man's statement.

The bomber was from 6/KG26, flown by Leutnant Kurt Weigel and two of the crew were dead, Oberfeldwebels Rost and Geedts. Weigel and Oberfeldwebel Rehbein were taken prisoner. With a real bomber right on the RAF airfield, it was not long before souvenir hunters were at work and within a day or two everyone was confined to barracks and an order was made for everything that had been taken to be returned. Some had found packets of cigarettes on the machine, another had taken what was described as a 10 lb bomb, which was discovered in his locker. Pieces of aluminium were taken and at least one airman made a ring from some for his wife. One airman, Paddy O'Kane, who was a guard over the bomber, was asked by a pal of his to get him a souvenir. Paddy came back with a huge oil gauge with about two feet of cable attached. Some Perspex jewellery was also made from bits taken from the Heinkel.

Frank's new squadron had been at Kenley for three years, an aerodrome situated on a hill above Whyteleafe, with that long hill road winding up from the railway station, although during 1939 they had moved to nearby Biggin Hill and then to Croydon and Hawkinge as their immediate war station. The squadron had returned to Kenley in January 1940 but with the imminent threat from Europe, a detachment was kept at Manston. In the last years of peace it had flown both the Bulldog and then the Gladiator biplane, but Hurricanes had taken their place in March 1938. Frank's new commanding officer was Squadron

Leader P Gifford DFC AAF.

Patrick Gifford had been another early recipient of an award, the Distinguished Flying Cross. He was a member of the Auxiliary Air Force – the famed weekend airmen – having been with 603 Squadron up at Turnhouse and Prestwick, Scotland, although unlike his command now, they had had Spitfires. When he hadn't been flying Spitfires he was a solicitor and town councillor.

Like Frank, 'Patsy' Gifford had been in action against German raiders, and had shared in the destruction of a Ju88 of I/KG30 on 16 October 1939, and shared a He111 of 1(F)/122 on the 22nd, which went into the sea. The result for him was the DFC.

It was a tense time now. Almost any unidentified aircraft plot radar picked up was investigated, the famous – or infamous – X-raids. Sections of fighters would be scrambled almost at the drop of a hat, and although the vast majority of these sorties proved fruitless, it did keep the adrenalin flowing and the practise helped improve the time it took to get aircraft into the air.

Pat Gifford, Flying Officer A R Ball and Frank had one such rush of excitement on 27 April, the three Hurricanes climbing into the early evening sky, but then later being ordered to land.

May 1st proved a red-letter day for Frank. Air Vice-Marshal Keith Park, now AOC 11 Group, came to visit Kenley and among his tasks this day was the presentation of Frank's DFM. Things however, were becoming serious as May progressed. There had been several rumours and mild warnings that the Germans were about to start offensive actions soon. They had been active in Norway earlier in the year and with that campaign drawing to its inevitable conclusion, Hitler would be looking for further glory. France and the Low Countries were obvious targets.

The 'balloon went up' at dawn on 10 May 1940. Scores of German bombers hit RAF and French airfields in France, while others attacked bases in Belgium and Holland. Parachute troops rained down on key points in a number of locations in the Low Countries. It was obvious that reinforcements needed to be sent across the Channel, and despite the CinC Fighter Command, Air Marshal Hugh Dowding, not wishing to dissipate his limited forces while he was charged with the defence of Britain, he was over-ruled.

At Kenley the call came quickly. Although some RAF squadrons would soon be sending sections across, 3 Squadron as a whole unit was to go. Following a mad panic in the morning, the squadron pilots were ready shortly after lunch. With orders to fly to Merville, where they would become part of 63 Fighter Wing, along with 79 Squadron, commanded by Wing Commander E S Finch, they took off at five minutes after two o'clock. Frank related the following:

'It all really began at 05.30 hours on 10 May after having been on night readiness. My section of the squadron was scrambled after a Ju88 which had been coming along the Channel from the west. It was a glorious morning – one of those rare days in England that do much to repay you for all the too frequent ones of drizzle and fog.

'We were sent out across the Channel and finally finished up chasing the still unseen Junkers near the Dutch coast before being recalled to base. Despite no contact taking place that particular flight will always stand out in my memory because, for me, it marked the change from the slow, easy pace of the first seven months of the war to the overwhelming speed to which it accelerated until after the finish of the Battle of Britain.

'After landing, we returned to the dispersal hut to hold the inevitable post-mortem and, so self-important were we feeling, that it was with no small measure of surprise that about a minute later we were aware of a huddle of excited pilots at the other end of the dispersal point. The topic amongst the huddlers, we quickly discovered, was more than sufficient to obliterate any further thought of our recent flight. Germany had invaded the Lowlands and the squadron was to move to France within a few hours!

'We were all tremendously excited at the prospect of real action at last, little dreaming that within a week those who had not been killed would be secretly, if not openly, looking forward to a respite from the mad holocaust into which we were clamouring to dive.

'The remainder of the morning was one of ant-like activity. The relief squadron and transport aircraft for essential ground crews and equipment arrived. Breakfast was left to go cold but numerous cups of coffee and cigarettes were finished and replenished. Our kit was hurriedly thrown together, guarded telephone conversations were had with friends and relations, until, some four hours later, after an abortive attempt to swallow some early lunch, the squadron departed. I did not leave with the squadron because my aircraft was unserviceable, so I was to follow about two hours later.

'Naturally I felt quite depressed following the excitement of the morning which had culminated in proudly watching the squadron form up and fly away southwards and, although I had many friends left at the station, I felt very much out of things. However, I took off about 1 pm and twenty minutes later was viewing the last of the English coast-line with very mixed feelings. Not least of these was wondering when I would next see the shores I knew so well, yet looking half-fearfully and half-excitedly to the uncertain future.

'My first trouble after crossing the French coast was navigational, as it was my first flight over the continent where villages sprawl along straight roads which looked to a troubled pilot remarkably alike. It must have taken me nearly 15 minutes after arriving in the vicinity of the aerodrome I was heading for before I saw the familiar plan-view of several Hurricanes parked in what merely looked to be a large field.

'After landing, I walked over to join the rest of the pilots who were all standing outside a solitary Nissan hut, which apparently was the only sign that this field was any different from its numerous neighbours. Our first interest after arriving was purely physical – where do we eat and sleep? Nobody seemed to know the answer to either question and there seemed little point in pursuing the thought that someone must know something. Therefore, as our ground crews had not yet arrived, we knuckled down to refuel our own aircraft. This procedure completed, three of us decided to take off and fly round the immediate locality and try and get to know the lie of the land, as I discovered that everyone else had experienced the same difficulty in navigation and locating the field. This flight was merely one of familiari-sation of the area, so it was something of a surprise not long after climbing up, to see some aircraft in the distance....'

The squadron had all landed safely but it was some time before the ground crews following in Bombay and Ensign aircraft arrived. The airmen were put into Nissan huts $1^{1}/_{2}$ miles from dispersal, while officers and NCO pilots were to be billeted in the nearby town. The RAF, 3 Squadron, and Pilot Officer Frank Carey DFM were now in the hot spot; just how hot he was about to find out.

Not long after 3 and 79 Squadrons had departed, volunteers to reinforce 3 Squadron were asked of pilots in 32 Squadron, who were also using Manston as an advanced airfield, from their home field at Biggin Hill. Jack Rose was one of those who volunteered, and he together with Pete Gardner, D A E 'Jonas' Jones and R T 'Chota' Ware, flew out in their 32 Squadron Hurricanes, guided by a Fairey Battle.

Things had not improved since Frank and the others had struggled over earlier, and Jack Rose noted that it took them two hours to cover the distance that should have taken no more than 40 minutes. They assumed the Battle crew either had no maps, or could not read the ones they had.

Once at Merville they, presumably like Frank and his colleagues, discovered they were at a great disadvantage compared to the Hurricane pilots already in France with the Advanced Air Striking Force (AASF) or the Air Component of the British Expeditionary Force. Their newly arrived Hurricanes did not have pilot armour behind the seats, nor self-sealing fuel tanks. They did not even have the same radio crystals.

Rose had been happy to volunteer because he imagined that, just like World War One, this war too would be fought over France and that having gained this initial experience he would soon be reunited with his 32 Squadron once they came over. In the event only Gardner and Rose returned to 32, the other two staying with 3 Squadron. Had they known that in less than two weeks the BEF would be kicked out of France their enthusiasm might not have been so great.

Jack's brother Flying Officer Frank 'Tommy' Rose was also in France, flying with 56 Squadron. On the 18th he would be shot down and killed, along with another pilot in his section, while the third pilot, Pilot Officer Barry Sutton, would barely escape with a badly shot-up fighter and wounded in one foot. Barry Sutton would later fly with Frank in Burma.

Chapter Four

France

Merville was in Flanders, south of Hazebrouck, east of Aire-sur-la-Lys, north of Béthune and west of Lille. It was right in the firing line, although at this precise moment the exact 'line' was uncertain. All anyone knew was that since dawn German bombers had been hammering every airfield they could locate. While the attack was not totally unexpected, the surprise when it came was absolute.

By the time the Hurricanes of 3 Squadron put down at Merville everything seemed to be in a complete shambles. It was a shock to the system as Frank later wrote:

'Initially somewhat bewildered by the rapid and dramatic change in circumstances in a little over 30 minutes, from a comfortable, well organised, disciplined and efficient RAF station to an isolated, deserted grass field with an empty Nissan hut and one telephone.

'Substantially short on facilities; no furniture, no beds, no catering, no intelligence about the general situation – we were just told to keep permanent patrols over the area along which British troops were advancing to meet the Germans.

'Mere patrols meant one Flight in the air, the other refuelling, re-arming, etc, to take over when the other Flight returned. It was all hands to complete this duty with little or no respite between sorties.

'Food was available only after dark when we finished, except very occasionally the ground crews would get something from a little store near the village. Sleep was on the bare boards in an empty house or in the Nissan hut in readiness for the dawn patrol the next day.

'My clothing remained on my back until I was shot down some days later. I suppose we didn't notice it as we must have smelt as bad as one another.

'The great thing, however, was that the air situation was Heaven! There were German aircraft everywhere and we met them almost every time we took off. Radar was both non-existent and totally unnecessary and the weather was fine and warm.'

Towards the end of the last chapter, Frank had written that he and two others had flown off to look at the locality and had spotted aircraft in the distance. He continued:

'We flew out to the east after taking off and had not been airborne many minutes before I noticed a considerable number of black specks to the north-east of us over Courtrai. We decided to investigate and, on approaching them, identified to our utter joy about thirty He111s circling individually and bombing, troubled only by a few sporadic bursts of AA fire. This was the first time I had seen more than one enemy aircraft in the sky at once, and I felt exactly like the dog who tries to chase a dozen rabbits at the same time – I wanted to fire at all of them!

'After two or three short attacks, first at one and then at another, I realised that if I really wanted to bring any of them down, I had better choose one and stick to it. This I did to good purpose and had the pleasure of seeing it "hit the dust" in no uncertain manner. I attacked two more, firing until the aircraft were obviously in real distress each time before, much to my disgust, my ammunition ran out. Shortly after we three had started to attack, I noticed three other Hurricanes from another squadron join in the fray, and I will always remember the polished manner in which these pilots delivered their attacks – perfectly executed as if they had been practising them with camera guns.'

Flight Lieutenant M M Carter had, in fact, led off two sections of three machines each at 19.30 and near Lille they spotted the gaggle of Heinkel 111 bombers from Third Gruppe of Kampfgeschwader 54 (III/KG54), that had already been in action with Hurricanes of 85 and 607 Squadrons. Bombs were falling from the Heinkels and the air was now full of exploding anti-aircraft shells.

Carey was no stranger to He111s and began firing at one as soon as he was in range, blazing away, as he recalled, at several. Finally smoke billowed back from one and it fell away. Already he was shooting at another, then another. One of these too began to trail smoke and go down. A fourth Heinkel received a burst, pieces flying off as it turned away and began losing height. Carey closed in, giving it the rest of his ammunition. The bomber staggered and fell earthwards on fire. Later Frank noted in his combat report:

'[The] R/T being useless, we chased after the EA independently. I attacked several EA, taking a different one each time, but eventually settled on to one, which I attacked until both engines were put out of action and [its] wheels were down, when it spun round to the right sharply and dived towards the ground. It eased out of the dive, but I observed what appeared to be a large cloud of dust as EA apparently hit the ground. I resumed attack on other EA until all ammunition was expended. During attacks, my fire was obviously damaging EA as several were emitting black smoke or had wheels lowered. Other squadron and remainder of section were still attacking and many EA observed losing height on easterly course and almost certainly did not reach their base.'

One of Frank's Heinkels was that flown by Unteroffizier Walter Zenner of the 8th Staffel. He was the only crewman to get out of the burning bomber as it dived towards the ground. Crunching into the ground on the end of his parachute, he was lucky to survive the attentions of a mob of angry civilians who were bent on stringing him up from the nearest tree, but the arrival of some British troops saved him. Frank was later credited with two He111s shot down (although he claimed three) and two more damaged. Despite two sections being involved, Frank only recorded one, or perhaps he was only recalling the actions of the one section he was in:

'After we had landed and started to re-arm and refuel ourselves the ground crews arrived and soon helped us finish the job, that had looked like taking us the rest of the week, especially as two of us had had [gun] stoppages. We three, feeling like veterans to the other pilots, did our best to impress them all with our recent daring and might have continued this all night, but, just before dark, the local AA boys opened up on something.'

So, not that long after landing, 3 Squadron were again ordered up, and at 21.10 Blue Section took off with Flying Officer Ball leading. It was not orderly, everyone just piled into a Hurricane and headed off across the grass field in whatever way they faced. Hostile aircraft were apparently approaching the airfield but the light was fading in the east so things would be difficult. The Hurricanes climbed to 15,000 feet and on meeting a large formation of Heinkel 111 bombers, everyone waded in. Frank's report describes the action:

'EA seen almost immediately after take-off and chased. EA flying in open vic formation at approximately 7,000 feet and climbing. EA constantly changing direction and full use of this was made by Blue Section cutting corners. EA eventually attacked at 15,000 feet and fire was opened at 300 yards, using up to 20° deflection. Blue One [Ball] and Two [Carey] concentrated on attacking wing aircraft and attack continued by Blue Two until engines were very badly damaged and emitting clouds of smoke, with EA losing height. Blue Two immediately returned to base owing to failing light. Possibly two EA shot down.'

In the event both Ball and Frank were credited with one bomber each, but Ball did not return. In the darkness, Ball was unable to locate Merville, so in desperation he headed for the Channel and England. Reaching Dover in the dark he was unable to find any airfield and finally had to bale out. He got down without injury, eventually got back to Kenley, and flew back to France in a replacement Hurricane the next day.

The other casualty was Flying Officer R B Lines-Roberts who while engaged with the enemy aircraft was hit, and had to make a forced landing near Fiefs, where his Hurricane (L1923) had to be written off. Frank was later to write of the action:

'We couldn't see what the AA boys were firing at but we didn't wait any more. The squadron, or best part of it, took to the air individually and a few minutes later were strung out over several miles, all clambering up to the bright AA shell flashes. The target of the guns turned out to be three He111s flying at about 12,000 feet, again without escort. I doubt whether we would have caught them before complete darkness set in had the German formation not twisted and turned, finally flying back due east in exactly the opposite direction. Leading the field of fighters by a very short head, I attacked one aircraft giving it everything in one long burst in order to finish the combat and get back to our strange aerodrome before dark.

'While I was attacking my target, the two others carried out similar tactics against the other two. The leading aircraft caught fire, strangely enough, just long enough after my ammunition had finished for me to begin to curse myself for missing, and I followed the Heinkel a short way down to watch him crash and explode with a terrific flash. That flash did two things to me – first of all, I had the satisfaction of knowing that I had definitely shot it down and then it brought home with a bang the fact that it really was dark downstairs and, flying at about 12,000 feet during the combat, it was still quite light at that height.

'I really had no idea at all where I was within a 100-mile radius of the aerodrome because of the erratic courses flown by the enemy bombers. I could, however, see the English Channel shining off to the north and that gave me a rough idea of my location. One other lucky thing proved to be extremely helpful. I had earlier noticed a peculiar looking and rather large wood, about ten miles north of Merville when I was first looking for the airfield. With the devil's own luck, about ten minutes later I spotted the wood. I eventually made a moderate, if heavy, landing with the aid of lorry head-lights which the ground boys had the good sense to switch on, and my own landing lamp.

'Once down I was told that everyone else was back except the two others who had attacked with me and it wasn't until the next day that we heard that one had been shot down by the rear gunner of one of the Heinkels and had crash-landed about 60 miles from base. He had been lucky not to have hurt himself in the process. The other pilot [Ball] had an extraordinary experience. He had been last to leave the bombers after watching one crash and the other force-land, and then searched for the aerodrome without success. Finally he decided to fly to England and land although in doing so he was met enthusiastically by our AA and searchlights. In the chaos of being blinded and endeavouring to get away from the gun-fire, he got into the dickens of a mess, and finally spun. He had little or no idea of his height or position so finally gave it up and baled out with a very few hundred feet to spare.

'The next bit of fun came after landing, as all the local people, assisted by the police, chased him for some way, convinced he was a German pilot. He eventually managed to establish his identity after they caught him, and got back to the aerodrome he had left that morning, without further trouble. He rejoined us the next day.

'After I had landed, the night having completely arrived, I found everyone in the squadron busy with car head-lamps trying to sort out their luggage which had been dumped in one big pile at the side of the aerodrome from the transport planes. It must have been nearly midnight before I had my own cases organised and one can imagine how hungry we all were as most of us, too excited to have anything at lunchtime, hadn't eaten since very early morning.

'We were carted off to the nearest French village in lorries, my lorry stopping at the largest estaminet we could find. After a few glasses of champagne – nothing less being good enough for us after such a hectic day – we settled down to a cooked meal which I ate with great relish.'

Jack Rose had a similar experience as regards equipment. Having left Manston, leaving all their personal equipment at Biggin Hill, he and the others had been told that some essential personal items would be collected and flown over to Merville in a Blenheim. Somehow in all the confusion, his batman at Biggin was told to pack all of Jack's possessions and send them over. Thus his uniforms, civilian clothing, mess kit – everything – was flown out and like Frank's gear, dumped unceremoniously on the ground. Most of it remained unpacked and Jack was to return home in just what he was wearing, the rest lost.

The day's action finally ended. 3 Squadron had arrived in the middle of a maelstrom but Frank had acquitted himself well. As far as he was concerned he had shot down four He111s this day and another one he thought had been probably destroyed. Not bad for an old chap three days past his 28th birthday! However, the pilots had yet to find somewhere to rest:

'After the inner man had been satisfied, my thoughts not unnaturally turned to my bed which had not as yet been organised, and after a fruitless half hour, with three other pilots, I rolled up in an Irvin flying suit on the floor of an empty house. Despite my utter fatigue, I spent a very restless night, to be awakened at about 4 am and told to get down to the aerodrome for dawn readiness.

'When we arrived at the aerodrome we found that several of the pilots had wisely settled themselves for the night in the dispersal hut. Shortly after first light, the AA guns opened up again – this proved to be our only warning system – and off we went again.

'Our targets were again three He111s flying in tight formation without escort, and again being in the forefront of the disorderly rush to get at them, I felt that once more I could look forward to an easy victim. I suppose I was within a mile of them when I saw the first Heinkel go down in flames, to be shortly followed by the other two, and slowly the disappointment dawned on me – another squadron had got to them first!

'After landing we were so put out about this that we had more or less decided to keep up a standing patrol to prevent a further occurrence when the CO called us all in for a conference. He wasted few words giving us the dope on our new duties. We were to keep up a constant patrol over the roads in the vicinity of the front lines to allow the army to bring up artillery and men to stop the mad rush of the German army, which, even as early as 11 May, was beginning to gain momentum. We were to patrol in sections of six, and would relieve one another from dawn till dusk. This was a pretty tall order as the distance then from our base to the front line was well over 100 miles and each section had to relieve the other over the patrol line. In other words, each patrol was roughly 2½ hours with only 30 minutes on the ground between patrols.'

After the hectic and immediate actions late on the 10th, the 11th was a bit more peaceful. Happily Flying Officer Ball returned to Merville from Kenley, but unfortunately a Bristol Bombay that was flying out with spares for the squadron, crashed and was burnt out.

In Frank's first patrol of the day, between Douai and Lille, three He111s were spotted over the latter town but, as he related above, all were shot down before he could get near enough to engage. A second patrol to Douai produced no action, but on a third sortie over the Louvain-Dieste road during the afternoon, Frank saw a He111 bombing the nearby aerodrome at Dieste and shot it down. This was a machine of KG54's Stabs-Staffel; its pilot, Oberleutnant Wilhelm Surborg and two of his crew were captured by British soldiers, the other two being killed. The squadron records the day as being 'quiet' and indeed, Frank was the only pilot to score this date. He continued his recollections of the 11th following the CO's directive:

'We left shortly afterwards to start the ball rolling and covered the roads just west of the Belgian-Dutch border. After patrolling for about half an hour without finding trouble, the flight commander decided it might be a good idea to go east and look for it. A few minutes later I learnt another valuable lesson. We had crossed over the Albert Canal, which the Germans were busy storming, flying in a nice tight flight formation at about 6,000 feet. I need hardly say more. We had barely reached the far side of the canal when everything opened up. It was the first time I had ever been under concentrated flak-fire and it took me several seconds to realise why the surrounding air had suddenly turned black. The next few seconds we had split up all over the sky and were busy trying to get back to the safety of the other side of the line. How those German gunners must have laughed. One second we were in a beautiful formation and the next we were wide open, trying hurriedly to retrace our steps. Anyway, none of us crossed the line after that except to chase enemy aircraft. We had no combat during that patrol, or on the subsequent one, which I did later in the day.

'In between patrols on three occasions we had to do a short local flight on defence work, thereby effectively upsetting the relief at the front line, but generally things went fairly smoothly. The only R/T we had was between aircraft and as our frequency was pretty well bang on the 'Forces' programme we usually got lulled into a semi-stupor by the music while on patrol, and several days later, being a Sunday, we were actually listening to a sermon on "...loving one's neighbours..." while in the middle of a dogfight. We would have switched it off but for the warning we could still give one another.

'Our meals were hurriedly devoured between flights while the ever-busy ground crews patched up our aircraft. The only cooked meal I had at that aerodrome, apart from the nightly one at the village estaminet, was an excellent steak, cooked in the airmen's cooking trailer. For all that, the squadron's morale was very high as up to then nobody had been killed, although several had been shot down, and the score for our side was steadily mounting.'

Frank was later to recollect more about this day:

'Later in the day I did more patrols to the front line and had two combats, both against He111s. The first one was really a fluke because I left the formation to check on a distant aircraft that turned out to be a Heinkel bombing Dieste aerodrome by itself and found it using only one engine! It crash-landed in a cornfield and two of the crew got out and as I was circling above I saw them start off across the field due east – back towards their own lines. I don't know what made me do it but I decided to put the wind up them so climbing up-sun, I turned and dived on these two little figures. At first they carried on walking but when I got well into my dive, I saw them stop, hesitate, and then run like mad back to their crashed machine.

'They just about made the aircraft as I reached it and I last saw them diving headlong under its fuselage. That sight cheered me up for days. Although I circled the aircraft several times after that I didn't see them emerge from their hiding place. I subsequently heard of another pilot who did a similar thing and was promptly shot down by the rear gunner of the downed aircraft for his pains.

'The other combat was whilst flying to the patrol line. Seven Heinkels suddenly popped out of a cloud just above us, much to their disgust and our joy. We each selected one and chased them individually in and out of the small broken clouds. The only incident in my combat was that I was flying extremely close behind one when one of the crew baled out of the top gunner's position and very nearly collided with my aircraft. The bomber then went slowly into a shallow diving turn, to explode on hitting the ground.'

On the morning of Sunday the 12th, Frank noted down sorties not mentioned in the squadron diary. It seems apparent that the diary – RAF Form 540 – was not dutifully maintained, or at least, was probably reconstituted later, upon the return from France, as several items are missing. Frank recorded a possible four sorties on the 12th. One was to Hannut and although the pilots met terrific anti-aircraft fire, no enemy aircraft were seen. On another mission to the Louvain area there was no action either, but later, south of Brussels, pilots intercepted 12 He111s and Frank shot down one and probably a second. He recorded:

'May 12th brought me one more Heinkel and one probably – the main thing of note being that for about the first time we tried using a co-ordinated attack instead of a series of individual ones as hitherto. These were also intercepted by chance, whilst on our way to the patrol line and out of the nine attacked, five were destroyed and three others were probables or damaged. It does give an indication of the number of unescorted bombers that the Germans were employing in Belgium, that we could constantly run into them without any help from ground control.'

The memorable action of the next day came, so the diary records, in the morning. No time is given, but other records note that the sortie began at 07.25 am. Either Frank's two earlier sorties were very much earlier, or he got them mixed up in his mind after returning from France – which was a month later!

In any event, B Flight's Flying Officer Walter Bowyer with Sergeants E Ford and J Sims (Blue Section), Flight Lieutenant Carter with Frank and Pilot Officer M M Stephens (Green Section), apparently went off at 07.25, again covering the Louvain-Dieste road area, and met a mass of Ju87 dive-bombers – numbering around 60. Also in view were a number of He111 and Do17 bombers.

Everyone attacked, into what pilots today would call "a target rich environment". Afterwards the total claims were totted up and it amounted to Pilot Officer Carey two Ju87s, Mike Stephens two Ju87s, Sergeant Ernie Sims two Ju87s and Sergeant Jimmy Ford one possible Ju87 – a total of seven. Mike Stephens described the initial sighting as like a seeing storm of midges. Attacking one Stuka – they were aircraft from I Gruppe of Stukageschwader Nr.2, together with an escort of Me109 fighters – it exploded in front of him, forcing him to fly through the debris that rattled off his machine. He then came upon a Dornier 17 bomber and following his attack saw it belly land onto a ploughed field. The Form 540 makes no mention of the Do17, and Stephens only records attacking one Stuka. German losses were not as great as 3 Squadron assumed. Frank however, had learned another valuable lesson, recalling that after pursuing one Stuka out to one side of the formation, it began jinking wildly.

> 'I came up behind lots of Stukas one day. This chap was weaving about so I left him and went after a much more obliging chap flying straight and level.'

In future, he decided, he would not bother with enemy aircraft whose pilots were taking violent evasive action, and seek easier targets with less animated pilots.

Later in the morning A Flight, led by Flight Lieutenant Walter Churchill, spotted two Hs126 observation machines and shot both down. Frank and B Flight were not on this sortie.

Frank later recorded three more sorties flown. According to the 540, the first was led by Squadron Leader Gifford at 11.20, with Ball and Frank making up Blue Section, Churchill, Sergeants Roy Wilkinson and Allen, Red Section. Patrolling Louvain to Wavre, they ran into bombers – He111s and Do17s – and attacked. Frank noted later there were nine Heinkels and Dorniers, and some biplane fighters. In fact the latter were Hs123s of II(S)/LG2. Results are confused to say the least. The squadron diary notes Frank with a Dornier, Wilkinson, Churchill and Allen a Heinkel each.

However, Frank later noted his victory was over a Heinkel and one biplane fighter, and the 'Heinkel biplanes' were in fact those Henschel 123s.

Flying Officer Ball was himself engaged by some Me109s while attacking a Dornier and failed to return. He was later reported badly wounded and a prisoner, and died of his injuries on 6 July. To add to the squadron's woes, at 16.00 that afternoon, whilst returning from another patrol, two Hurricanes collided about five miles from the aerodrome. Flying Officer Adams had just signalled the section to close up and it was assumed that Flying Officer Lines-Roberts, blinded by the low sun, crashed into Adams' machine. Both aircraft exploded in the air and both pilots were killed. Frank's later recollections make things a little clearer:

'The 13th was a Sunday and it was to give me my biggest bag. I did three patrols during the day and had combats during two of them. On the first one, whilst on patrol, the Flight ran into hordes of Ju87s with a number of He111s and Dornier 17s. Once again our luck held – there were no escorting fighters.

'I can't remember exactly how many we shot down but it must have been between 15 and 20 with many others either probables or damaged. The Ju87 Stuka has always been a particularly desirable opponent in a dogfight because it almost invariably bursts into flames as soon as fire is opened. It was so on this occasion and I had shot down two 87s, practically before I was aware of it – then a Heinkel 111 appeared in my sights and that followed the other two. Back to the 87s to make two more stand abruptly on their noses (I did not see the end of either of these) and finally, as I was breaking away from the second of these, I found myself beautifully positioned out to one side of a Dornier 17. I really had little option but to open fire and can only have been firing for about a second when an ominous silence occurred again – I was out of ammunition.

'I could only see evidence of damage to the port engine of the Dornier which had started to emit the usual black smoke and caused the aircraft to slew slowly to the left. This Dornier, however, for some reason or other, was all silver with beautifully polished cowlings, making it rather conspicuous and the next patrol that flew out, came back with the story that it had crashed a few miles east of the engagement, so I was able to claim it as destroyed.

'Later in the day, the Flight was patrolling somewhere to

the south east of Brussels when suddenly, somehow – enemy aircraft always seem to make an abrupt entry into view – nine Heinkel 111s appeared in beautiful tight formation and once more we selected one each after a certain amount of jostling. On this occasion I remember I was extremely careful with my ammunition as I seemed invariably to run out of that very necessary commodity just when it was really needed most. This care, of course, had just the opposite effect and it took me nearly all my ammo before it blew itself to pieces with its own bombs uncomfortably close to an inoffensive farm house.

'Four of the six of us managed to rejoin after this and we continued with our patrol. The other two had run out of ammunition and left. We had only been patrolling for about ten minutes when I spotted five biplanes astern of us. They looked very much like Gloster Gladiators but we never did identify them for certain.

'Enthusiastically I called to the others over the R/T and whipped round to meet them. In fact, I was so enthusiastic about it that I was in the middle of a hornet's nest before I could organise myself. This was the first time I had ever met an enemy aircraft more manoeuvrable than myself and it didn't take me long to realise things were a trifle uncomfortable. The arrival of the other three Hurricanes squared things up and we soon paired up with individual opponents. I didn't learn who the unfortunate one was who left over with two, but anyway we all got back.

'I think my opponent must have been one of the best pilots I ever met in combat and it took some time before I was able to press the gun-button at him, but, when I did so, only about four or five rounds fired – ammo trouble once more. The biplane by now was doing remarkable tricks round the sides of woods, houses, etc., and I was diving and zooming, using him as a moving ground target. I carried on doing this after my ammo had run out. On one occasion he tried to turn up and round to fire head-on at me and he was so nearly successful that I almost collided with him and I was in a great panic as I hauled back on the stick. I didn't see him again after that because when I had got over the palpitations and looked for him all that could be seen was a mushroom of fire coming up from the ground.

'He must have stalled in his frantic endeavour to twist round and I have always felt very sorry for that fellow because we must have been fighting for well over 15 minutes before he had the misfortune to spin in. Had he only known that I was by then unable to fire at him, after the fright he gave me I would most likely have called it a day and gone home.'

Frank's last day of action in France came on the 14th. Was it only four days since they had been rushed to Merville? Frank later wrote:

'We patrolled the front line, wherever it happened to be at the time. German aircraft were all over the place – you just took off and there they were. If you flew anywhere in the Pas de Calais or east over Belgium, there were lashings of them, absolutely asking for it and they had very few fighters about at that time. Over the first four days after my arrival, I must have had about 20 engagements. I shot down what I think was about 14 aircraft in that period. Still without a proper place to sleep I was finally given a billet on the last evening.

'I picked up my kit – which was still among a big pile of stuff at the edge of the airfield – and took it to this place. I was on the dawn shift the next morning so I couldn't sleep there then but I thought that the next night I would finally get a bath, have a change of underwear and get some real sleep.'

Next morning he was off early – 04.04 – with B Flight, led by Mark Carter, with Walter Bowyer, to patrol the front lines. As usual they found enemy aircraft and Frank went after a Dornier. He recalled:

'We had reached the patrol line almost without incident. I say almost because we saw our first squadron of French fighters on our way, Morane Saulniers, both squadrons making a dart at each other, then gained recognition, and continued on our allotted tasks.

'The beginning of my end was, strangely enough, an inoffensive Westland Lysander, doing its work quietly right up on the front line. How I always admired the crews that flew them. One minute they were there, then a fight would develop and they would vanish. No sooner was it clear than they would pop up again and carry on as though nothing had happened. Two or three times other pilots in the squadron had taken the trouble to take a close look at them as they appeared awfully like Henschel 126s, their German counterpart.

'At around 5 am, I thought I would do the same. The first thing that went wrong was that this Lysander didn't change into a Henschel as I got near it, so I thought I would fly alongside and give the pilot a cheery, reassuring wave to let him know that there were some friendly fighters about. This I did and received an equally airy answer, and as I pulled up into a climbing turn above him, I spotted my Waterloo! About 3,000 feet above me was a Dornier 17 – all alone. It looked too good to be true, so I stalked it carefully from underneath, checking very warily for enemy fighters as it looked such perfect bait.

'All this time I was steadily climbing up to it, and finally, as I was getting close enough to get into a firing position, it suddenly turned round. At first I thought the crew had seen me, but apparently they must have been on a photographic reconnaissance, because, after the turn, it flew straight again but in the opposite direction. Being able to wait no longer I plunged in from astern and below, not more than 100 yards range. The effect of my burst of fire was electric because this large twin-engined aircraft did practically a perfect half-roll.

'It was an extraordinary thing to do. They were very fast – a lot faster than a Hurricane in a dive – so I followed it down, almost vertically. I imagine the pilot had been hit but before it crashed, the rear gunner fired back and hit me well and truly. It gave me such a shock that I noticed I was still pressing the gun button although my sights were nowhere near the Dornier.

'First of all my Hurricane was on fire, so I pulled it up into a near vertical stall, deciding I should get out. Levelling out I just caught sight of the Dornier going vertically into the ground. Checking my instruments I could see my oil pressure had disappeared and smoke was pouring back from the engine. I had been hit just below the knee by a bullet that subsequently passed between my legs and into the parachute pack. Nevertheless I decided I must bale out, so reduced speed and unhooked myself. I slid back the hood and stood up but was hit by a 100 mph slipstream and was thrown back, my parachute pack getting caught in the hood. I was also having trouble getting my good leg over the side of the cockpit. The aircraft went down into a vertical dive making it difficult to get out at all. Eventually I managed to get back into my seat – the fire having gone out – selected a nice large field and was able to make a reasonable crash landing, despite not having had time to strap myself back in again. After the bumping and scraping of the belly-landing had subsided, I could only hear the sound of the horn blaring, warning me that I had not lowered my wheels as my speed dropped off. It was with no small measure of vindictive pleasure that I pushed open the throttle to silence it!

'I imagined I was in what in World War One would have been called "no man's land". After a curiously morbid inspection of the bullet damage to the engine, the aircraft and my leg, I tied up the latter with my handkerchief and began to walk eastwards, coming then to a farm. Almost as soon as I set off I realised I was leaving my Hurricane unguarded, possibly in enemy country, so I went back and removed the maps and a code card, but decided not to set it on fire. My decision was no doubt motivated by a very recent talk we had been given explaining how valuable our aircraft were owing to their shortage. Also, the countryside, as far as I could see, was completely devoid of humanity.

'Once again I set off, this time taking out my revolver and looking at it in an entirely different light. Here at least was a friend. I didn't get far before I heard aircraft overhead and, looking up, found them to be the other five aircraft of my Flight. I raced back to the Hurricane, even forgetting my damaged leg, feverishly pulled on my helmet to call them up and tell them where I was, but to my utter dismay, they didn't answer my repeated calls. I left the aircraft for the third time, now feeling very lonely and despondent.

'I must have walked about half a mile across a large ploughed field when I heard a couple of motorcycles nearby and turning saw them heading towards me, so I pulled out my revolver, determined to "sell myself dearly", and greeted these two chaps, calling for them to halt. I was gripping my gun in both hands to keep it steady.

'It now became confusing because I discovered they were Belgians, who'd been out on patrol trying to locate the advancing Germans, so my schoolboy French had little effect. They had spotted some tanks and were in the process of racing back when they saw me coming down and had bravely motored across some ploughed fields to try and find me, only to be greeted by me pointing a gun at them. However, I recognised them by their helmets and so got on the back of one of the bikes and we roared off. Meeting up with some of their companions I was transferred to a sidecar and the driver took me back with him.'

The Dornier, from 3(F)/11 (3rd Staffel of Aufklärer 11 – a

reconnaissance unit), crashed near Wavre. Its pilot, Oberleutnant Kopetsch, his observer and gunner all suffered wounds, but survived the shoot down, and were taken into captivity by French troops. Frank had come down near Hamme-Mille, about eight miles south of Louvain. He continued:

'We got over the River Dijle in Belgium and then they dropped me with four or five British sappers who were preparing to blow up a bridge. These chaps then drove me back some way until I eventually had to join a column of refugees and began walking, despite my leg wound. I then experienced first hand being strafed by German aircraft and wished desperately that I was in my Hurricane.

'Then a British truck came along and they took me to a village somewhere south of Brussels where they said there was a medical officer in one of the houses. I found him and he gave me some brandy, then cleaned up my wound. I then walked back into the street, looking down the half-deserted village and suddenly a door opened. An old lady appeared with a cat in her arms which she deposited outside and, after a quick look up and down the street, went back inside and closed the door.

'I was then put into another truck together with two other RAF chaps. They were the survivors from a Blenheim. The pilot had had a face full of Perspex, the gunner had been killed and the observer had lost a hand.[4] However, despite powdered Perspex in his eyes, the pilot had managed to get his aircraft down.

'The three of us then transferred into a WW1 Crossley ambulance and I was asked to hold onto a poor chap who had a badly shattered pelvis. It was a hellish journey for him but finally we arrived at a casualty clearing station just across the French border. It was a tented camp but long before I was dealt with I fell fast asleep. While out of it, I was put into a bed, someone sorted out my leg and knew nothing at all till late the following day. I was then taken to Dieppe, that was being used to evacuate wounded at that stage, being put into

---

[4] This was a 57 Squadron crew shot down that morning too – and by another Dornier 17. They were forced down at Termonde. Pilot Officer W G Spencer and the wounded Sergeant R Pike had gone looking for some petrol so they could fly back to their base at Poix but while doing so someone came across the apparently abandoned Blenheim and set in on fire. Frank remembered being impressed that despite everything, these two men had brought their parachutes back with them – and the aircraft's rear Lewis gun.

a commandeered infant school in a small village above the town. Four of us ended up in a classroom used as a ward, me, the two Blenheim guys and Bernard, the Duke of Norfolk.[5] He was a nice fellow but he was in hospital because of gout! We got on famously and used to play rummy over the next couple of days.

'Finally we went into Dieppe itself, by train, but once in the docks I heard aircraft and some Heinkels come in and begin bombing the harbour – and our train. It looked as if we were going to board *The Maid of Kent* that was at the quayside but she was hit and sank. As the bombs began to fall we started to run and the interesting thing was to see who ran for cover the fastest, me with my wounded knee or the Duke with his gout.

'The raid over we came back and found the driver had disconnected his engine and had gone. Part of the train was burning so we unhooked the burning section and a number of us began pushing the remaining carriages a short distance from the fire. The engine reappeared so we hooked-up again and persuaded the driver to head west. Two or three days later we ended up at La Baule, on the Atlantic coast, near the Loire estuary by Saint Nazaire.

'There, a very posh hotel named *The Hermitage* had become an officers' hospital so I spent a few days there. It was quite impossible to believe there was any war going on at all, everything seemed so calm. All the lights remained on at night and we enjoyed strawberries and cream; we were suddenly in a totally different environment.'

By this time, of course, the British army in the north had been pushed back to Dunkirk and under miraculous circumstances had been evacuated back to England helped in no small measure by an armada of small ships. These small boats, many commandeered by the navy, and often crewed by their civilian owners, worked in liaison with the navy, ferrying troops from the beaches to larger ships in deeper water off shore. Other vessels came in to the Dunkirk harbour to pick up waiting soldiers, sailors and airmen. Meanwhile, British troops still in France had been retreating back to Cherbourg or to ports on the Atlantic coast, such as Saint Nazaire, where FRC had been sent. Frank resumed:

---

[5] Bernard Marmaduke Fitzalan-Howard, 16th Duke of Norfolk; Major, Royal Sussex Regiment, who was approaching his 32nd birthday.

'Much to the Duke's and my own disgust, we were discharged back to our respective force, he to the army, me to the RAF, and I was sent off to a tented stores depot near Nantes. Here I met up with another couple of pilots, one of whom had "acquired" a fine old Citroen car, so we used to drive into Saint Nazaire most evenings for a drink. After we'd been there a while we got a message to say that there was a British aircraft on an adjacent airfield that had apparently been abandoned some days earlier. The CO of the depot suggested we go and take a look at it, which we did. As far as I recall the date was 5 June.

'It was a Bristol Bombay – a bright yellow painted transport aircraft. We gave it the once over – kicked the tyres and so on – and it seemed intact. Borrowing (!) some aviation fuel from the French contingent based at the airfield, we checked the engines thoroughly and the next morning took off for England. I was put in the back because the others said that I was the only one among them who had fired at a German aircraft, so I had better man the gun. If a German aircraft had attacked it would have been interesting, for during most of the trip I was trying to find out not only how it fired but how to load it. There were four of us and feeling very conspicuous in this bright yellow twin-engined machine, which appeared to have only a top speed of 120 mph, we headed for England, although we cut across the French coast around Le Havre.

'Luckily we didn't see a thing till we neared the English coast, where some RAF fighters came alongside and took a look at us. We continued on and eventually landed at RAF Hendon. I then had to find out where my squadron was and discovered it had pulled out of France a few days after I'd been shot down, with nothing much left. They had then been sent up to Wick where it relieved 43 Squadron which had now flown back to Tangmere. I therefore asked Air Ministry if I might rejoin 43.

'George Lott, the CO, had two days earlier taken the squadron on a patrol to Abbeville and arrived back with just two – himself and a flight commander. He was naturally keen to get replacements, so I got my wish.'

This fateful day for 43 had been on 7 June, Lott and John Simpson being the two who had returned. The Dunkirk evacuation had ended but there were still British forces in other parts of France. Ten squadron Hurricanes had flown out, in company with 601 Squadron, and while

43 did not lose eight pilots, four Hurricanes were shot down by Me109s and two pilots killed. The rest had landed at Rouen. In a later patrol from there, whilst heading back to Tangmere, another scrap with some 109s and 110s had resulted in four more losses, although all the pilots survived.

Three Squadron had not faired well in France. Later on the day Frank was shot down they had lost Sergeant Allen, and three other pilots had been forced to land after a combat. On the 15th Squadron Leader Gifford had force-landed due to an accident, Mike Carter and Sergeant J L C Williams had been killed, while another pilot had been captured and two more Hurricanes damaged. Then on the 16th Pat Gifford had been killed, Walter Churchill taking over the reins. Two more pilots were shot down on the 17th, one safe, one badly burned. By the 20th they had more pilots than aircraft, so when the call came to evacuate, the pilots had to toss-up to see who would fly out and who would go by road to Boulogne (shipped out on the MV *Mona's Queen III*), although finally a transport aircraft got the rear party out.

At Wick, the squadron were advised of several decorations to pilots. It was an impressive list.

Squadron Leader W M Churchill – DSO and DFC
Flight Lieutenant M M Stephens – DFC and Bar
Flying Officer C A C Stone – DFC
Pilot Officer F R Carey DFM – DFC and Bar
Flight Lieutenant M M Carter (Missing) – DFC
Sergeant R C Wilkinson – DFM and Bar
Sergeant A H B Friendship – DFM and Bar

To receive one Distinguished Flying Cross would have been a good result, but Frank had also received a Bar, both citations together recording at least nine enemy aircraft destroyed in France. Both awards appeared in the *London Gazette* dated 31 May 1940 (even though they got the name wrong – see Appendix B).

Following a quick visit home to see his wife and daughter, he went down to Tangmere. Frank had lost his first log book and all his kit following 3 Squadron's pull-out from France. Starting a new log, the first entry referred to his being shot down on 14 May, the second entry, the flight back to Hendon from Nantes in the Bombay, dated 6 June. His next flight is dated 24 June in Hurricane P3786, a thirty-minute solo trip which he noted as a 'local thrash!' In other words, putting himself through his paces, his first flight in over four weeks.

There were different personnel in 43 Squadron when Frank returned to it. Caesar Hull and Peter Townsend had both left, Hull to an adventure in Norway, Townsend to take command of 85 Squadron. However, Hull would return to 43 in the summer.

John Simpson now commanded A Flight, Flight Lieutenant Rowland B, although he had been injured on the 7th and was about to be replaced by Flight Lieutenant T F D Morgan. Of Frank's two old NCO buddies, Darkie Hallowes was still going strong but Peter Ottewill had been badly burned, again on the fateful 7 June.

The Battle for France and the evacuation from Dunkirk had now passed into history. Everyone in Britain awaited Hitler's next move, which no one doubted would be an air assault followed by an invasion. Britain's only defence was her fighter pilots. Bloodied from the two recent fights against the Luftwaffe they might be, but they were ready and able to ward off the next blows. What has now become recorded as this country's greatest challenge – the Battle of Britain – was about to begin.

Chapter Five

The Battle of Britain

The RAF's fighter aircraft had been drained away in France and above Dunkirk and many of its finest regular air force fighter pilots had been lost in both actions. Many of the latter had been killed due to poor foresight in training, the thinking of the day being that the RAF would only meet unescorted bombers over England. It had not been envisaged that France and the Low Countries would fall; the surmise was that if anything, this present war might easily fall into a conflict similar to the Great War, being fought across the whole of France.

The use of aeroplanes had meant this would simply not be the case. The German tactic of *Blitzkrieg* had been successful. Dive-bombers blasted the way ahead, with troops and armour pushing forward before any form of defence line could be established. Once the momentum of advance was begun, it had been almost impossible to oppose its inevitable conclusion. Now, however, the English Channel made a far more formidable line to defend. To cross it the Germans would have to gain total air superiority over this expanse of sea before an invasion fleet could realistically be launched. That air superiority would also be necessary to thwart any attempt by Britain's Royal Navy to intervene against such a fleet.

Hugh Dowding however, was painfully aware of how small his defending force had become in recent weeks. It had never been at full strength as promised by the government, and despite his urgent appeals to the Prime Minister, Hurricanes had been poured into France, while the consequent loss of Spitfires and Hurricanes, forced to help protect the evacuation from Dunkirk, had reduced his force still further. Not only that, but in France and above the evacuation, his pilots had met an aggressive force of German fighters, whose pilots were on a high. RAF tactics had been found wanting. Squadron commanders leading their men in classic vics of three were easy targets for the fast, nimble Me109s. Wingmen being so careful not to run into their leader, could not watch the sky adequately and were open to surprise attacks.

Squadron commanders too, in many cases, were senior pilots, whose rank and position had been formulated due to natural progression upwards though their career. In WW1 the majority of combat leaders had been flight commanders who had gained experience in battle. Very few really good WW1 squadron commanders led their men high over the trenches. It had been left to the experienced flight commanders. But early in WW2 the relatively inexperienced squadron commanders had been leading their men in battle.

Things were beginning to change, however. The quick thinkers now were realising that younger men were better equipped to lead squadrons into battle, and these men ideally must also have experienced battle. Not that everyone had fought in France or over Dunkirk, but in the coming weeks, battle experience would be gained quickly – if one survived.

George Lott was 33 years old and while an experienced pilot, and well liked by his men, he was of an earlier generation. In 43 Squadron John Simpson was 27, and already an ace, and Frank's flight commander. Tom Dalton Morgan was 23, and while he would become a successful fighter pilot, had yet to see action. Much would fall on the shoulders of men like Frank Carey, Darkie Hallowes, and Tony Woods-Scawen. It must have been strange for Tony Woods-Scawen, for only a few months before, Frank had been a sergeant pilot while he was an officer, now Frank was back and about to be his flight commander.

By the time Frank had returned to 43 Squadron – on 24 June – it was still a period of calm before the expected storm. New pilots who arrived found themselves thrown into some intensive training, all the while expecting something big to happen. There was no reason, they thought, why the Germans couldn't come over immediately, but of course, they were busy bringing their squadrons into their newly acquired aerodromes in northern France and assembling their invasion fleet. They hoped the British might yet see sense and sue for peace. A victorious army and air force were on their doorstep, so why, they thought, wouldn't Churchill and his government consider this move?

Newspaper editors were becoming more and more enthusiastic about reporting stories of Britain's new air heroes, and Frank had his share of – for him especially – unwanted publicity. When he returned to 43 Squadron one newspaper reported:

AIR ACE TOASTED
Pilot Who Shot Down Ten Has Double Distinction
Pilot Officer F Carey DFC and Bar, DFM, 29 year old fighter pilot, took his place yesterday in the Officer's Mess of a

Fighter Squadron which six years ago he joined as an ordinary mechanic.

He was toasted by the mess as the only airman in this war to have the Distinguished Flying Medal – awarded to non-commissioned officers and men – and the Distinguished Flying Cross with Bar.

Pilot Officer Carey has ten enemy aircraft officially credited to him. When the war broke out he was a sergeant pilot. He was awarded the DFM in March last after engagements against the enemy over the North Sea.

Like many such reports, there always seemed ambiguity or complete errors, many of which therefore quickly became indisputable facts. In this case it reads as if Frank was the only pilot in the RAF to have the DFM, whereas the writer meant to say he was the only pilot in 43 Squadron to have been so honoured.

RAF Tangmere, still part of Fighter Command's 11 Group, commanded by Keith Park, had nearby Portsmouth to help defend as well as the south-west approaches to London. They were right in the front line. 43 Squadron were hastily bringing themselves up to fighting strength and fighting efficiency. Between 8 and 11 June seven replacement pilots and eleven new Hurricanes arrived. From then until the end of the month time was devoted to returning the unit to a fully operational standard. The whole ambit of training was gone through: fighter area attacks, with variations (no doubt changed due to recent lessons learnt), flight and squadron formations, aerobatics, dog-fighting, cross-country flying, airframe and engine tests, cloud flying, D/F homings, ciné-gun attacks, low flying, map reading, dusk landings, searchlight co-operation and so on.

One glaring problem for Fighter Command was the almost complete lack of night fighter defence. It had never really been addressed and although twin-engined, radar-carrying aircraft would soon be available, there would be few of them. To help this situation, day fighter squadrons were being encouraged to gain experience of night operations, although over a blacked-out country, it was anything but welcomed. However, Frank noted in his log book two night patrols on 28 June.

A couple of squadron stragglers had turned up from France, Sergeant Buck on 9 June, Woods-Scawen a week later. On the 12th George Lott flew down to Farnborough in order to fly against a captured Messerschmitt 109. Sergeant Pratt was killed on the 15th, low flying over the sea.

As July began the squadron once more flew over France, escorting a recce machine to Abbeville – twice – on the 1st. The next day it was back to shooting down loose barrage balloons, which Frank did in his P3786.

The Germans now started testing British defences with flights over the Channel, coastal shipping an obvious lure. The famous 'X-raids' began appearing in his log again, which meant scrambles from Tangmere, which were interspersed with patrols, flights into the areas of activity where there might be the chance of an engagement before any hostile aircraft turned back for France. Action came at last on the 9th, starting off the Isle of Wight.

Lott was leading Frank and Sergeant Mills, taking off at 11.40 am, and met six Me110s of III/ZG26 head-on. Everyone began firing and in the fight two Messerschmitts went down off Littlehampton. However, George Lott was wounded as a cannon shell exploded on his armoured windshield. He was blinded in one eye and his machine caught fire. Turning for home, the fire intensified forcing him eventually to bale out over Fontwell racecourse. Losing his right eye he was out of the battle and had to leave the squadron. Lott was later awarded the DSO and DFC for his recent efforts.

Most accounts credit Lott, Frank and Mills with the two 110s shared between them, although in his log book Frank only acknowledges one 'damaged'. Jack Mills was RAFVR, called up as war was about to be declared. He had been with 43 for exactly one month now. He would end his RAF career as a squadron leader DFC post-war, having served on Malta, in North Africa and Italy too.

The new commanding officer was Squadron Leader J V C Badger, who fortuitously was on attachment to the squadron as a supernumcrary to gain experience. John Badger was the same age as Frank, and also a former apprentice. Selected for pilot training he had gone to Cranwell and won the Sword of Honour in 1933. He had already served a period with 43 Squadron in the 1930s. After that he had been active with the Fleet Air Arm and then with the Marine Aircraft Establishment at Felixstowe.

Frank now began flying P3468. On the 18th, coming back from a trip to Weston-Super-Mare he was warned of a raider nearby and spotted a He111 but lost it in cloud. On the 19th he flew P3527 five times, three X-raid scrambles, and two patrols. On the fourth sortie the squadron met enemy aircraft off Selsey – Me109s from III/JG27. The scramble came at 16.55, John Simpson, John Cruttenden, John Crisp, Tony Woods-Scawen, Jimmy Buck and FRC. This is another action Frank recalled:

'Another odd scrap I remember was over Bognor against some Me109s. The squadron were at it and I had just finished engaging one which I don't think I got – it just went down into cloud – and although I saw some muck on the sea afterwards, it was reckoned to be one of our own aircraft. I then climbed up to get back into the scrap and there I saw a Hurricane flying along, quite upside down, with no one in the cockpit. I flew up alongside it and had a good look – it seemed totally undamaged – and I could see by the aircraft letter whose it was, Sergeant Buck's. I had heard him on the radio earlier saying he had a bad wound in the leg and that he was baling out, which he obviously did over the coast but by the time they picked him up he had drowned. He had been a strong swimmer too.'[6]

John Simpson, after despatching one Messerschmitt and hitting another, was wounded in the left foot in this fight, and baled out near Worthing, breaking his collar bone as he landed on a roof and then crashed backwards through a garden fence.

By now the Battle of Britain had well and truly begun. Convoy patrols and scrambles occurred daily. Four on the 20th, and during one there was a fight with a Heinkel 59 German rescue floatplane and some 109s. Before any damage could be inflicted, they disappeared into cloud, but a 109 picked off Flying Officer Joe Howarth, and like Buck, he also baled out but drowned.

At this stage there was no properly co-ordinated air sea rescue organisation in being. Fighter pilots did not even have dinghies until the early summer of 1941. If a man came down in the sea and was lucky enough to be seen to do so, there was a chance a lifeboat or naval launch might be sent out to find him, but even being seen was no guarantee. Time was always of the essence and time was generally against a swift rescue. All they could rely on was their 'Mae West' life jackets to keep their head out of the water, but it was the cold that killed.

On the night of 22/23 July, Frank was again on a night patrol, raiders having been reported over the south coast. In the air he saw a Dornier go down in flames, noting it in his log book as '...possibly the first aircraft to be shot down by an aircraft using airborne radar – confirmed for F.I.U.' This had been a Do17 of 2/KG3 that the Fighter Interception Unit shot down south of Brighton, and Frank was able to give this experimental night fighting unit confirmation of their victory.

---

[6] James Alan Buck was 24. His brother Flight Lieutenant H A Buck would die on active service on 27 April 1945 aged 31.

Frank now took over another Hurricane, P3202, which he used for most of the rest of the month. However, despite a number of sorties, it was to be August before he and his new machine would be in combat and it was its last with Frank. In July his flying hours had topped the 1,000 hour mark.

August 1940 began what historians now regard as the start of the Germans' main assault. Till now the Luftwaffe had merely probed. With an invasion date provisionally set for mid-September, the task now was to eliminate the RAF, particularly the fighters. This would need successful actions against the Hurricanes and Spitfires in the air and also the destruction of their airfields.

The limited range of German bombers meant that only airfields in the south of England could be targeted and it says much for the RAF's senior staff that withdrawing units further north was never an option. Public morale would have suffered badly had Fighter Command conducted its air war against the Germans from well north of London, so the risk of bombs knocking out RAF airfields had to be taken.

Tangmere and its satellite, Westhampnett, were among those very vulnerable being just a short flying distance in from the south coast. Radar, of course, gave reasonably good warning of approaching raiders, and most RAF squadrons had learnt to be off the ground within minutes of an alert being sounded.

Thursday 8 August has often been cited as the official date for the start of the Battle of Britain. The assault began with an attack on yet another Channel convoy. The squadron put up Badger, Cruttenden, Crisp, Johannes Oelofse, Jack Mills, Woods-Scawen and FRC, take-off 15.40. Frank recalled to me:

'Over the convoy code-named Peewit we had seven aircraft up and as we arrived we could see a huge mass of aircraft seemingly stretching back to Cherbourg. There were Ju87 dive-bombers, above those were Me109s in great big ovals covering the distance, and above them Me110s.

'On the way up the CO called to me, telling me to do the fighter protection part at the back; myself and two others! It was so ridiculous – almost laughable – and I could not help thinking how bloody peculiar, just three of us to take on that mob. It was like throwing Christians to the lions.

'Having absorbed this order I then noticed that we were not going to be around for very long. The other three went into the dive-bombers and within seconds I'd lost my two companions and the only advantage was that I could fire at anything near me because it was bound to be the other side.

I got nothing, but my aircraft was damaged – then suddenly I was alone.

'Looking round I saw a formation so headed towards it, seeing they were 109s. I hooked myself onto the last chap, firing away quite merrily when I got an awful wallop from a 110 with its four cannons. I got one shell in the port block of my guns and ammunition so there was quite a big bang and a hole appeared. I was thrown right over onto my back. By the time I'd sorted that out and straightened out I found I was almost to Cherbourg. I'd also collected some splinters in my left arm and blood was seeping down to my hand.

'Some more 109s were near me and I came up behind them but again a 110 came down and blew off my rudder, one whole elevator one side, and the canvas covering the other. I thought I'd better get back and once in the circuit of Tangmere, the ack-ack opened up on me. All I could see in the mirror, of course, was a lot of fabric flapping about. Somehow it all seemed to work, although landing was difficult without elevators, and I got it down.'

Back in 1940, Frank Carey had written the following account of this engagement:

'For my part, I didn't have so much luck on this occasion although it was quite a busy trip. We were on convoy patrol off the Isle of Wight when a most formidable and orderly array of enemy aircraft arrived to interfere with things. First of all, at the top level – around 15-20,000 feet – came formations of Me110s escorting roughly oval patrol flights and eventually stretching from the French coast to the Isle of Wight. About 5,000 feet below them, squadrons of Me109s came out taking up station at intervals also stretching right back across the Channel. Then underneath this "umbrella" came a sizeable force of Ju87s.

'We did nothing about the fighters to start with except that with my section of three above the rest of the convoy patrol, I climbed up to gain height. When the 87s appeared on the scene, those in the squadron lower down went in to attack them while I was trying to keep the 109s from interfering. This I managed with only partial success, but in the fight that followed, I lost contact with my other two aircraft. On my own I spotted a squadron of 109s in Vic formation which I took, at first, to be Hurricanes and I went off to join them. On discovering my mistake I was happy to note that I had not been seen by them and I continued until I had got behind one of the outside members of the 109 formation. I had just settled down to fire at this aircraft with some success, as bits started to fly off it, when a very large explosion nearly blew me upside down. A Me110 had seen what was happening, had come down and was sitting about 30 yards behind me and his explosive 20 mm shots had blown up all the ammunition in my port wing, leaving a hole big enough for a man to crawl through.

'By the time I had righted the aircraft, all the 109s had disappeared so I laboriously climbed back up to get back over the convoy when I was once more jumped by some Me110s. This time they blew one elevator and the rudder off and the aircraft did a half "bunt" before I collected my senses. I had been hit in the arm on the first occasion and what with that and having only about three quarters of an aircraft to control, I thought discretion was the better part of valour and slowly brought the remains back to base. As if I hadn't had enough, the Tangmere ack-ack opened up on me as I entered the circuit – I suppose my silhouette must have looked a bit odd. Fortunately they didn't hit me.'

Despite the damage to his Hurricane, P3202 was repaired on the squadron and air tested just four days later. 43 did not fair well with their encounter with V Gruppe of LG1. From this action Cruttenden and Oelofse, a South African, were missing and Tony Woods-Scawen crash-landed at Tangmere with 'multiple foreign bodies in both legs'. In another action nearby, Sergeant C A L Hurry had his fighter damaged, while later, Pilot Officer H C Upton had his engine seize on a flight from Ford to Whitnell, forcing him to crash land.

For the next few days there were constant scrambles. Four on the 9th, two on the 10th, four more on both the 11th and 12th. No contact was made until sortie number three on the 12th, although on the first sortie the squadron had been chasing large numbers of vapour trails. Frank was now flying R4109, and he met Ju88s on this mission. His Flight comprised: Crisp, Mills, Cliff Gray, Woods-Scawen and Roy Lane. Frank's combat report read:

'I was Red Leader and left Tangmere at 12.15 to patrol base at 10,000 feet, afterwards changed to Selsey at 15,000 feet. On reaching patrol point I noticed large numbers of Me110s circling at 20,000 feet and being attacked by some other Squadron. I saw isolated aircraft leaving Portsmouth and after detailing Yellow Section to attack EA that they had sighted I selected a Ju88 below me and dived to attack. After delivering four attacks using up to 20° deflection, no return fire from rear gun was noticed. After third attack both engines emitted considerable clouds of black smoke. EA lost height fairly rapidly. As I was looking round to watch out for possible escort I lost sight of EA and did not see it again, but my Red 4 who did not fire states that it dived to sea level and flattened out, flying straight but smoking in engines badly. I returned to Portsmouth but all EA had left the vicinity so landed at Tangmere 12.55. Red 2 and 3 lost me.'

Frank was credited with a probable, a category only introduced during this week. Up till then these sorts of claims were generally regarded as 'possibles'. However, the German unit – KG51 – lost a number of aircraft in this raid on Portsmouth, engaged by 43, 145, 152 and 213 Squadrons, and had others badly damaged. There is every reason to suppose one was Frank's victim. It certainly didn't look as if it was going to get back across the Channel. The reader will also note that 43 were now operating in sections of four – rather than three – but this was not always the case (see below).

Only two sorties occurred on the 13th but the first, in company with Crisp and Mills, resulted in a fight over Littlehampton – in fact he referred to it as a 'dogfight' with Me109s, Me110s, and Ju88s. He also noted that he shot one 88 down, damaged two and got another probable. There may be some question about the Ju88 recorded as destroyed in his log book, but Frank did tell of one unusual incident that may help explain it:

'Going into attack some Ju88s one day, while above we could see the fighters we thought we could get a nice burst in before they got near us. I sat behind this one 88 and pressed the button, and to my utter amazement bits flew off all over the place. The damage was massive and I thought, good grief, it has never happened like this before. I was then aware of some stuff going over my cockpit canopy and looking in my mirror, saw a fighter right behind, trying to hit me but his fire was missing and knocking hell out of this 88!

'Once I realised this, I was off like a shot. Luckily his fire went straight over me, but it was very interesting. The trouble with our .303 guns was that they weren't really heavy enough and of course, you have to conserve your ammunition. We only had just 15-seconds of fire, then you were finished. Shortage of ammunition was always a worry – to me anyway.'

His combat report tells us some of the story, although not about the German fighter's part in it:

'I was leading Red Section and took off at 06.15 with orders to patrol Brighton at 15,000', afterwards changed to contact remainder of Squadron and patrol Tangmere at 18,000'. After joining up with them I sighted a large bunch of EA approaching Worthing at same height and gave a Tally-ho. Leader turned Squadron to left to use sun as background, but EA were too close and we attacked in waves, each section in line astern, from the EA's starboard bow. I followed in and attacked the Ju88 formation, "jinking" about in between each burst to watch [for] EA fighter escort and to foil EA rear gunners. After first wave of attack it became mainly individual combats. After firing at the 3 Ju88s on starboard of formation, they each showed signs of distress with smoking engines and falling back from main formation. Leading aircraft and left hand aircraft continued, though losing height slowly but right hand aircraft dived steeply into layer of cloud, with black and white smoke coming from engines and fuselage. I was attacked then by 3 Me110s so had to break off attack on Ju88s. Me110s pulled up and refused to mix it although I appeared to be isolated at the moment. When I had a moment to spare to attempt to look for EA formation, they had disappeared. I patrolled above and below cloud waiting for EA to return and later saw one Me110 flying just above cloud heading south at coast between Bognor and Littlehampton, but ammunition gave out after short burst and EA was lost in cloud. I returned to base and landed at 07.00.

'While waiting for return of EA, I noticed large palls of smoke at following places:

2 miles N of Arundel

1 mile N of Bognor, about 10 miles NW of aerodrome, in hills.'

Further sorties took place on the 13th, and 14th, one on the latter Frank recorded as: 'Looking for isolated bandits over Southampton.' Two pilots from the squadron baled out on the 13th, Tom Dalton Morgan in the morning, shot down over Petworth and receiving a slight wound. Then Tony Woods-Scawen in the afternoon, over Southampton. The squadron lost Sergeant H F Montgomery on the 14th, hit by return fire from a He111 he was chasing, 40 miles out from Beachy Head.

The 15th was a big day. The Germans had begun *Adlertag* – Eagle Day – on the 13th, which called for the final destruction of the RAF's fighters. This, the third day, found the enemy no nearer to achieving this goal. But the 15th was to witness perhaps the bitterest fighting thus far. 43 however, were not as involved as other units, although Frank was in action, shooting down a Ju88 encountered near Selsey Bill. Frank, Badger and Upton all had a go at it. It was a machine of the 4th Staffel, II/LG1 which finally went down at Priors Leaze, Breach, Southbourne, West Sussex, at 18.30. Frank had described it as a sitting duck, although its gunner had put bullets into Squadron Leader Badger's machine, one of which had hit the heel of his shoe. The observer, Oberleutnant Harald Möller, and gunner, Gefreiter Erhard Anders, were killed, Oberfeldwebel Wilhelm Richter, pilot, and Feldwebel Heinz Dittmann, radio operator, taken prisoner. Möller in fact was the Staffel Kommandeur. Frank related:

> 'I had no engagement personally over Southampton on this day. The only engagement I had was when I bravely shot down one isolated Ju88 with the assistance of about five others. This was such a sitting duck that it gave us all a perfect chance to practice large deflection shooting – the aircraft eventually crashed just north of Thorney Island.'

Some local people had seen the 88 coming down. Leaving a trail of smoke, it had turned back towards land from the sea after being damaged. One of the crew had attempted to bale out as it came across the A27 road, to make a belly landing, then to slide some 200 yards, at Woodmancote, Westbourne. It went over a ditch, into an orchard before ending up in a potato and carrot field. As it came to a halt it slewed round to face southwards. From pictures of the crash it is obvious that the starboard engine had been on fire, the engine and most of the wing having been burnt through. The bombs had been ripped off as it careered along the ground, but none exploded. They were left for six days before finally being blown up by the army.

The German airmen gave the locals the impression of being dirty and unwashed, but having ploughed through some rough ground which had smashed the nose Perspex and showered them all in earth and dirt, while filling the nose compartment with vegetables, there is little wonder at it. The bomber had also scythed down 55 apple trees. One of the two survivors had started to crawl away, and had managed to get some 200 yards south of the wreckage before he was spotted.

Jim Cheeseman, one of those at the scene, was the son of farmer Don Cheeseman, on whose land the Junkers had come down. He took away a parachute, but made the mistake of talking about it in his local a few days later. This led to the arrival of an armed RAF Intelligence Officer who demanded to see it. After inspecting it closely and making certain there was nothing new about it from its markings, he allowed Mr Cheeseman to keep it. It was later cut up by the local womenfolk who turned the silk into underwear.

On the night of the 15th Frank fitted in two night patrols but saw nothing. The next day, however, was to see much more action and Tangmere was among the German targets. Frank was flying R4109 exclusively now.

Early morning mist delayed operations by the Luftwaffe while the RAF flew a few coastal patrols or moved squadrons down to advanced bases. Mid-morning some Dorniers attacked West Malling in Kent and then, shortly before noon the first radar signs hinted that further raids were imminent along the south and south-east coasts. Within half an hour these radar plots had firmed-up to show some 300 enemy aircraft coming in, the RAF scrambling over 80 fighters to intercept.

These raiders made for Hornchurch, with others going for Harwell and Farnborough. The third bunch of aircraft headed in nearer one o'clock – an estimated 100 Ju87s from Stukageschwader Nr.2, leading a dozen Ju88s of KG54 and an escort of Me110s from III/ZG76. To meet this threat, eight RAF squadrons were scrambled. As the Stukas reached the Nab, on the eastern end of the Isle of Wight, signal flares came from the leading dive-bombers and the force split into groups, the largest of which headed directly towards RAF Tangmere. Hurricanes of 1, 43 and 601 Squadrons dived upon the Stukas, while 602 Squadron tangled with the Messerschmitts.

The squadron consisted of Squadron Leader Badger, FRC, Woods-Scawen, Gray, Lane, Hallowes, David Gorrie, Upton, Roy du Vivier, Albert van den Hove and Dennis Noble. 43 Squadron's Form 'F' records what happened next:

> Intelligence Patrol Report of 43 Squadron, 16.8.40.
>
> 11 Hurricanes of 43 Squadron took-off at 1245 hours and intercepted 50 to 100 Ju.87's travelling North off Beachy Head at 1255. The Squadron was at 12,000 feet and e/a were at 14,000 feet in flights of five, seven, in close vics, vics stepped up. A head-on F.A.A. No.5 attack was made at once, some turned straight back to France, jettisoned their bombs and the leading e/a was shot down by S/Ldr. Badger, who was leading the Squadron as Green 1 and two people baled out. There were escorting Me.109's at 17,000 feet or higher, but they took little part in the engagement, some of the pilots never saw them at all. The Squadron then turned and

attacked from astern whereupon the combat developed into individual affairs and lasted approximately 8 minutes. Some of the e/a made no attempts at evasion while others made use of the manoeuvrability by making short steep climbing turns and on account of their slow speed and tight turns one pilot at least made use of his flaps to counteract this.

The writer has seen Yellow 2's front windscreen which has been rendered almost opaque by the bullets which struck it. The bullets penetrated three parts of the way through before being stopped.

Blue 4 noticed an object which resembled a cube box falling away from a Ju.87 he was attacking. It appeared to follow the bomb out which was jettisoned, but may not have as pilot cannot be sure where it came from. It did not appear to be aimed at him for e/a was below at the time. It was very small by comparison to the bomb.

All e/a noticed appear to have carried one bomb only, slung between the wheels; and Green 2, very observant pilot, states the bomb was approximately one quarter or one fifth of the total length of the aircraft. A Ju.87 is 35 feet long.

The camouflage and armament of both sides was standard and nine pilots returned to base at 1310. Pilots state the Ju.87's catch on fire and go down comparatively easily.

Our losses: 2 Hurricanes (P/O Upton and P/O Woods-Scawen forced landed)

Enemy losses: 17 Ju.87's destroyed.
4 Ju.87's Probably.
4 Ju.87's Damaged.

Signed: F J Cridland F/O
Intelligence Officer,
No.43 Squadron.

The claims were a trifle over-optimistic, StG2 losing just nine aircraft with seven more damaged. Frank claimed two destroyed; his actual combat report recorded:

'I was leading A Flight behind the leader of the squadron, having taken off at 12.45 hrs. We were patrolling Selsey Bill at 11,000 ft when I gave the Tally-Ho on sighting waves of Ju87s. The leader ordered the squadron to attack one formation of '87s from the front, and immediately on closing the leader of the enemy aircraft was hit by the squadron leader and the crew baled out.

'I pulled my Flight over to the left to attack the right hand formation as we met them. Almost as soon as I opened fire the enemy aircraft's crew baled out and crashed into the sea, just off Selsey Bill. I turned to continue my attack from the rear as the enemy aircraft had been completely broken up by the frontal attack, and several other waves behind them turned back out to sea immediately, although we had not attacked them. I picked out one Ju87 and fired two two-second bursts at him and the enemy aircraft burst into flames at the port wing root.

'I did not wait to see it crash as I turned to attack another. After one burst at the third enemy aircraft two large pieces of metal broke off the port wing and it seemed to stop abruptly and go into a dive. I did not see it crash as two other Ju87s were turning onto my tail.

'I eventually picked on a fourth, but after firing two bursts and causing the engine to issue black smoke, the enemy aircraft turned out to sea and I ran out of ammunition. Noticing fire behind me, I turned round to see a pair of Me109s behind me, one firing and the other apparently guarding his tail. After a few evasive actions the enemy aircraft broke off and I returned to land and re-fuel and re-arm at 1340 hrs. During the attacks I noticed many enemy aircraft jettisoning their bombs into the sea.'

Frank also remembered:

'This was the first time that Tangmere itself was attacked – with considerable success too. We met the raid head-on just about over Selsey Bill. Due to our positioning, we were only able to fire on about the second wave, leaving the leaders more or less undisturbed in their bombing. However, we were very lucky that our head-on attack so demoralised the Ju87s that they, and the successive waves behind them, broke up. Some dropped their bombs into the sea in an effort to get away.

'The Ju87 was my favourite target. One of the great difficulties in air fighting is that you very quickly run out of ammunition. So if you have a target such as a Ju87, the moment you hit it, it bursts into flames, and of course, once that's started you know you've got it.'

As well as Woods-Scawen, who crash-landed at Parkhurst, on the Isle of Wight, slightly wounded, and Hamilton Upton, who crash-landed on Selsey beach, Pilot Officer D G Gorrie's Hurricane was damaged by return fire from the Stukas. Tangmere itself was badly hit and several Hurricanes caught on the ground. Four of 43 Squadron's machines were destroyed and one 19-year-old airman killed. Frank described what happened at Tangmere on this day:

> 'Tangmere was always regarded with much affection by all who served there and many like me would say that there was never another station to touch it. Furthermore, it had hitherto miraculously escaped any damage, as other stations had received. We felt at the time that perhaps it had been ear-marked for invasion landings by the Germans.
>
> 'So our horror can be imagined on returning from this particularly successful hammering of dive-bombers over Selsey Bill, to see all the vast smoke pall, fire and debris that was once our attractive and peaceful base.
>
> 'Avoiding the craters as we landed and returning to our dispersal area we could see just how much damage had been caused. The hangars with one notable exception had been destroyed or badly damaged, the sick quarters were reduced to rubble, sleeping quarters, messes, all had some damage and few windows remained anywhere. Bushes and trees were adorned with bits of curtains, clothing and underwear, while bits of furniture were strewn about. There were quite a number of human casualties too, including some German aircrew prisoners who were in the sick quarters from previous air actions in the area.
>
> 'Tangmere was never to look quite the same again – even when all the facilities had been replaced. It's character seemed to have suffered irreparable damage. It lives now only in the Museum and in some measure in the nearby 900-year-old village church.'

After the mauling of the 16th, the Luftwaffe was quiet on the 17th, but they returned in force the next day – Sunday. The Ju87 dive-bomber was already proving fairly non-effective in combat over southern England. The tactics employed by these machines in land actions were devastating, but they were vulnerable to fighter attack. The 18th saw their vulnerability exposed still further. Over previous weeks the eight Luftwaffe Stuka gruppen had suffered almost 40 casualties, mostly to anti-aircraft guns and fighters. Today they would lose 18 more, shot down or written off, with five others damaged.

Early reconnaissance aircraft sent over by the Germans tried to determine which of Keith Park's airfields still had fighters on them. The task was still to destroy Fighter Command and knock out its airfields. Shortly after mid-day the radar plots began to multiply and it was soon apparent that perhaps the biggest effort so far by the Luftwaffe was about to begin. By 12.30 virtually all of 11 Group's fighter squadrons had been called to readiness, as the first wave of raiders – some 300 – approached Kent.

At around 1 pm Biggin Hill was targeted by a small force of Do17s, followed by some Ju88s that should have attacked simultaneously but had missed the rendezvous. Then Kenley came under an attack which severely damaged the base. At around 2 pm four large formations of aircraft were seen approaching the Isle of Wight area. These consisted of Ju87s from StG77 and a formation of Ju88s. It was feared that Tangmere would again be the target so its squadrons were scrambled and told to fly above the airfield to provide protection. Frank led North, Mills, Gray, Lane, Woods-Scawen of his Flight, and Hallowes, Upton and Noble of B Flight.

However, Tangmere was not the target. The bombers were going for the radar station at Poling, near Littlehampton, the naval air station at Ford, west of Littlehampton, the naval airfield at Gosport and the Coastal Command airfield at Thorney Island. (German intelligence failed to appreciate that not all airfields were used solely by Fighter Command.)

While the Ju88s headed for Gosport, the Stukas were approaching Poling. Only three miles away, 43 Squadron's Hurricanes suddenly spotted them and headed straight into the attack. Frank remembered:

'I was leading the squadron for the first time. A couple of days earlier our airfield had been attacked and everyone was pretty sensitive about further raids. We had already been up once and were re-fuelling as the next alarm came, so we had taken off in a bit of a hurry. I had just about got everybody together somewhere between Tangmere and Chichester, and at about the right height.

'Warned of approaching aircraft I told the pilots we were going in from here and to pick off what we could, in fact to do anything to prevent them bombing. It looked as if they were going for Tangmere again, although in fact they weren't. So when we spotted them, I turned in and was suddenly right in the middle of fighters, Ju88s and dive-bombers; the fur was flying everywhere!'

Frank went after a Stuka, fired and saw it going down, streaming flame, but was then in trouble:

'Somebody stitched me right across the cockpit area and I caught another bullet in the right knee, but the aircraft seemed alright, though the engine wasn't sounding too happy. It must have been an almost spent round, for if the bullet had been anything else, I shouldn't have had a knee left. As it was the slug was right under the kneecap.

'I had to drop out of the fight as my knee seemed to be locked and I wasn't feeling too well. The wound made it awkward to control the aircraft and although one did not use the rudder that much in the Hurricane, there were times when one needed to waggle it a bit. I handed over the squadron to the number two and called base to say I was returning. They immediately told me not to as they were expecting to be bombed at any second. I therefore eased my way slowly north to get away from the fun and games and commenced to circle, losing a bit of height all the time. I called Tangmere again but they still said no, because enemy aircraft were all around – in fact they were bombing Ford.

'I saw a field that looked as if it didn't have any anti-invasion obstructions on it, certainly I could not see any poles sticking up, so I came in for an ordinary landing. Wheels and flaps down, which in retrospect I should not have done; everything was working beautifully. I had just sat her down and was saying to myself – you're a wonderful pilot – when I was suddenly thrown forward with terrific force.

'The next thing I remember was lying out in the field, blue sky above, and two women were slitting up my trouser leg, looking for bullet holes. They said they couldn't find any more, and seemed quite disappointed I had only the one.

'What had happened I discovered later, was that I had landed OK only to run over a semi-concealed trench which had been dug across the field and covered with grass. There was a Royal Observer Corps post just over in the next field, and also a machine-gun position nearby. I was very lucky because usually a Hurricane going over resulted in a broken neck for the pilot. Luckily too the machine hadn't caught fire. Anyway, the observer chaps ran over and managed to get the tail up sufficiently for someone to pull me out after undoing my parachute harness and seat belt.

'I was carted off to the Royal West Sussex Hospital [Brighton], which was a lovely old building. In fact we had four of Tangmere's pilots in one little ward so had great fun. The squadron adjutant would come down with a basket full of beer. Further along the corridor was the maternity ward, the occupants moaning quite a lot about the noise we made!'

One of the other pilots in the ward was Tim Elkington of 1 Squadron, who remembered '...an affable time.' Others were Pilot Officer Roy 'Lulu' Lane and Flying Officer H L 'Gerry' North, who both arrived on the 26th. Roy Lane, as a squadron leader in Burma later in the war, came down with engine trouble and was captured by the Japanese and beheaded. The Lane family lost three sons during the war, two with the RAF, the third with the Fleet Air Arm.

The combat effectively put Frank out of the Battle. He had come down near Holme Street Farm, Pulborough. His Hurricane (R4109) was salvaged and repaired, later going to 1 RCAF Squadron, and later still to 213 Squadron. It was finally written-off following a collision with another Hurricane during a practise dogfight near Castletown, on 18 March 1941. Again the Squadron's Form 'F' that was made out gives the overall action report for 18 August:

> Intelligence Report on Patrol of No. 43 Squadron, 1412-1455 hours. 18.8.40
> The Squadron had just come down from a patrol when the order to 'Scramble' base was given and as Green section had only just landed and was not refuelled, nine Hurricanes from Red, Yellow and Blue sections took off from Tangmere at 1412 hrs. and were vectored to Thorney Island where Ju.87s were sighted just crossing the Coast from the South. In the formation attacked there must have been from 40 to 60 Ju.87s but there were others seen in the distance. They were escorted by Me.109s at about 18,000 ft. over Selsey, but these latter took little part in the Combat and some pilots never saw them. The Ju.87s were at 10,000 ft, slightly below our fighters and were in no particular formation when the Squadron went into line astern by sections to attack from above and astern at 14.20 hrs. Enemy objectives appeared to be Thorney and Ford aerodromes and at least one pilot was able to fire just as e/a were going into line astern preparatory to diving on objectives. Three of the nine pilots claim no casualties. One of these approached a Ju.87 from astern closing slowly right up, but nothing happened when he pressed his guns owing to a fault in the air pressure. When 50 yards astern of e/a and about to break away, enemy rear gunner took hold of what appeared to be [the] perspex hood of his turret and hurled it at our pilot's machine but missed it; so far as pilot knows he was not fired at and several pilots state that no fire was directed at them when they might have

expected it. An unfortunate example was F/Lt. Carey leading
the Squadron as Red 1. who was seen to approach the leader
of enemy formation when he broke away sharply down-
wards. It appears a bullet had passed through his knee and he
is now in Hospital suffering also from concussion as a result
of a forced landing.

Frank did not fly again for over a month. However, he was eventually
discharged from hospital and returned to the squadron but not allowed
to fly. It was no doubt a frustrating time for him, with his brother pilots
daily going into action.

Remarkably there were few casualties while Frank was away. Pilot
Officer H L North was wounded and baled out on 26 August but then
on the 30th Sergeant Dennis Noble was killed while Squadron Leader
Badger was forced to bale out. However, he was badly injured falling
into the branches of a tree and although he survived, his injuries finally
proved fatal and he died on 30 June 1941. His DFC had been gazetted
on 6 September 1940.

On 2 September they lost two aircraft, one pilot killed and two
wounded. Tony Woods-Scawen was killed, Pilot Officer Leroy du
Vivier wounded and his aircraft lost. Mike Carswell was also wounded
but got down. Tony Woods-Scawen's brother Patrick, flying with 85
Squadron, had been killed (reported missing) the previous day
although his body was not found until the 6th. Both boys had just
received DFCs. Tony had baled out too low, Patrick had died due to
parachute failure. More disaster came on the 7th as Frank recalled:

> 'Caesar Hull and a number of us were sitting outside the
> Mess at Tangmere, including George Lott, a patch over his
> missing right eye, just discharged from hospital, and Jack
> Boret, the station commander. That afternoon the squadron
> took off and Caesar and Dick Reynell were both killed. When
> Tubby Badger was shot down the whole squadron thought
> everything was starting to fall apart. Everyone thought that
> Caesar would become CO and there had been a party in
> anticipation.'

There had been photographs taken of the officers outside the Mess that
Saturday afternoon. A semi-formal group in deck chairs, and others
with everyone standing about holding tankards. Frank was there, back
at Tangmere but not yet operational. Hull and Killy Kilmartin had only
recently returned to the squadron too, Hull after his Norwegian
adventures, Kilmartin following a rest after his service with 1 Squadron
in France. Dick Reynell, an Australian, had been a pilot in the

squadron pre-war and had then become a test pilot at Hawkers. He had managed a posting back to 43 in order to gain first hand knowledge of the Hawker Hurricane in combat. Hull was 27 years old, Reynell 28.

It had been a late afternoon scramble – German bombers had been raiding London for the first time. Both men had fallen to attacks by Me109s at 16.45. Hull had crashed in the grounds of Purley High School, Reynell had baled out badly wounded but died before he hit the ground at Blackheath.

It was a shattering blow. 43 were now pulled out of the Battle and sent north to RAF Usworth, near Newcastle upon Tyne, on the 8th. If only that decision had been made a couple of days earlier.

Chapter Six

After the Battle

Tom Dalton Morgan now took command of the squadron. Frank was back in the air on 23 September for some local flying. Then it was a matter for him and other surviving pilots with experience to impart their knowledge to the new pilots who began to arrive. Frank gave any number of them training in air-fighting, formation flying and attacks. Among them were several Czech pilots, and another newcomer was Pilot Officer K W Mackenzie.

Ken 'Mac' Mackenzie was to be with 43 for just a week but he was impressed by the pilots who were on the squadron, especially Frank Carey, Jim Hallowes and Killy Kilmartin. Mac flew 17 sorties in five days, beginning with flight formations led by Carey. It was an intensive training period as Mac related in his book *Hurricane Combat*. Today, he recalls:

> 'Frank Carey was a great chap. We met in 1940 when I was on 43 Squadron at Usworth for a whole week. He was a very capable chap and pilot. Very likeable, he was excellent at his job – an able pilot and meticulous in all he did. A man of relatively few words, he was a great leader in the air and on the ground – truly a man's man. Unassuming, good at his job.'

Ken 'Mac' Mackenzie went off to join 501 Squadron and later won the DFC and AFC. He also gained fame by knocking the tail off a Me109 with his wing after he'd run out of ammunition. He retired as a wing commander.

In December came a move to Drem, to the east of Edinburgh, with a detachment at Crail, south of St Andrews, near Fifeness. From both bases they could help guard the Firth of Forth approaches to Edinburgh. What operational flying there was, comprised convoy patrols and a few night sorties. On 20 January 1941 there was a bit of excitement. Soon after lunch, Frank and another pilot – Pilot Officer Tufnell in P3776 were sent off to intercept a reported Ju88. Frank found it briefly, and fired three bursts at it before losing it in cloud. He claimed it as damaged and put in the following report:

> P/O Tufnell took off as my number two from Drem to look for an X-raid off the coast near Dundee. We went out low over the sea so as not to be seen by approaching aircraft as there was plenty of cloud cover about. As we came to Bell Rock Lighthouse, we saw a Ju88 heading out to sea and gave chase. We managed to get fairly close beneath it before it [they] saw us so that I was able to get one or two good bursts into it before it climbed frantically into the cloud layer. The cloud was broken so that a game of hide and seek began in and out of the clouds in which one was never quite sure how near or how far one would be from the target as we popped out of each cloud. After this highly frustrating game had gone on for some minutes, I saw Tufnell, who was searching more or less independently of me, heading back for the coast. I called him but got no answer and had to return my attention to getting in behind the Ju88. In the event, after a chase lasting nearly 15-20 minutes, I was getting a long way out in the North Sea with little or no chance of getting a long enough sight on it to be able to open fire. I returned to base to hear that Tufnell had crash-landed on the Scottish coast and had lost an eye. I think that he must have come out of the cloud close to the Ju88 but not able to see it and it had hit him before he could do anything about it.

A German He111 was reported badly damaged this date, but it was due to a flying accident at Vaernes, Norway, not combat.

Things droned on during these winter weeks. In the new year Frank had left A Flight and taken over command of B Flight. More training, more convoy patrols, the odd scramble, then came 16 February with Frank doing some local flying in Hurricane R4196. He related:

> 'Early in the period I had an amazingly lucky escape in an aircraft collision. I was taxi-ing a Hurricane out for take-off on the rather humped-back grass airfield at Drem, near North Berwick. In most fighter aircraft all vision directly forward is obscured by the large frontal engine cowling and to cater for this blindness one has to swing the nose of the

aircraft from side to side as you taxi forward.

'I was suddenly confronted by the startling sight of a Spitfire with wheels retracted coming straight at me head-on at only about 20 yards away! I believe I said to myself – 'Duck!' – but things happened so quickly that I doubt whether I did anything at all except gaze in horror at the sight.

'There was an almighty clang as the two noses met. Some seconds later when all movement ceased I was utterly staggered to find that I was completely unscathed in the battered and twisted tin-box that surrounded me. Unfortunately the Spitfire wreck, which was still travelling at flying speed – unlike my almost stationary 2 to 3 miles per hour – spun right up in the air for some 75 feet before crashing back onto the ground. The pilot[7], who was a friend of mine, only lived for a few hours.'

Finally it was time to leave 43 Squadron, a unit he had been associated with for so long. Frank had arrived as an AC1, and now left as a flight commander, having, on occasion, even led the squadron in the air. His flying hours are recorded as 1,161.45. Upon leaving 43, Tom Dalton Morgan had written an assessment in Frank's log book, which was: "Above the Average."

His new posting was as an instructor, at No.52 Operational Training Unit (OTU) at Debden, which had been formed in March 1941. Its Chief Flying Instructor (CFI) was Wing Commander John Grandy DSO, who had commanded 249 Squadron during the Battle of Britain. 52 OTU had Hurricanes and Miles Masters, the latter for dual instruction. In April, Frank became OC A Flight.

'In March 1941 I was posted to an OTU to do a spot of flying instruction at Debden, near Cambridge. This provided a comparatively quiet and somewhat relaxed spell. After a while we were required to accept a batch of young Czech trainee pilots and to introduce them to fit into RAF customs and flying practices. Suddenly we found that even their basic knowledge of English was almost nil (as was our Czech!) and the thought of handling this, even on the ground, was bad enough, but it quickly became mind boggling in the air

---

[7] This was Flight Lieutenant John C Boulter DFC, who, like Frank, was a pre-war pilot. When the war began he was posted to 603 Squadron and in March 1940 was lucky to survive a collision with an Avro Oxford when taxi-ing. He had shot down a number of enemy aircraft in the Battle of Britain, for which he received his decoration. He was 28 years old.

situation. Somehow we managed but to recall some events still leaves me wondering how we were able to live through it. I was later presented with the gift of one of the Czech Air Force's beautiful silver pilot wing badges in appreciation.'[8]

A good many successful fighter pilots went through this unit during this period. Squadron Leader C F 'Bunny' Currant DFC was one, Squadron Leader Flying. Keith Lofts DFC was another, and Richard Barclay DFC – not surprisingly both the latter had been in 249 Squadron. In May Flight Lieutenant Manfred Count Czernin DFC arrived as an instructor, in from 17 Squadron. Despite his name, Czernin was British even if his background was rather complex. Father Austrian, mother a daughter of a British Baron, born in Berlin and lived his early years in Rome before coming to England for his education. Other well known pilots at Debden were Gerald Lewis DFC, Pete Matthews DFC and Andy McDowell DFM & Bar, all 1940 veterans. No doubt there were plenty of great stories in the Mess bar.

The unit also had a Dominie aircraft (X7343) and on one occasion Frank flew Bunny and Keith around the locality, while on another day, he flew Barclay and Lofts down to Duxford and back. The unit boasted some 60 Hurricanes and 25 training machines.

There was a new aircraft on show too, a North American P40 Tomahawk. On 26 June, Frank (in W9143) had a mock dogfight with one, the American pilot showing off its paces being a then unknown 1st Lieutenant Hubert Zemke – known to everyone as 'Hub' – who would later in the war lead and command the US 4th Fighter Group to great things – and 18 personal combat victories. The following month Frank had another dogfight with a P40, this time flown by 1st Lieutenant J R Alison. Hub Zemke and Johnny Alison were both visiting from the States to promote and instruct RAF pilots onto the P40 that the RAF were having under the Lease-Lend Scheme. Alison later became an ace flying P40s in China with the US 23rd Fighter Group.

Towards the end of July Frank was posted to 245 Squadron at Ballyhalbert, east of Belfast, on the coast. The squadron was commanded by Squadron Leader W P Blackadder DFC. In the Battle of Britain he had commanded 607 Squadron, and it had been this unit which had replaced 43 at Tangmere on that fateful 7 September. While Frank was back with an operational squadron, Northern Ireland seemed even further from the enemy than had Drem. One of the few exciting things to happen was Frank being scrambled to investigate a 'bogey' and locating a huge four-engined Liberator over West Freugh.

---

[8] This has now been turned into a brooch, Marigold Carey giving it to his daughter Jane.

He was now flying a much improved Hurricane, the Mark IIC, and some IIA types. The IIC had four 20 mm cannon. However, his time as a squadron commander was just around the corner and on 25 August 1941, he was given command of a brand new squadron – 135.

'At the end of August 1941 one of my dreams came true. I was posted to Baginton, south of Coventry, and promoted to squadron leader. I was to form No.135 Squadron and have it ready for overseas posting by the end of the year – barely three months away. As it was we sailed from the Clyde in November. Arriving at Freetown, we finally heard about the Japanese attack on Pearl Harbor. This changed our destination from the Middle East, to the Far East.'

Number 135 Squadron was formed on 15 August, Frank arriving to take command on the 26th having been appointed CO three days earlier. At the beginning of September Flying Officer E J Watson was posted in from 605 Squadron as an acting flight commander. Although Eddie Watson, from Dundee, had no way of knowing it, he'd been shot down by the German ace Werner Mölders on 6 September 1940, and wounded.

Then 135 moved to Honiley, a few miles to the west. More pilots started to arrive and by 3 October the squadron was made operational. Immediately there was a scramble – an unidentified aircraft was flying over Coventry. Frank was already airborne and turned to investigate. It turned out to be a Fleet Air Arm Martlet (an American F3F Wildcat) fighter. A few days later came another scramble – this time the 'bogey' turned out to be a Spitfire. Other scrambles also turned out to be a fruitless waste of petrol.

Flight Lieutenant D H T Dowding was posted in as B Flight commander on the 7th. Derek Dowding was the son of CinC Fighter Command, Sir Hugh Dowding. He did not feature long with 135 and was not scheduled to go overseas with it. Another of the new pilots posted in was Eric Batchelor, who would have a long association with Frank, both as a pilot and friend:

'After receiving my wings in Canada, I was fed into the Hurricane OTU at Debden, where I first met Frank Carey, who was on the staff there. He was not one of my instructors, I had a Czech flight lieutenant, but of course, we new boys were very much in awe of FRC with his decorations and Battle of Britain experience. I think his presence brought a sense of grim reality and purpose to our training, despite his very friendly and modest, approachable manner. Those of us

who then joined 135 under his command felt very privileged
and in the very best of hands.

'On completion of my course, Frank was forming 135
Squadron at Baginton, and I was posted there. We worked-up
at Honiley and got ourselves to an operational status. There
were a few scrambles, chasing things around, but we rarely
had the chance to catch anything. Then the squadron was ear-
marked for shipment overseas. So 136, 135 and 17
Squadrons all embarked at Greenock on the same troopship,
destined, we were told, for the Caucasus or somewhere.'

By the end of October the squadron became non-operational as the
time for departure overseas drew near. War in the Middle East was
becoming serious and reinforcements were needed urgently. 135 was
scheduled to be a part of them, together with another new squadron,
136, and the experienced 17 Squadron.

Orders to sail came and in early November under the command of
Flight Lieutenant T P M Cooper-Slipper DFC, the squadron entrained
at Berkswell, except for 20 pilots who would fly out. At Greenock the
squadron embarked on HMT (His Majesty's Troopship) A6 – *Duchess
of Bedford*. There were now four squadrons heading east, the first
three having been joined by 242 Squadron. As far as was known the
plan was for 136 Squadron to go to Persia on the *Durban Castle*, 135
and 17 to the Middle East, 242 for Singapore. Other pilots were
aboard the SS *Strathallan*, (of the P&O Line) while many of the ground
crews had all left on an earlier convoy.

Number 136 Squadron was commanded by another Battle of Britain
veteran, Squadron Leader T A F Elsdon DFC, while 17 Squadron was
led by Squadron Leader C A C Stone DFC, who had been in France
with Frank in 3 Squadron. Despite Stone being the senior man, Frank
was put in charge of RAF troops and as the convoy reached the West
African coast, he was in fact manning a machine gun on the ship! A
Hurricane from nearby Hastings flew by at low level, cockpit open and
a grinning face poking out. Frank immediately recognised Iggy
Kilmartin's Irish good looks. Kilmartin was now with 128 Squadron,
under the command of another friend, Billy Drake DFC who led this
squadron and who had been with 1 Squadron at Tangmere pre-war.

No sooner had the ship anchored than a small boat came out to it
with an urgent request for Squadron Leader Carey to attend an
important conference. It had been sent by Drake and Kilmartin, their
way of getting him away for a party.

Flight Lieutenant M C 'Bush' Cotton, with 17 Squadron, recalled in
his book *Hurricanes over Burma*, similar stories about this particular
arrival:

'Being the senior flight commander of 17 Squadron I was one of the fortunate ones to be off-loaded and, on landing at Freetown, found to my delight that an old friend from 43 Squadron, "Iggy" Kilmartin, was there in command [sic] of a fighter unit at Hastings aerodrome [128 Squadron]; protecting the allied interests. Through the grapevine, Killy had got to know that we were coming in to port and our anchor chains had barely rattled out when we saw a Hurricane appear low amongst the shipping. He then turned on a hair-raising display of low-level aerobatics culminating in a fly-past ten feet beneath us as we stood on the bridge and gazed into his grinning face.

'The ship's captain had by now become very agitated so Frank Carey signalled Killy with an Aldis Lamp... "For God's sake piss off." Half an hour later an RAF launch arrived alongside with Killy on board and our COs and flight commanders were invited to join him for an hilarious [pre] Xmas lunch, which was interrupted by Iggy being scrambled to intercept a Vichy French aircraft which had strayed into our territory. This he shot down and then rejoined us at the table to indulge in an even merrier celebration.[9]

'After a night or two at Freetown, basking in the tropical warmth, we were all ushered on board a Pan American Douglas DC2 and flown to Takoradi in Ghana. Here we were taken in RAF DC3s over the African continent to Khartoum, staging via Kano and Fort Lamy. The boredom of droning away over the limitless wastes got to be too much for Frank Carey who wheedled his way into the cockpit to try his hand at flying the DC3. I am not sure who thought up the skulduggery that followed but somebody (I think it was Bunny Stone) organised us all to leave our seats and creep to the back of the aircraft, thus upsetting the centre of gravity so that Frank had to level the aeroplane with the elevator trim control.

'When Frank got things back into equilibrium we all moved forward, making the machine nose heavy, thus requiring more work on Frank's behalf to trim it again. After this happened several times he got suspicious, opened the cockpit door, and saw the horde of grinning faces at the back of the machine. This brought forth an admirable string of air force invective.'

---

[9] In fact it was Billy Drake who commanded 128 Squadron and who shot down the Martin M-167F – 13 December 1941. Kilmartin was Senior RAF Officer at Hastings and took command of 128 the following year.

As mentioned earlier, while the convoy was at sea the attack on Pearl Harbor had occurred, and destinations had been changed. Ground crews of 135 and 17 were consequently diverted to Rangoon, Burma. 135 arrived at Durban on 19 December, and had their feet on land for the first time in five weeks. They sailed again on the 24th and had Christmas at sea. On the 26th the squadron lost 19-year-old Corporal Peter Baldwin overboard.

While it was known that 135 was heading for Rangoon, the formal announcement only came on 6 January 1942, upon reaching Bombay. At Bombay they changed ship, boarding HMT *Lacdy* on the 12th for Rangoon. Four days later they disembarked at Rangoon harbour, and boarded motor transport for nearby Zayatkwin airfield. On the 19th Frank and Pilot Officer W J Storey arrived at this airfield by air to be met by Flight Lieutenant Hartley from Group Headquarters. Another person Frank knew here was A W Pennington-Legh, who had been in 43 Squadron pre-war and was now OC 267 Wing. Frank, of course, had travelled to Burma by another route entirely. Remaining at Freetown while his men had sailed for Durban, Frank was ordered to get himself and a few others to Burma post-haste. That was easier said than done, but Billy Drake got to work and organised a Pan Am aircraft to fly Carey, Stone and a few others eastwards. This small advance party headed off on 26 December. Before that however, Frank had managed to celebrate Christmas as Barry Sutton recalled in his book *Jungle Pilot*. Sutton had flown with 56 Squadron in the Battle of Britain and was now a flight commander with 136 Squadron:

> 'I remember too that Christmas Day we had spent in Sierra Leone and how after that gastronomic nightmare of a Christmas dinner (roast pork, curries, spices, plum pudding with brandy sauce, and fruit) we had slept like glutted beasts until tea-time and then had gone for a swim in a pool of spring water at the foot of some rocks. We swam naked and sported about in the sun like native boys.
>
> 'Frank Carey, the CO of one of the squadrons which had travelled out with us, who was one of the party, lost a small gold chain carrying his identity disc and some lucky charms in the water. The water was so clear that once we had all got out of it and allowed it to settle, we were able to see the chain and the charms, three small elephants, lying at the bottom which was at least ten feet down. "Bush" Cotton, the best swimmer amongst us, dived down and recovered the lot.'

Frank recorded his trip out and the subsequent flight east, right across the African continent, then on towards the Far East:

'The sea voyage itself was more or less uneventful until we learnt at Freetown, Sierra Leone, that the Japs had entered the war. It was also at RAF Hastings (a few miles upstream from Freetown) that we were told that our destination was being changed. We were required to make our way, by the earliest possible method, and to report at Air HQ in Cairo. We managed to get seats in an American DC3 which flew us from Hastings to Khartoum, via Lagos, Accra, Kano, Maiduguri [Nigeria], El Genina, El Fasher [Sudan] and thus to Khartoum. From there we managed a lift by an Empire Flying Boat to Wadi Halfa [on the Nile] and then on to Cairo – ten flights. Some 14 days later we flew, again by Empire Flying Boat, from Cairo via Tiberius, Habbaniya, Basra, Dubai, Karachi, Gwadlior, Calcutta, to Rangoon – eight flights. I arrived on 19 January 1942 – in the middle of an air raid.'

Frank's pilots, once he could finally get them all together in one place, would consist of:

F/Lt E J Watson	F/Sgt W H F Dean RNZAF
F/O A Whitby	F/Sgt C G Beale RNZAF
P/O W J Storey RAAF	F/Sgt W D Dunkley RNZAF
P/O E Batchelor	F/Sgt A R Campbell RNZAF
P/O R E Stout RNZAF	Sgt C H Fox RNZAF
P/O G W Underwood	Sgt M A McRae RAAF
P/O J W Monk RCAF (US)	Sgt D P Robertson
P/O L C C Hawkins	Sgt A W Bedford
P/O R A Prince	Sgt A W Arrowsmith RNZAF
2/Lt G A Booysen SAAF	Sgt J R Sergeant

Chapter Seven

Rangoon and Burma

Everything was a shambles. For over a month the Japanese had been in almost complete control of events in the Far East having caught Allied forces on the wrong foot. No sooner had they attacked the US naval base at Pearl Harbor, Hawaii, plunging America into the war as well as forcing war onto the British, than they had struck at Malaya, a British protectorate.

They had bombed the British base at Singapore, then sunk the Royal Navy's capital ships the *Prince of Wales* and *Repulse* by air attack. Hong Kong island had surrendered on Christmas Day, and the same day they bombed Rangoon for the second time in three days. Then came the invasion of Malaya, landings made north of Singapore effectively cutting off the British garrison from the north. On 8 January 1942 the Japanese landed on Borneo and two days later Kuala Lumpur, Malaya, was evacuated. On the 12th came a major daylight air attack on Singapore and then targets in Burma were hit.

Jimmy Elsdon had had a struggle to get to Rangoon. Initially left in Cairo to oversee the arrival of Hurricane aircraft, he eventually got hold of eight machines – in desert brown camouflage – and led by a Blenheim for navigation headed for Burma on 14 January, along the route, Lydda, Habbaniya, Bahrain (where one Hurricane was lost while landing), Sharjah, Jiwani, Karachi (second Hurricane lost due to oil pressure problems), Jodhpur, Delhi (where a 'famous' formation flight was requested over the city by the CinC India to uplift civilian morale), Allahabad, Dum Dum (Calcutta), Toungoo, Mingaladon. The first four machines landed on the 24th at about 10 am local time. The Blenheim had become u/s somewhere in India, so the last section of the flight was achieved without its navigational help.

One of Elsdon's pilots was Alan Kitley, and it was he who had the unfortunate crash at Bahrain, as he recalled in his book *Take Mary to the Pictures*. It is worth mentioning that Kit Kitley had just 250 flying hours in his log book:

'We had considered the implications of the trip to Rangoon. The journey envisaged landings at [various] airfields. The distance was some 5,500 miles and each stage was between 5-600 miles.

'Our radios would not be fitted until we reached Karachi so it was essential that we stay in close flight so that we could, if necessary, communicate by hand signals. If we had to force land in the desert we would need water, so we had put bottles of water in any space available. We did not even have one complete set of aeronautical maps to cover the journey and would have to rely on picking up maps as we went along.

'The real drama of the journey, as far as I was concerned, was landing at Bahrain in the Persian Gulf. Bahrain was a small airfield with no runways and subject to tidal flooding. A wall varying in height from, I believe, some one to two feet had been built to stop the sea encroaching onto the airfield; it would have been helpful if someone had told us this. Anyway, I approached the landing in a section of two, led by the squadron commander, and in open formation. My eyes were on his aircraft as we landed, with my Hurricane some thirty yards behind and to the right. I looked ahead on touchdown and congratulated myself on a smooth and safe landing. The next second all hell broke loose. I hit the wall, which I believe was some two feet high at this point and hidden by drifting sand, at some 100 mph; the undercarriage was ripped off, the nose of the aircraft tipped into the ground shattering the propeller and, if I recall correctly, the Hurricane somersaulted with bits breaking off leaving me at rest in the cockpit protected by the engine.

'The squadron commander, upset that he had lost a Hurricane, was not in "star worshipping" mood. He did however concede that the accident was not entirely my fault. The next day we set out for Sharjah with me as a passenger and cramped up in the gun turret of the Blenheim.'

A couple of airfields later one of the other pilots became ill, so Kit was able to get back into a Hurricane cockpit and complete the journey in happier fashion. Just as well once the Blenheim became u/s. Another problem on the way was the lack of petrol at one stop, the pilots having to wait until a train of twenty camels turned up carrying the precious liquid. Even then the small airfield only had a couple of hand operated petrol pumps and the pilots had to refuel the aircraft by hand – some 1,400 gallons.

Some way behind – by about three days – was another small

formation of 136 Squadron, being led out with Barry Sutton in charge.

The first three of 17 Squadron's Hurricanes arrived from the Middle East on 23 January – Mark IIA which carried twelve .303 machine guns rather than the usual eight in the Mark I. This was fine from a hitting point of view but did not help manoeuvrability. Possibly acceptable in a ground-attack role, but unhelpful in fighter combat, so four of the guns were immediately removed. Later Hurricane arrivals were little better, and were certainly not new. At least one had recorded in its Form 700 – 'unfit for operational flying' – while in another it was noted, 'fit for training use only'. A case of air commanders in the Middle East getting rid of their unwanted rubbish.

It should be remembered too that all these pilots arriving at Rangoon found conditions very different from what they had been used to. All had seen some sort of operational flying in England or over France, but Burma was vastly different. The weather was tremendously dissimilar from northern Europe for a start. The sun shone brightly from a piercingly blue sky in which enemy fighters could lurk. It was hot and humid. On the ground one was almost constantly bathed in sweat, clothes clinging to the body with irritating regularity. Those early arrivals had to adapt to these conditions quickly if they were to have any chance of survival. The airfields too were generally pretty primitive, and dusty.

Within a couple of days there was an attack on Mingaladon, as Bunny Stone recalled in his memoirs:

> '...we were in the mess on the aerodrome having a mid-day drink (all pilots regardless of rank) when someone looked around the corner and shouted, "Christ, Bloody Nips. Scramble!" About 30 fighters coming in over the trees with their guns firing. Frank Carey dashed over to man the Ack-Ack Lewis gun and we baled out into the slit trench outside. I was the last one in, with bullets nipping at my heels, and landed right on top of dear old Seton Broughall, our Canadian Group Captain. I remember him shouting above the racket, "Bunny you silly bugger, you've spilt my pink gin!"'

It is fascinating to imagine Frank Carey manning a Lewis gun on the airfield, but there is no other information about this event unfortunately. Once the first few Hurricanes had arrived, Carey and the pilots set themselves up at Mingaladon airfield. No sooner had they done so than they were called to a conference with the AOC at 221 Group HQ – Air Vice-Marshal D F Stevenson CB DSO MC – who proposed that the four newly arrived Hurricanes, as soon as they could be made ready, should take off and attack the Japanese airfield at Bangkok. The four pilots looked back in shocked silence, then started to protest, but the AOC justified his plan on the grounds that Jimmy Elsdon had adequately demonstrated the suitability of the Hurricane for such a role during a formation display over HQ at Delhi two days earlier! Just how the AOC came to this conclusion is not recorded, but probably it was really the distance they had flown which had impressed him. Another reason the pilots were not keen was that long-range tanks used for the recent trip were bolted on, not ones that could be jettisoned. They quite understandably did not relish mixing it with enemy fighters over Bangkok with such an adornment.

The AOC, taken aback, said he would reconsider his idea with his staff and the pilots were dismissed back to Mingaladon, but they were not to un-bolt the tanks until told to do so. What happened next, of course, is not difficult to guess. A report of approaching enemy aircraft, with four Hurricanes still with fixed tanks at readiness. Jimmy Esldon, Bunny Stone, Fuggy Fuge and Pennington-Legh scrambled, along with some P40s from the AVG – known as the Flying Tigers. These were American volunteer pilots fighting as mercenaries for the Chinese. This American Volunteer Group had three squadrons, but only two were based here, the other was in China. They flew Curtiss P40 Tomahawks.

It took the Hurricanes a quarter of an hour to reach 6,000 feet because of the tanks and then above them the pilots saw a mass of Japanese aircraft. Stone pulled up to engage but then the enemy fighters – they were Army 97s of the 50th Sentai – were coming down on him. While he tried to engage them, the other three – seeing themselves at a disadvantage – wisely headed down. Stone's Hurricane was hit in the starboard long-range tank – thankfully empty – and then one of his ailerons flew off. With other fighters queuing up to attack, Stone did his utmost to provide a difficult target, quickly discovering how manoeuvrable those enemy fighters were. Finally he pulled up into the sun, stall turned out of it and dived over the estuary, hiding amongst the shipping, before making a shaky landing at Mingaladon without further injury to his precious aeroplane.

The 50th Sentai lost two aircraft, both claimed by the Americans, while 67 Squadron's two Buffalo machines that had been in the air, got caught and lost one. The Army Type 97 was what the Allies called the Nakajima Ki-27. It was a low-wing monoplane with fixed spatted undercarriage. It had already been used by the Japanese in China and Manchuria, having proved a versatile and very manoeuvrable fighter. It was armed with two 7.7 mm machine guns.

The new pilots were not overly impressed with their immediate superior officer. This was not an unusual trait amongst operational pilots, but they seemed to have a point as Bunny Stone recalled in his memoirs following that first combat:

> 'I then insisted that the AOC come and see my aircraft. Having not fired a shot, there was the bottom of the starboard long-range tank ripped out, the starboard aileron and God knows what else. He gave me reluctant permission to remove the tanks. He had a bomber command mentality, having been AOC No.2 Group, Bomber Command in England, and had little or no knowledge of the role of fighters.'

However, the saga was far from over. The AOC may have agreed that the tanks could be removed – in case the aircraft needed to be scrambled – but having reconsidered his desire to attack Bangkok, ordered them to be re-fitted. Bunny Stone calculated that with their target being 350 miles away, the time the Hurricanes could be over the target in order to have enough fuel to get back, was three minutes.

Headquarters thought Bunny should lead the mission and that he should nominate the other pilots. He chose one of the senior flight commanders, Frank, and one other. Common sense prevailed in the end, helped by someone in HQ realising that there was every chance of losing the three most experienced fighter pilots then in Burma, and the operation was quietly forgotten.

Bunny later recounted his first brush with the AOC, describing him as a 'bland individual whom everyone quickly nicknamed "Old Boy"', this being the way he greeted everyone. His 2 Group Blenheim squadrons had called him 'Butcher' after suffering several casualties on raids he sent them on.

On the day Frank had arrived at Rangoon, Tavoy fell to the enemy, a base just across the Gulf of Martaban from Rangoon.

Jack Storey, an Australian, who had arrived at Rangoon with Frank, wrote:

> 'Frank Carey and I were the first of 135 Squadron to arrive; we flew in by flying boat. There were also the COs of 136 and 17 Squadrons, with just three or four Hurricanes. Other aircraft were ferried in subsequently from the Middle East – the Hurricanes with long-range tanks and escorted by a Blenheim.
>
> 'The situation was confused. Some of the senior officers went up on a scramble to meet the Japs and some of the aircraft had been damaged. There was great consternation as

to how to deal with these Japanese fighters which were quite extraordinarily manoeuvrable. The conditions were so different from the Battle of Britain type of combat. New tactics had to be evolved.

'We had a nucleus of RAF, the AVG and the Buffaloes of 67 Squadron but it took a long time really for the Hurricanes to get going – about four or five days – because the spares situation was bad.

'Our warning system was very primitive. The initial part consisted of spotters over on the Moulmein side of the Gulf of Martaban, who would telephone by land line across to Rangoon. They would tell us if Jap squadrons were building up and setting off towards us. That gave us about 20 minutes' warning and we would take off and endeavour to meet them. The Rangoon radar would take over but I think they had their serviceability problems because they found it almost impossible to give us vectors or heights.

'On the quality of Japanese pilots, we had been told and we had read – in rather silly articles – that they couldn't fly and they couldn't see! But we quickly found out that we were up against some of the most experienced pilots in the world. These men had been fighting in China for up to six years and many of them had long lists of victories. They were superb shots, because even with their very limited armament they seemed to be scoring hits on our aircraft repeatedly, and of course, shooting the odd aircraft down. It came as a great concern to all of us that many of our experienced pilots were shot down in the first few days.'

Frank, Jimmy Elsdon, Bunny Stone, Jack Storey, Alan Kitley and Fuggy Fuge – with the first handful of Hurricanes – were keen to get started but were utterly overwhelmed by the task that confronted them. Aircraft were still in short supply, ground crews and spares were still stretched out across various routes heading for Rangoon, and while on paper there were four squadrons available plus the AVG, there were hardly enough pilots, men or aircraft, to equip a single flight. Frank recalled much later:

'What I remember most of the Japanese campaign was the appalling lack of facilities we had to deal with. No spares, no tools, no equipment. Sometimes to get an engine out we wheeled a 'plane under a palm tree, pulled the tree down, tied it to the engine and slowly released it. Much of the time we had to "cannibalise" one aircraft for spares. The main ops room at Rangoon was in a road culvert under a little bridge and control had to look out to see what was happening in the air above. Our mobile radar vehicle had barely more than a few miles range.

'Originally we had to use the ordinary telephone system to get warnings: some brave local chaps used to sit and watch the action at Moulmein airfield, because in the early days the Japanese had no other aerodrome available within fighter range of where we were at Rangoon. These chaps used to report by telephone when there was flying activity. It was important for us to know if there was any flying at all, because the Japs would often retire back into Thailand for anything up to about a week and then come forward and throw everything they had at us again.'

Some years ago, Jimmy Elsdon gave me a copy of the squadron history he had written. He refers to the poor conditions facing him and his brother squadron commanders:

'The ground crews, few in number, were very hard pressed to keep such aircraft as the squadron had in a serviceable condition and they did a marvellous job with very limited facilities and tools at their disposal. Replacement parts, when needed, were taken off other aircraft which were unservice-able for some other reason and very soon the squadron possessed two "Christmas Trees" – aircraft used solely for spare parts.

'As much work on the aircraft as possible was done in the early morning, before the sun dispersed the early morning mist and the aircraft became almost impossibly hot to work on.'

In Frank's case, with his previous knowledge from being a fitter, it was not unknown for him to buckle down and help service his own Hurricane, thus releasing an airman for other work.

In Frank's flying log book he records his first flight and first action in Burma as being on 3 February 1942, in Hurricane BM914. How-ever, for some reason this is in error, no doubt because he was far too busy to write-up his log daily and by the time he got a moment to do it, times, days and dates had become something of a blur.

The actual date of his first action was 26 January, squadron records noting that the CO flew an operation with 17(sic) Squadron, although it was, presumably, 136 Squadron. The diary also records that a Japanese aircraft had over-flown Zayatkwin on the 23rd followed by a bombing raid the next day which killed two members of the Burma Rifles (airfield defence) and wounded two more. This, they were to find, was a routine Japanese tactic; reconnoitre one day, attack the next. Then came Frank's first sortie on the 26th, a scramble in company with Flight Lieutenant F B Sutton, of 136 and with whom Frank had swum on Christmas Day, but they saw nothing. On the 28th 135 Squadron moved to Mingaladon.

On the 29th – Thursday – came Frank's first combat. Bunny Stone wrote of Frank at this time:

> 'He (Carey) was browned-off with seeing everybody else shoot things down and could he do some of my readiness? I was only too pleased as Barry Sutton and I were on most of the time. He had no sooner taken over when the old sirens started their dismal noise. The same mad scramble into the air – it always gave me the jitters as everyone took off from their own dispersals and it was only by the grace of God there were no accidents. We came to an arrangement with the AVG in the end – we held down to the end of the runway and they pulled up over us – this worked very well in practice but was extremely hair-raising. I got into a trench behind the mess and waited.
>
> 'There was about 6/10ths cumulus cloud at about 5,000 feet. Soon the air began to vibrate with the beat of high-flying aircraft; the long-drawn-out crescendo of diving fighters; the deep crash of the .5s; the slow staccato rattle of the Jap's two 'Vickers', and occasionally the tearing calico of the Hurricane's Brownings. The fight got nearer – just south-east of the field; now and then two aircraft would dive down between the clouds, one to go into the paddy and explode in a mushroom of black smoke, the other pulling up and away.'

Six Hurricanes got off plus some P40s. Frank was in BE171 and Jack Storey was flying BD921. This was Frank's second sortie from Rangoon, and Jack Storey's first. Jack Storey told me:

> 'We went into action, Squadron Leader Carey and myself, flying through cloud to 22,000 feet. Saw six enemy fighters below against the surface of the cloud at 12,000 feet. Rolled over and dived at 400 mph to attack. As we approached their range, they went into cloud. We swept up into the sun, rolled over and saw them come up through the cloud again. They now started circling and two seemed to get separated from the rest. At this moment the AVG and their Tomahawks

started dog-fighting. As we swept down for our second attack, I saw three enemy aircraft behind one P40 that was easily out-turned. We came down in a steep right-hand spiral at 310 [mph] this time and selected one enemy aircraft each. I got two steady bursts into mine, hits were observed and it slipped off into the cloud to the left. Our ground crews could hear the firing and saw an enemy fighter dive out of the cloud and crash near a Blenheim. The rest got away in the cloud. Two AVG were lost, one force-landed at base with bullet holes in the head and leg. Neither of our Hurricanes was hit.'

Meantime, Frank had latched onto his victim, fired as his sight encircled the fighter, and watched as it turned over on its back then went straight down. On the ground, Bunny Stone was still looking at the action above and later recorded:

'Things were more or less over when a "97" came gliding down with his motor stopped. He suddenly winged over and with his guns going, made straight for one of 113 [Squadron's] Blenheims in a pen – he must have missed it by inches and piled himself up in the corner. There was a line of .303s right across the left-hand side of his torso, so it was given to Frank.'

The AVG had had two P40s shot down but claimed to have knocked down an amazing 14 Japanese aircraft. The Ki-27s had been from the 77th Sentai, led by Major Yoshio Hirose and had lost four aircraft. They in turn had claimed at least ten 'Spitfires' and some P40s, not bad considering there were no Spitfires yet in Burma.

The Japanese pilot that had tried to crash into the Blenheim, had been Sergeant Major Nagashima, one of four Japanese losses. Inspecting his remains afterwards, five bullets had been found in his side. It is not certain if he had been hit by Frank or Jack, but in any event, they were both credited with two of the Ki-27s shot down over the airfield, and Frank had claimed a second one damaged. At the time Frank was of the opinion it had been him who had hit the fighter that tried to crash into the Blenheim, as he later recalled:

'The enemy aircraft were incredibly more manoeuvrable than we were. If we got down and mixed it with them at low altitude we were in trouble because we couldn't accelerate away from them unless we had a bit of height to dive away and therefore they could run rings round us. The Japs were at that stage flying fixed undercarriage monoplanes called Army

97s [Ki-27]. They were extremely light for their weight and had very powerful engines, but not much in the way of gunfire. They also didn't have any armour plating behind them. If you got a good squirt at them they used to fold up. Later they re-equipped with Army 0.2 Oscar fighters. These were faster, more manoeuvrable, but also suffered from the same lack of guns and armoured protection.

'They really worked those Jap pilots. One I shot down and then followed, deliberately crash-landed trying to dive into a revetment with a Blenheim in it. He missed. We got the whole aircraft and body and everything else. He'd got 27 bullets in him and he was still flying that thing round the airfield looking for a target. Incredible. They were always trying to dive into something; that was what we were up against.

'The big difficulty with the Japanese aircraft, though, was trying to find them. Frequently they seemed to disappear from the area altogether and then re-appear in some strength for several days. I personally never had any success at night, not even on moonlight nights. It used to make me mad. I just couldn't find them although other chaps seem to have got the knack. They used to fly from about full moon to half moon. We used to call it a "Japanese moon" period. In Burma you could navigate easily at night and land without any flares during those periods.'

Another sortie not written-up in his log book is a scramble on 31 January. Six Hurricanes were sent up, four being flown by Messrs Carey, Kitley, Stone and Elsdon, who were ordered to patrol above Mingaladon until told otherwise. Five Ki-27s were suddenly encountered, one of which shot away the aerial mast of the Hurricane flown by Kit Kitley. He had been climbing, the Ki-27 diving on him from out of the sun. The others saw no sign of the Japs and eventually landed.

On 1 February Frank had a mock dogfight with a Buffalo of 67 Squadron (once again not recorded in his log), flown by Sergeant Gordon Williams. Frank found the performance of the stubby Brewster machine amazingly superior to his Hurricane above 20,000 feet. At around 16,000 feet they were on a par, below that the Hurricane was all over the Buffalo.

Two more sorties on the 3rd, neither of which Frank thought to enter into his log book. The first was an escort to three Blenheims with four Hurricanes against Moulmein airfield. Then Frank and Jack Storey flew a recce mission, while later still came a scramble over

Top left: Frank Carey as an angelic choirboy, aged 10.

Top right: When Carey arrived on 43 Squadron as a pilot, his flight commander was F/Lt R I G MacDougall, seen here in the centre. Others are from left to right: Lorry Lorimer, Caesar Hull, T J Fitton and A R L Griffiths.

Middle: Hawker Fury machines showing 43 Squadron's chequered markings. Note that the bottom fuselage square next to the roundel, has the reflection of the lower wing, confirming that the 'white' squares were actually the silver-doped fabric.

Left: Squadron formation – the famous 'vics'.

Top left: On the back of this picture Frank had written: 'Yours truly burning up the skies and shooting up an Avro Anson which took this snap – good shooting eh?'

Top right: Last days with the Fury, which have now been camouflaged. Preparing for the final Fury formation flight, A Flt on left, B Flt on right. L to r: H J L Hallowes, G P Christie, FRC, J I Kilmartin, C A Rotherham, C B Hull, Pennington-Legh, J L Sullivan, M K Carswell, S/L R E Bain, F E Rosier, J W C Simpson, P Folkes, P A N Cox and F G Berry.

Middle left: One of the first two Hurricanes to be delivered to 43 Squadron – L1725. It was lost on 15 December 1939, Sgt Arbuthnott baling after losing control in cloud.

Middle right: 43's Hurricanes during Daily Express Show.

Bottom: NCO pilots, May 1939. From left to right: J Arbuthnott, F F G Berry, P G Ottewill and A C Shawyer. In front: H J L Hallowe

left: Some of 43's officers, May 1939. J W C
~pson, -?-, C A Woods-Scawen, W C Wilkinson
~ P Le Rougetel.

~right: Flight Lieutenant F R Carey DFC & Bar,
~M, 1940.

~dle left: Acklington dispersal, winter of 1939-40.
~ T A H Gough (KIA Dunkirk), Tony Woods-
~wen on guitar (KIA Battle of Britain) and FRC.

Middle right: FRC's Hurricane L1932 which he
used exclusively in France with 3 Squadron,
May 1940.

Bottom: A familiar picture showing FRC's
fellow pilots during the Battle of Britain.
L to r: John Arbuthnott, Robert Plenderleith,
Jim Hallowes, John Simpson, Peter Townsend
and Hamilton Upton.

Top left: The Ju88 of 4/LG1 shot down by Frank and others on 15 August 1940. By the tail is farmer Jim Cheeseman, Mr Cousins by rear fuselage, then two RAF airmen, Don Cheeseman (dark jacket) the farm owner's son, unknown, then unknown RAF men. The civilian rear right is Harry Bowler.

Top right: Officers of 43 Squadron outside the Tangmere Mess after lunch on 7 September 1940. Left to right: Upton, Marshall, Caesar Hull, George Lott, FRC, FL R C Reynell, D G Gorrie, W/Cdr Jack Boret (station commander), I G Kilmartin, and an army liaison major. Later that afternoon, Hull and Reynell were both killed in action.

Middle: Squadron Leader Carey with his pilots, 135 Squadron, Honiley 1941. FRC is first left on the wing, while next to him in his dark Australian uniform is Jack Storey. The first five identified in the front row are: Guy Underwood, Lee C C Hawkins, R A Prince, E J Watkins and R E Stout.

Above: FRC was among those pilots drawn by war artist Eric Kennington, the date being 31 January 1941.

*: FRC in front of his Hurricane at Honiley
·1. Note the Czech flying badge on his right
ast pocket.

ldle, left: Squadron Leader A C 'Bunny'
ne DFC, OC 17 Squadron, Rangoon.

ldle, centre: Squadron Leader T A F 'Jimmy'
·lon DFC, OC 136 Squadron, Rangoon.

Middle, right: Two of the early pilots of 136
Squadron to arrive in Burma were D E 'Fuggy'
Fuge (left) and Ken 'Ting' Bunting.

Bottom left: One of the first Hurricanes to arrive at
Mingaladon – with fixed long-range fuel tanks.

Bottom right: Another early 'Woodpecker' (136
Sqn) pilot to arrive in Burma was Alan 'Kit' Kitley.

Top left: Australian 'Bush' Cotton,
17 Squadron and 136's Barry Sutton.

Top right: FRC at Mingaladon. Far
right is Jack Storey. The other two
are believed to be Ken Bunting and
Barry Sutton.

Middle left: The Japanese fighter
which after being hit in combat
attempted a suicide crash into a
Blenheim on Mingaladon airfield,
29 January 1942.

Middle right: FRC in jeep at
Mingaladon with S/Ldr R H 'Bob'
Neale of the AVG. Note Curtiss P40
Tomahawk in the background.
Despite the serious situation Frank
never lost his smile.

Right: Guy Underwood, 135
Squadron, shot down over
Moulmein, after knocking a Ki-27
off of Carey's tail, 26 February 1942.

op left: Smoke rising from Mingaladon airfield.

op right: Officers' quarters at Rangoon where RC and others lived for 17 days until the retreat n 7 March 1942.

Middle left: Despite desperate and harassing times, RC can still smile at the camera – Magwe, urma, March 1942.

Middle right: Alipore, April 1942. Left to right: FRC, His Excellency the Governor of Bengal, Sir John Herbert, Air Vice-Marshal D F Stephenson CBE MC DFC, AOC Bengal; at the rear is Air Commodore J L Vachell MC, SASO, Air HQ, India.

Bottom: Flight Hut at Alipore, May 1942.

Top left: Dispersal, Chittagong, April 1943.

Top right: Quite a variety of dress! Ken Hemingway, Bush Cotton and FRC ready for tennis.

Middle left: Three senior staff at Jessore, after the retreat: S/Ldr B L Duckenfield AFC, OC 615 Squadron, G/Capt Seton Broughall MC DFC, who had been station commander at Mingaladon, and Wing Commander H M Stephen DSO DFC, Wing Commander Flying at Dum Dum.

Middle right: Hurricane landing on the Red Road, Calcutta.

Right: Hurricanes dispersed among the trees by Red Road, Calcutta.

Top left: A burst tyre and the camber of Red Road, let Gordon Conway of 136 Squadron down, and he careered into the balustrade.

Top right: Taking a break. FRC off for a ride while at Darjeeling. The building is the Planter's Club.

Middle left: Pilots of 136 Squadron, a few of whom are mentioned within these pages. L to r: D J 'Barney' Barnett, Frank Wilding, A N Constantine (CO), A Gordon Conway and Dennis Garvan.

Middle right: FRC hobbling round after injuring his ankle during a football match, Amarda Road, 1944.

Left: FRC in the Officer's Mess at Amarda Road. Note the scene of London on the wall mural.

Top left: Robin Hedderwick, one of Frank's instructors at Amarda Road, with Frank in the latter's jeep. Marcus Townsend and Willetts sit in back.

Top right: FRC after an aerobatic demo, Amarda Road.

Middle left: 'Big White Hunter' – that leopard, Orissa, June 1944.

Middle right: 'FRC – the well-dressed wingco' – by his car (note RAF roundel on the bonnet's nose) with local dignitaries, Orissa, 1944.

Right: 'All work and no play …' FRC, in his well-worn slouch hat, helping to play the fool at Amarda Road, although unhappily the reason for the event is unknown.

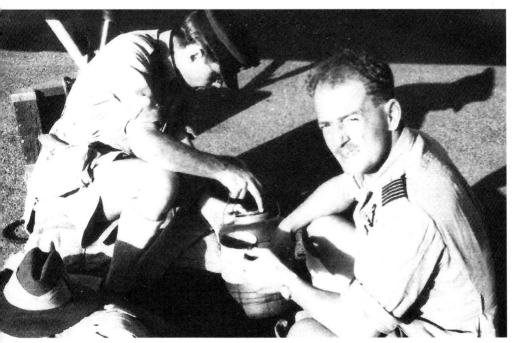

Top: Frank's Spitfire VIII (JG560) at AFTU, 1944. It had a red nose and a red fuselage flash to aid identification in the air – by his pupils!

Bottom: A look which says it all. Frank caught having a brew on 26 October 1944, the day he left India in a Liberator for the Middle East.

Top: FRC's quarters at Fayid – with bearer!

Middle: Nobby Clark DFC was the CFI at Fayid. Here he instructs a sergeant pilot in the arts, in front of a Harvard.

Bottom: Frank's all-black Thunderbolt (KJ348) at Fayid, again with a red fuselage stripe, red nose and ace of spades marking.

Top left: F W T 'Bill' Davis was one of Frank's instructors at Fayid, seen here in front of a Thunderbolt with a better view of the ace of spades marking, plus skull.

Top right: FRC up in the rafters in the Officer's Mess during a party at Fayid.

Middle: FRC in a Tempest II (PR674) at Gütersloh, 1948. Note wing commander's pennant. The practise rockets have concrete heads.

Left: FRC at Gütersloh by a Vampire V, in 1949.

Top left: Frank noted on the back of this photo: 'Fully legalised low flying by self over Nottingham Town Hall to advertise Battle of Britain Show at RAF Newton, September 1950'.

Top right: A post-war 136 Squadron reunion. Jimmy Elsdon and Frank talk about old times.

Bottom left: Frank's loyal driver – and friend – in Australia, Ted Evans.

Bottom right: FRC in full war-paint, Australia.

Top left: At the Rolls-Royce stand in Sydney, talking to Governor-General of Australia, Lord de Lisle. Frank wrote on the back: 'His Excellency Lord de Lisle looks very disbelieving of my story!'

Top right: FRC fishing on Lake Taupo, New Zealand, February 1969. His daughter Jane was not at all surprised to see he is wearing jacket and tie!

Left: Frank and his nephew, S/Ldr David Carey, who was with Search and Rescue. The helicopter is a Sea King, and they had just flown over RAF Tangmere, September 1990.

Above: Frank talks to Ken Cresswell, one of 43's pre-war ground crew, at a 43 reunion at the RAF Club in London.

Top left: Frank and Kate, Peurto Pollenca, Majorca, October 1991.

Top right: FRC and Heather Franks, the author's wife, Majorca, May 1992, shortly after Frank's 80th birthday.

Middle: Frank back in the cockpit of a Hawker Hurricane, Brooklands, June 2000.

Right: Frank's medals and flying log book. CBE, DFC and two Bars, AFC, DFM, 1939-45 Star with BofB clasp, Air Crew Europe Star, Burma Star, Defence Medal, War Medal, Coronation Medal, American Silver Star.

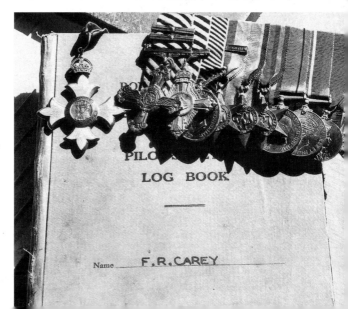

Rangoon. Frank did note this one in his log. Jack Storey related:

'3rd February 1942: The CO and I patrolled Moulmein on a reconnaissance. Approached the area at 25,000 feet, did figure of eights down to 3,000 and swept down to nought feet, and returned across the sea to base. Led Red Section on a scramble at mid-day; orbited base up-sun at 25,000 feet – no joy.'

Bunny Stone came to grief on this day. He had flown up to Toungoo with Sergeant D C Cropper, where they were subjected to a bombing raid. Stone's machine was then found to have a glycol leak so he took Cropper's aircraft for the flight home, leaving his companion to follow once the leak had been repaired.

Heading back to Mingaladon, Stone lost his direction and with his fuel running out had to make a landing somewhere. He chose a sand bar alongside the Irrawaddy river, with wheels down, and was just coming to a halt when the undercarriage collapsed. He had hit a ridge of soft sand that he had not observed from the air. He organised some local villagers to look after the sorry-looking Hurricane, and returned by various routes to Rangoon, which took him some days.

There was a scramble and a recce mission on the 4th, but with Frank making an error in his log for this date, it is unclear if he was involved in either. However, on the 5th, Frank led an escort mission with three other fighters to three Blenheims attacking Pa-An, a Japanese base just north of Moulmein. No enemy aircraft were encountered and in consequence Frank was able to confirm some good bombing results. That same afternoon Frank and his pilots escorted five Blenheims in a raid on Moulmein, Frank reporting 'a good beat-up'.

Next day came another escort followed by strafing runs by the Hurricanes on the airfield at Pa-An. That afternoon he flew to the satellite airstrip that had been named 'Johnnie Walker', situated just north of the city, which RAF light bombers used. The squadron were using it to disperse their aircraft rather than risk damage from night bombing. However, the Japs visited the main airfield at 09.00 but did little damage. Jack Storey and some others scrambled and three raiders were claimed shot down with three more damaged.

Frank and Jack were on night readiness on the 7th and although scrambled twice, made no contact. Little help came from fighter control.

This day Frank was promoted to a wing leader, handing over 135 Squadron to Barry Sutton. The AOC was making some changes starting with Frank. He was made acting/wing commander in charge of 267 Wing, but as he himself recalled, it was hardly a wing in the normal sense:

'I was made wing commander ops., which was silly really as we didn't have enough aircraft to form a wing. One day I recall, we had one aircraft on defence at Rangoon, one aircraft escorting two or three Blenheims on a raid, and another flying a patrol covering a boat. However, the AOC decided he wanted it and he was going to talk to Claire Chennault who ran the AVG, that he wanted me to run all the aircraft of the RAF plus the AVG for a period of a week, then hand over to a chap called Bob Neale, one of his COs, so he could run it for a week, although they weren't going to promote Neale to [an equivalent rank of] lieutenant-colonel.

'It was crazy. How could we work together in the air – we had no common radio frequency? After some thought we started with a Hurricane flying in a formation of P40s while we took a P40 with us, and we communicated with each group that way. Of course, only the two odd pilots would have any idea what the other formation was doing, and that pilot could not tell the pilots flying about him.'

Jack Storey recalls that farce too:

'Because the RAF and AVG operated on different radio frequencies, once the aircraft were airborne, we could not speak to each other. On one or two occasions this led to an embarrassing encounter where we had dived down to attack what we thought were EA, only to find they were the AVG. In order to get over this problem it became advisable for a single Hurricane to fly with the AVG formation. I did this on a few occasions and in that way you would keep R/T contact and if things looked as if they would become complicated – a flight of Hurricanes diving towards you – you could tell them that this was the AVG and they'd better fire elsewhere.'

A few days later the AOC set up 'X' Wing Headquarters in order to control all fighter and bomber operations to support the army, giving command of this to Group Captain N C Singer. Meantime, 221 Group became Norgroup. The three Rangoon Hurricane squadrons, 17, 135 and 136, plus 67's Buffaloes, could now boast 31 aircraft between them, although 67 was down to a mere five! The two Blenheim squadrons were 45 and 113, with some 27 aircraft.

Frank led a bomber escort and sweep to Pa-An and Moulmein on the 9th, ending up with a strafing attack on the airfield but was then kept on the ground for a few days whilst trying to set up the wing thing. He was back in the air on the 15th, for another bomber escort and strafe on Thaton and D'zeik, on the coast west of Pa-An.

Life was becoming busy and hectic. He flew to Zayatkwin for a conference on the 17th, then flew back in order to escort Blenheims on a raid upon Chieng Mai, well over 200 miles north east of Rangoon, in Thailand. They all made it, but Frank noted in his log – 'landed with 2 gallons petrol – phew!' The problem was that they had not appreciated or been told that due to the heat, fuel evaporated at a greater rate than in the UK so that flight duration was much less. His next flight to Chieng Mai – in March – was to prove even more of a problem as we shall read.

A night scramble on the 18th gave Frank no joy, only grief. He was bombed while taking off and whilst landing back! This was followed by yet another bomber escort on the 19th with more strafing runs, this time to Martaban and Moulmein. Two sorties on the 20th, a raid to Bilin Basin, north of Kayaikto, and Poonjis, then another night scramble during which he was again bombed whilst taking off.

An unpleasant target was presented to them the next day. The Japanese were still moving relentlessly northwards up the Malay coast using every type of transport they could get hold of. Many troop movements had been spotted in the Salween area, the Japanese using elephants through jungle trails, and barges on the Salween river, which ran north from Moulmein. Neither were difficult to hit but to strafe elephants....!

Something of a respite followed, with just two flights to and from another airstrip, 'John Haig' (someone liked their whiskey – there were others strips named 'Black & White', 'Highland Queen', 'Dewar' and for those who didn't take it neat, 'Canadian Club') again just north of Rangoon. His main Hurricane since early February was BM914, which in Air Britain's list is noted as only being with 261 Squadron and was eventually 'struck off charge' in July 1944. Presumably it was given to 261 after the retreat from Burma and I wonder if they knew which illustrious pilot had used it before them.

The Japanese were now advancing rapidly and the British were, if not in full retreat, heading north fairly fast. The RAF at Rangoon were told to maintain air superiority for as long as possible and give as much support and air cover to the army as they could. Hurricanes were now going out and strafing any Japanese troops and transports they could find, inflicting some heavy casualties in doing so. The Sittang river was now the only major barrier to the Japanese coming up from the south. Once across that, Rangoon was not far to the west.

Frank scored again on the 23rd. He led a fighter sweep over the Sittang bridge following a report of Japanese aircraft to the south east. They found seven enemy machines over Kayaikto, but just before these were spotted, Frank saw an aircraft below and went to investigate. He found what he later thought was a Navy 97 two-seater recce plane, which he promptly despatched into the jungle. It was in fact a Mitsubishi Ki-51 (Army type 97), another machine with fixed spatted undercarriage, and used for tactical reconnaissance. It was flying only about 50 feet above the trees, obviously keeping tabs on both the retreating British and the pursuing Japanese soldiers. The machine was from the 70th Independent Chutai, flown by Captain Tadao Ohhira, who was following orders to reconnoitre the east bank of the Sittang. The Ki-51 crashed in flames, Ohhira and his observer both being killed, and later buried by advancing Japanese troops.

Meantime, Jack Storey, flying above with other Hurricanes, shot down one fighter whose pilot seemed unaware of his presence. It was not all one-sided, for in a later sortie led by Barry Sutton, there was a skirmish with some Ki-27s from the 50th Sentai, which led to the loss of Flight Lieutenant Watson, last seen with two Japanese fighters on his tail. Jack wrote up this action in his diary:

> 23 Feb 1942. Scramble. Seven EA over Kayaikto – Flight Commander was killed. My luck to get an Army 97 fighter which crashed at Kayaikto. This was interesting because we first found a single recce aircraft – a two-seater – down at 50 feet. He must have been patrolling over the army, seeing the situation there. Carey went after it and got him and while this was going on I happened to notice out of the corner of my eye, six fighters coming in from my left. I and my No.2 set off after these. My man was a bit of a push-over for he was out to the right of the formation, curving around slowly, away from me, looking to see where the recce aircraft had gone and I got him very smartly. I got in an astern attack – I don't think he even saw me – and he was set on fire, crashed and burned in the trees, from about 50 feet.'

Frank began a second sortie on this day, a bomber escort, but his engine suddenly cut out as he took off; however he managed to get back down without too much difficulty. Because of this, Frank was flying BM842 the next day, leading a raid on Moulmein airfield, in company with AVG P40s.

At mid-day the AVG attacked Raheng airfield, claiming two bombers destroyed on the ground. An hour later, Frank, Jimmy Elsdon and Bunny Stone, plus a fourth Hurricane, flew out with two Tomahawks to attack Moulmein. Coming in over the airfield boundary, Frank spotted an aircraft that he described as '...similar to a Dakota...' in the act of taking off. As it cleared the runway, Frank's bullets found it and it plunged back onto the ground. Almost immediately he saw a Ki-27 lifting off and giving this a burst as he flashed past, claimed this one too as it ploughed into the ground.

Stone also claimed a bomber and a fighter destroyed on the ground, but records of the 47th Independent Chutai note just one Ki-27 damaged, although there does not appear to be any 'transport' unit records that survive to confirm Frank's first claim. From his description, it could possibly have been a Mitsubishi Ki-57, or even a Nakajima Ki-34.

Yet another bomber escort on the 25th, Frank flying BE743, but later that day he got his BM914 back – flying it on a scramble as an enemy fighter sweep came in at around noon. In all 21 Japanese Ki-27s from the 50th Sentai and 23 from the 77th, plus three Ki-44s from the 47th Independent Chutai, ranged over Mingaladon. It seems the Japanese were taking a leaf out of the RAF's book.

Three AVG pilots got off plus six Hurricanes from 17 Squadron. In the mêlée and dust, one Hurricane narrowly missed a collision with a P40. In some very confused fighting both the AVG and the Japanese over-claimed on victories, neither side suffering losses although five of the enemy had been claimed, while the Japanese recorded shooting down more than 25 Allied aircraft.

In the afternoon Bunny Stone led his squadron to attack shipping in the Gulf of Martaban, strafing two boats crammed with soldiers, one being left on fire and the other being abandoned. Just as these Hurricanes were landing back another Japanese fighter sweep headed in at around 17.00 hours, bringing with them a dozen bombers. Every available aircraft was scrambled and an air battle ensued, the AVG claiming 21 fighters and one bomber shot down. In fact the 50th Sentai lost just two fighters, and no bombers had been lost (losses by the 77th and 47th are not known but would not have been too great). The RAF claimed a bomber and a fighter, the latter by Barry Sutton. On the ground 45 Squadron had five of its Blenheims destroyed or badly damaged.

The Americans, of course, were being paid for results, by the Chinese, so had a vested interest in claiming victories. Frank had an interesting encounter with Bob Neale[10] of the AVG not long after he and Jack Storey arrived, as Frank described to me on one occasion. Frank was invited into their mess building:

---

[10] Robert H Neale had been a former US Navy pilot but resigned to join the AVG in June 1941. He joined 1 Squadron as vice Squadron Leader and then became CO on 7 February 1942. When the Flying Tigers were disbanded in July he had been credited with 13 victories, the British awarding him a DFC.

'Immediately one of the Americans pulled out a six-gun and fired a shot into the lintel above the door as I entered, shouting, "Get out, you Limey!" Bob Neale instantly grabbed the pilot and knocked him out cold, then asked if any one else "... had a beef?!"

'Many of the AVG pilots were fine and exceptionally good and experienced, but they all had the mark of the mercenary about them – which of course they were. They did, however, impart what experience they had to the RAF pilots which was very welcome.

'A local man thought it unfair that the RAF were not also rewarded for each Jap aircraft they shot down and volunteered to pay them, just as the Chinese paid the AVG. The RAF didn't think much of that and said so, but suggested the cash might go into the RAF Benevolent Fund. This local chap, in turn, didn't think much of that so it all fell through.

'Bob Neale suggested to me that if I pin-pointed where the RAF shot down their enemy aircraft, they would claim the money from the Chinese and go fifty-fifty. At the bar I pretended to be very upset by the RAF ruling, and so when asked if I would tell them where any Jap crashed and get some money, amid much hilarity I said, "Done!" It sounded good but it never happened but the story went the rounds, although my mock agreement was not regarded by anyone present as anything more than a light-hearted retort. I was often asked later how much we'd made, much to my annoyance. Most certainly I did not pass any pin-points to the Americans, neither did I receive any cash – perhaps I should have done.'

Chapter Eight

The Retreat to India

It was now appropriate to return the favour to the Japanese and attack once again their flying base at Moulmein. All that was needed was a sign that their aircraft were there. Things were getting desperate at Mingaladon, however. Almost everything was in short supply, especially aeroplanes, which were being dispersed all over the place, as Frank once told me:

'We had to disperse all our aircraft off the airfield. We got so little warning that we could never leave our aircraft on the airfield so had to disperse them widely. We taxied them out along tracks and roads, then under the trees. Others we flew out to nearby airstrips for the night. This was rough on the already ancient Hurricanes. Most had been ferried in from the Middle East and none of them were new aircraft. The slightest problems kept them grounded because of the lack of spares and tools. The dust too caused many mechanical problems. The Japs could also see the dust rising from the runway which helped them navigate to our airfields and airstrips. By this time we had plenty of pilots, just too few aircraft.'

Frank briefed the pilots chosen for the next raid on Moulmein, set for the early morning of February 26th. His section would consist of Pilot Officers J Monk and G W Underwood. Glop Underwood – he had picked up his nickname during his training – had been among four pilots who arrived on 2 February, including Eric Batchelor, with Sergeants M A McRae and D P Robertson. Batchelor, it will be remembered, had been at 52 OTU during the time Frank was an instructor there. He told me:

'FRC was my mentor and inspiration virtually throughout

my four years in the Far East, 1941-45. I have always had the greatest respect and admiration for him as a pilot and fighter leader, and feel very privileged to have served with him for so long. He was very human and compassionate in command, had a great sense of humour and fun, and had a natural flare for generating team spirit and getting the best out of others. He led by example and inspired great loyalty.

'I arrived in the second batch of Hurricanes flying across the Gulf and India to Rangoon. FRC was already there of course, with small numbers of Hurricanes and the American AVG's Tomahawks. He was a courageous and fearless leader; a great inspiration to young pilots.

'When we arrived we were desperately needed. Frank had Jack Storey and Watty Watson with him already, and life became pretty hectic for the next few weeks. Raids were pretty frequent and we were also mounting what sweeps and escorts we could, across to the other side of the Gulf of Martaban.'

Within days, Eric Batchelor's aircraft was hit by two Japanese fighters but he got away with it. Guy Underwood shot down a fighter in his first real action, on the 6th, and McRae damaged another. For Guy Underwood, the attack on Moulmein on the 26th was going to be his last mission. Frank Carey:

'We suddenly got the message that the Japanese had flown back into Moulmein, so I said, "Right! We'll catch those devils. We'll have a dawn patrol." This particular morning we got into our dispersed aircraft at dawn and as usual, hoped we could all form up once airborne. By the time we had done that, the other side had already got his stuff together.

'So there we were, trying to join up and the Japs were above us. Why they didn't come down and attack us I don't know. If they didn't see us then we had been lucky. Maybe we had managed to get off just early enough. There used to be a deep thick haze at various times which severely reduced horizontal visibility. I had ordered that we were all to make for Moulmein independently, chase them back down the line and catch them short of petrol and going into land.

'So that's what we did. We got to Moulmein and there they were, all ready for landing – a whole mass of them like a loose hive. I saw two planes ahead, and by the time I had closed in they were about 50 to 100 feet off the ground and on their final approach. That told me that they were locked in that position. My number two [Underwood] and I went down like a couple of hawks onto these two. The first one fell in a bit of a heap at the end of the runway – which was only to be expected. My number two was quite a bit behind me, so I got tucked behind the leader – precisely the moment when he realised something had happened to his wingman. He started to turn and I caught him at about nought feet. His wing scraped into the grass and he went into a whacking great arc and crashed straight into a hangar and blew up.'

Bunny Stone was on the mission and later wrote:

'We followed them down from 7,000 feet and then it was a free-for-all. I saw Frank Carey (whom I regard as the finest fighter pilot I have ever seen) coming in behind one as the enemy aircraft was touching down. He gave him a burst and the Jap hit the ground, skidded to one side, and then went straight through a hangar in flames. Frank zoomed after that, but I lost him.

'I went down on two of them and got one chap after he turned around and started to climb in the opposite direction. He was about 2,000 feet above the ground and someone must have warned him because he turned right round. I got in a full beam shot into him and gave him about a one-second burst. He flipped right over and went straight into the ground just by the edge of the aerodrome. After that I pulled up to about 5,000 feet and started getting mixed up with two of them and after getting a few bullets through my rudder, did a spiral dive, got away from them, pulled out between a couple of low hills near the aerodrome and, as I zipped across the aerodrome, shot one up as he was touching down.

'The Jap swung round, stopped, and as his aircraft was starting to burn it was enveloped in a cloud of dust. As I left the scene I counted five columns of smoke arising on and round the aerodrome.

'I had to stay right on the deck and get back home at full throttle because I could see two of the Japs chasing me in the rear vision mirror and we were out to the limit of our range and could not afford to stick around. I caught up with Frank Carey, who said afterwards that he thought he was going as fast as any Hurricane could but was intrigued to see me go past him like a rocket before slowing down. We crossed the Salween and flew in formation together and pointed out each other's bullet holes. I had about six and he some big ones in his machine just behind the cockpit, obviously from ground fire while he was in the circuit area.'

Frank continued:

'Then I started to look for my number two; I knew he'd be in a hell of a mess. I pulled hard round and there I was, right in the circuit with Japanese aircraft all around me, so I had certain things to attend to. One fighter came nicely across my bows and I gave him a burst and he went right into the deck – number three. Then I had to do a 180-degree turn, so I was at least heading in the right direction for home, and then they really hammered me. Enemy aircraft came in from all directions and all angles, filling my 'plane with holes, but they didn't do any serious damage. Nothing touched me – sheer luck again. Moments later I was out over the sea, heading north west, and going like the clappers and jinking wildly as I pulled away from my antagonists.'

Meanwhile, Glop Underwood was indeed in trouble as he once explained to me:

'Frank Carey asked me to act as his number two in a fighter sweep which he was carrying out to attack Moulmein aerodrome. The objective was to do as much damage as possible if we found any aircraft on the ground. It was a hairy take-off that day. I took off [from 'John Haig'] in the morning mist and we joined up in the air. We picked up John Monk on the way over – he wasn't officially with us, we just picked him up halfway across the Gulf where he was stooging about. [Monk had simply been out on a training flight.] We came down to see what he was doing, then he joined us. I remember thinking that had we been a couple of Japs, he'd have had it!

'On reaching Moulmein, Frank Carey dived his aircraft down to ground level to sweep across the aerodrome. I followed and noticed a fighter had just taken off and was pulling up as though it was about to fire at Carey's Hurricane, which was by then ahead of it. I succeeded in shooting the aircraft down (it crashed into the trees at the far end of the aerodrome) but I was then hit myself in the engine from something of fairly heavy calibre as I pulled away at low level over the trees. I was virtually blind from oil and smoke so pulled the stick back, stuck my backside into the breeze and pulled the rip-cord of my parachute. How I cleared the aircraft without hitting the tail I don't know but within a matter of seconds I was on the ground feeling somewhat lonely, very battered and a bit burned. Being relatively close to the aerodrome, it was not very long before I was "in the bag".'

The fighters they had bounced included not only Ki-27s but Army Ki-43s – Army 01s – known later as Oscars. Frank, unaware of the drama being enacted behind him in his initial run had caught the returning fighters as he'd hoped. When they arrived over the airfield, four Japanese fighters had already landed with eight more in the circuit.

Other Hurricanes came in. Bush Cotton and Pilot Officer Warburton of 17 Squadron began a strafing run, Cotton hitting two of the milling fighters, both seen to crash into the ground. Looking back as he flew out, Cotton, like Stone, counted five rising columns of smoke. Some AVG P40s now raced in, later claiming two fighters destroyed on the ground – and 11 more in the air!

Glop Underwood was picked up, stuck in a room, and tied to a chair, despite his burns, cuts and bruises. He stayed sitting there for some while, during which time further attacks were made on the airfield, and each time his captors disappeared, leaving him *in situ*. Luckily the hut he was in was not hit. Later, as he was being taken away, he saw a hangar that had been blown half apart. There were still aircraft inside it, obviously damaged. Had this been the same hangar into which Frank's second victim had plunged? In any event, Underwood had been lucky to survive, and his luck held, surviving three years of captivity in Rangoon jail.

The Japanese fighters had been from the 50th and 77th Sentais. The former had lost one and four damaged, but losses for the 77th are unknown. Frank got his damaged Hurricane back to Rangoon, where it was viewed by Jack Storey:

'Wing Commander Carey landed his aircraft with dozens of bullet holes through the fuselage and wings. How he himself or a vital part of the machine escaped damage had amazed everyone.'

Barry Sutton recorded the events of the day in his book (*Jungle Pilot*):

'Frank Carey, who had been promoted wing leader at the same time that I had succeeded him as CO of 135 Squadron, led a mixed force of Hurricanes and Tomahawks which beat up Moulmein.

'As leader of the attack, he set the ball rolling by shooting down a fighter as he made his approach on to the target. He went across the landing strip and dispersals flying just above the ground, spraying any parked aircraft he could get his guns to bear on, and, by way of a neat climax, on break-away caught a second fighter which was trying to take off. A wheel came off the Jap, who then swerved and blew himself to bits against the side of a hangar. The Hurricanes and Tomahawks following wrote off a dozen or more dispersed bombers and fighters.

'One-three-five lost "Glop" Underwood, which meant that we had lost one of the oldest members of the squadron and also one of its best pilots. I wrote to his father next day and wondered if the letter would ever reach a place as far away as Bournemouth.

'The effect of the beat-up was to compel the Japanese air force to quit Moulmein, which must have been a great inconvenience to them. "Glop" had gone two days after Watson, our only flight commander, who also had been his closest friend. Watson had last been seen going down with a couple of Jap fighters on his tail.'

Bush Cotton got back safely from the raid but received a leg wound in an air fight later in the day. He went on to command 17 Squadron later, and received the DFC. Frank did not fly BM914 again and on the 28th took BG297 from Mingaladon to Magwe. The RAF were now in the process of pulling out of Rangoon and to begin operating further north, from Magwe.

March began with Frank flying over to Zigon, then, with one other available pilot, he headed south to carry out a fighter sweep over Rangoon. Luckily they did not run into any trouble. Later he flew cover for the army over the Hlegu cross-roads, before heading back to Magwe for the night.

Next day saw three more sorties after landing at Zigon to refuel. This time he was flying cover along the Prome road and Hlegu again. On the 4th he got himself a new Hurricane – BG829. He tested it and did some aerobatics, and all seemed fine, but on the 5th he was going to use it for a special operation. Frank later elaborated on the story:

'After nearly a month of heavy air activity the Japanese began to close in on Rangoon, at the same time making a number of serious blocking raids on the Mandalay road which was our only overland escape route. We reduced the RAF element in the Rangoon area down to the smallest possible size, to just sufficient pilots and ground crews to operate the ever diminishing number of serviceable aircraft. We put all ranks into a former mission building for personal safety.

'Martial Law had been declared; the prisons had been opened and inmates set free; guns and ammunition were fairly freely available to anyone looting. Our food and provisions had to be acquired by a team of gun-toting ground crew whilst we were flying. Frequently we were shot at from the jungle as we drove to and fro from the airfield. Finally the order was given that we were only to move about in convoy with plenty of cover from our own weapons.

'About dusk one day, disobeying orders for reasons I can no longer recall, I went from the airfield to the mission building. About half a mile from it I came across two local Burmese men pouring gallons of oil on the road at a particularly sharp bend. Of course, everybody knew the Japanese were coming in and we would be unable to stop them, so these fellows wanted a little something in the way of dead British bodies to offer them as a sign of "friendship". I stopped and chased them into the jungle, firing after them. I heard them yell, but don't know if I killed any. I then rushed back to the airfield to warn everyone. This was pure luck again, for I don't know why I should have been at that particular place at that precise moment.

'Meantime, with the additional use of a small cleared strip just out of the danger area, named Zigon which had a telephone line, a small native hut and some fuel supplies, we were able to continue operating, albeit at a somewhat reduced rate. We had also begun to set up a base at Magwe, some 250 miles north from Rangoon in central Burma. By using Prome as a stepping-stone we could be sure of a way north if it came to it. This gave me some chance of providing cover for the retreating ground forces while at the same time being capable of carrying out offensive strikes against the Japanese. Most of these were usually quite effective but we had one very abortive attempt to attack the main Japanese airfield in western Thailand.

'It was from Magwe that we chose to try a raid on Chieng Mai which was almost at our maximum range; the raiding force would consist of just one Blenheim and six Hurricanes. The CO of 45 Squadron, Wing Commander C B B Wallis, had kindly volunteered to escort us – that is, navigate for us. It was over 300 miles away.

'Except for myself the other five pilots were very inexperienced on type having just come off a Buffalo squadron – ex-Singapore. We had only two maps of western Thailand, of which I had one and the Blenheim's navigator had the other. The plan was to use the Salween river which could be clearly identified at a large bend. Although this diversion added almost another 70 miles to our target, it was an essential checkpoint. Promising signs for a disaster were rapidly emerging.

'We took off and as we were forming up my engine cut out. By the time I had managed to get back safely on the ground engineless, the rest had set off obviously unaware of my absence, as I hadn't been able to contact them on the R/T to call off the raid. Nor had we any R/T communication with the Blenheim crew. Despite being suddenly bereft of the one man who could talk to them, "my" pilots set off without me.

'During the flight to Chieng Mai the five Hurricane pilots actually lost contact with the Blenheim. The situation at this moment could scarcely have been worse, with no idea at all where they were nor how to get back to base. By some absolute miracle the Blenheim, in doing a square search, managed to re-sight the Hurricanes and they flew then to what was thought to have been a deserted re-fuelling airfield called Namsang where, despite knowing nothing of the strip, they landed safely.

'Meanwhile, I waited frantically at Magwe trying to find out what had happened. Late that evening, Namsang managed to get a line through to us at Magwe. As all were OK and my engine had been serviced, we planned to join up at Namsang at first light. It so happened that the CO and his No.2 of the AVG squadron, who happened to be temporarily at Magwe, volunteered to join me.

'Heading off, we landed at Namsang and after refuelling set off once more for the elusive Chieng Mai, after a very careful briefing about visual signals and emergency plans, to make up for the lack of R/T exchange.

'We soon discovered that the two maps we had were very incomplete in coverage, showing some areas covering the approaches to Chieng Mai with little more than large patches of white – which seemed to be mostly mountains – with just some cryptic comment such as "insufficient information". Once again we all got very low on fuel before we found our target and were forced to return, but we did drop some bombs on an airfield at defenceless Phoane. I expect the locals are still mortified.'

Most of the RAF were now out of Rangoon. There were only three serviceable Hurricanes at Mingaladon and the AVG had already departed. Jimmy Elsdon, Barry Sutton and Jack Storey – now promoted to flight commander – were the last of the pilots. These three flew the odd scramble, strafed the enemy across the Sittang and helped destroy the last of the unserviceable aircraft on the ground. This was achieved simply by rolling a 44-gallon drum of aviation fuel under a wing, standing clear, then firing a Very flare into it.

Elsdon and Storey flew out the last two Hurricanes to Prome, while a 135 Squadron pilot flew back in a Lysander to fly out Barry Sutton. It did not take long for the Japanese to find them at Prome and subject them to more air raids. Meantime the Rangoon radar boys had been moved north to Magwe, while the surviving Blenheims had also been flown there, using it and a small satellite airfield called 'Highland Queen'. What remained of 136 Squadron flew into Magwe on the 6th and 'X' Wing HQ arrived the next day.

Rangoon was finally evacuated on 7 March 1942. Whatever was left at Rangoon, Zayatkwin, as well as the RAF HQ buildings, were blown up. The gallant if desperate defence of Rangoon was at an end. Frank recalled:

> 'Life out in the East was very much a matter of being between rags and riches. One minute we'd be in some awful mud hut beside a makeshift runway and the next in some Raj's palace. Once I was sharing the Lord Justice's house on Kohine Hill, a residential area of Rangoon, with Group Captain Seton Broughall, the Justice, and his lady, who were leaving in the face of the Japanese advance. This lady's last words to Seton and me contained a plea not to use the better quality fine china in the house! Well, she had some justification. The men used to move into one of these grand houses, stay until all the crockery was dirty and then move on. But the Japanese were going to be coming in after us, so it was rather immaterial whether we used the best crockery or not.'

From Magwe the RAF could still help cover the retreating British army and attack the pursuing Japanese and their lines of supply across and along the Sittang river. As an additional aid, small landing strips were set up along the main route north known as 'kutcha strips'. These were literally cut out of rice paddy fields but as it was virtually impossible to flatten them out totally because of the rock-hard ditches and banks, a number of Hurricane tail wheels were often damaged. As spares were used up, the RAF ground crews resorted to fitting bamboo sticks as tail-skids.

The main task now was to set up two air defence wings. 17 and 135 Squadrons formed the MagWing at Magwe, whilst 136 and some of 135's ground crews formed AkWing at Akyab Island, on the coast. Here some of 136's pilots were re-united with their ground personnel, who had been kept back to help service aircraft still staging in from the Middle East. Not that conditions were any better here than they had been at Rangoon or Zigon, as Jimmy Elsdon related in his squadron's history:

> 'Insofar as 136 Squadron was concerned, the first stage of the move northwards was to provide an air defence system based at Zigon, a paddy strip landing ground carved out of central Burma rice fields. The aircraft warning system was fairly rudimentary consisting of a line of small "wireless units" along the hills to the east which reported any sightings of Japanese aircraft flying westwards over their sites towards the British held areas of Burma.
>
> 'There was no radar and so, once a raid had passed over the line of wireless units, alterations of course by the raiders could not be reported to the fighters scrambled to intercept. However, visibility was good at this time of the year and some successes were achieved. The squadron moved to Akyab on 16 March by which time AkWing HQ under Group Captain Noel Singer had been established on Akyab Island.
>
> 'There was petrol available and one refueller, but most of the refuelling of the aircraft was to be done [by hand] from 4-gallon cans using a chamois leather filter, a painfully slow process.'

Busy on the ground for the next few days, Frank's next sortie came on the 13th. From Magwe he led a handful of Hurricanes to Prome from where he led a sweep along the Irrawaddy, searching for Japanese river transport. The next day came another similar sortie, landing first at Prome then leading a flight of fighters down the Prome road, making sure no Japanese were moving north along it. That same afternoon he led a sweep to Toungoo and Swegyin, once again searching for enemy movements north.

Then Frank was given another task as he later recalled:

> 'At Magwe we were trying to make another stand but

although we had pilots we were still desperately short of aircraft. So Group Captain Broughall commanding the wing, said, Frank, you're due a couple of days off, fly back to Calcutta and chase up the AOC and see what there is. Obviously I could not take one of our precious Hurricanes, so looking around found an old dusty Tiger Moth in the corner of a hangar, so taking a young pilot with me, I flew over the mountains to Akyab. When we got there, rather than continue on in the Tiger, I found there was a Vickers Victoria there. It cruised about 73 mph, max speed about 80! It was waiting for someone to fly it, so I thought that because we'd be flying over water, it was a better bet, it having two engines to the Tiger's one. I told my companion to ask if Magwe wanted him back, while I went off in the Victoria, crammed full of senior Indian officer's wives and kids all being evacuated. I headed for Chittagong, landed to refuel, then flew on to Calcutta.'

No sooner had he arrived at Calcutta – putting down at Dum Dum – than he began seeking advice as to how more Hurricanes could be flown down to Magwe:

'However, I quickly discovered that the reason for my mission had already disappeared. Soon after I departed Magwe it was subjected to several heavy air attacks, which soon reduced the small number of Hurricanes to nothing. In the face of the current situation, where the chance of receiving any more aircraft was nil, plus the fact that the Japanese army was well on its way north, they were left with no alternative but to retreat up the Burma Road to China.

'When I reached Calcutta, I was beginning to feel rather unwell and malaria was diagnosed. After some days in hospital I was given the job of forming a Defence Wing for Calcutta. Obviously this would be the next target for the Japanese. It was now that I was informed that I had been awarded a second Bar to my DFC.'

Many of Frank Carey's contemporaries still wonder today why Frank did not receive a DSO for his recent actions. He had done exceptionally well over the last few weeks, accounted for at least eight enemy aircraft, and since being awarded a Bar to DFC after the Battle of France, his personal score had doubled. There had been no reward for his actions over England during the Battle of Britain. Whether such a recommendation for a DSO was ever made, and then downgraded to a second Bar, is not known, but these things did happen. Many top awards were rationed, and if too many DSOs were recommended, someone's name slipped off the end of the list. Then again, it was a retreat, and nobody likes to give rewards for being involved in retreats. The only reference I found to this further award was a signal from NorGroup dated March 1942, to Admin (R) AHQ India:

> Further to my P.208 6 March – Wing Commander Carey 43132 has shown the greatest qualities of leadership both in command of his Squadron and as Wing Leader. He has destroyed at least 5 enemy aircraft and has set a very fine example to all his pilots by his devotion to duty and by his courage.
>
> Copy to: S.10.A (Action)

Action on this must have taken a very short time for his citation to his award was promulgated in the *London Gazette* on 24 March 1942 – less than three weeks after this signal was sent to Delhi some time after 6 March and is more or less what has been written above (see appendix B).

News of this, Frank's fourth gallantry award, was soon in the newspapers, although yet again there were errors in the reporting. In one article it praised the 'Aircraft Boy to Triple DFC' winner but in listing his achievements in date order, one read:

> *1940 (June): Shot down wounded, landed by parachute; bombed in hospital ship at Dunkirk; wins DFC and Bar at same time.*

Then with another error came exaggeration:

> *1941-2: Fights on every other British war front as flying officer, flight lieutenant, squadron leader and wing commander.*

Frank never baled out of any aeroplane and he was nowhere near Dunkirk, let alone bombed in a hospital ship there. Every other British war front? Malta? North Africa? New Guinea? Darwin? If this was not enough, he was now being called *Cockney Bill – No.1 Fighter Pilot.* How Frank must have loathed that sobriquet.

However, this was all mainly for UK consumption and perhaps Frank didn't see it for some time. In any event, he was now busy with his new task of defending Calcutta.

Free from the recent hard fighting it was a time to get back into training, and Frank's log book indicates that he led several wing and individual squadron formation flights during April. He was now flying Hurricane BG700. There were moments of excitement, such as flying through one of the early monsoon storms on his way to Alipore on the 6th. He had just flown up to Cuttack because Japanese warships had been attacking a convoy, but his log book entry noted that the convoy had been annihilated before they could get to it, as Frank later recounted:

'On 2 April, almost as soon as I had recovered from malaria, we began to get the wing set up and were faced with a daunting task. A convoy was sent from Calcutta to try and sneak down the eastern coast of India in an attempt to avoid being seen by the Japanese navy, which was in full command of the entire Bay of Bengal. As the convoy moved south they were not only seen but attacked by a full set Carrier Task Force, which proceeded to finish it off. We were told about the situation and requested, at this stage, to try to rescue them. This meant we had to collect a band of some half dozen Hurricanes to meet the situation. The mind boggles that we had to fly down the coast, refuel by hand at an airfield near Cuttack supply station and then fly out over the bay with no idea of the whereabouts of the Japanese. As we were getting ready to set off from Cuttack an RAF bomber came in, having spotted the carrier force some hundreds of miles away heading south. We were rather grateful that this force was now well out of our reach! The monsoon was beginning about this time and on the way back we were forced down to ground level under conditions of heavy storms, and I couldn't see how the engines could possibly still get enough air to run.'

Then on the 18th came a scramble, but no contact was made. Another scramble on 2 May, south of Calcutta, but again no contact. Then Frank was busy with a new project:

'The first big task was to find sufficient hard ground for airfields. During the monsoon period of torrential rain that was fast approaching, the whole of the large Ganges delta would soon be under water.
'There were two airfields in the immediate Calcutta area. The main one was Dum Dum, the normal city airport, with one short runway and a small hard standing area. The other was Alipore, civilian part-time airfield used by a small

number of civilian flyers with one reasonable concrete runway and a further small one at an angle across it. However, the main runway at Alipore had the distinct disadvantage that the entire rubbish dump for Calcutta was at one end! This attracted the inevitable mass of vultures, pye dogs, carrion crows, humans, etc., which made flying in that immediate area (i.e. take-off or landing) quite tricky, if not downright deadly.

'The small runway was also very interesting as it possessed a railway line across it. To this rather depressing total we were offered an even more extraordinary feature. It was the main road – called Red Road – which ran right through the middle of Calcutta. Luckily one side at least was flanked by the main city park, situated just behind a small wall. With some ingenuity we quickly got this into a very efficient air defence organisation.

'I do not remember who first thought of using a road, least of all plumb in the centre of Calcutta, by St James Park, but someone did – to their credit, and our novelty.

'I felt distinctly dubious about the whole idea at first, especially as it was to be the operational base for a fighter squadron and in my position as wing leader, I was responsible for their training and, in an indirect way, their accidents.

'My initial doubts may be well understood when it is appreciated that the Red Road had houses approximately 200 feet high at the north end, trees up to the edge of the road, was little over half the width of a normal runway, had an appreciable camber and between the two monuments that marked its beginning, measured only 800 yards. To further enhance its dubious value balloons were perpetually flown within 300 to 400 yards of its western side, while the south end had more high trees and the impressive Queen Victoria Memorial (itself at least as high as the houses to the north). The air in the immediate vicinity was clogged with those "guardian angels" of the east – kites and vultures. This feathered "top cover" was a constant source of worry as they took a light but regular toll of aircraft and sometimes aircrew. A collision with a 60-pound vulture can be a bit upsetting in more ways than one, so, altogether not a happy picture.

'There were, however, lighter sides to the project, which were quickly appreciated, as apart from the novelty of operating from such a place, Chowringhee, the main street of Calcutta ran parallel to the Red Road only a matter of about a 100 yards or so away. It was quite possible to sit in Firpo's, the leading restaurant and "RAF watering hole", and yet be capable of taking off should there be a raid, within three or four minutes. This I can vouch for because I managed it on several occasions. Another bonus was that with a neatly timed signal one could almost order a "chota-peg" on the way in to land from a number of catering establishments, and in later months it became quite the recognised thing to read the cinema advertisements when just leaving or arriving back, to see if anything worth seeing was playing.

'The road needed a bit of preparation for its war-time role. The statues had to be removed from the wall, the tram lines which cut across the south end had to be diverted, while a flag-pole on a house dead in line with the north end came down. A rough, plaited bamboo fence was erected to keep people out (although it only needed the gentlest of caresses to collapse it) and an adjacent tree-lined road had to be converted into a dispersal area. Many refinements were added after we had officially taken it over until finally we had one of the best equipped and superbly camouflaged landing strips that we experienced in the Far East.

'An additional 300 yards at the south end was constructed later, bringing its length to an acceptable 1,100 yards, but this was at a slight angle to the rest of the strip and was mainly used when one ran out of runway and provided a slightly better approach from the south. Taking advantage of my rank and position I selected myself to do the initial landing test on the morning of 25 May 1942 [Hurricane BG975], Red Road being officially closed to the public at midnight the previous evening.

'I took off from Alipore in great excitement at the idea of landing (safely I hoped) in the middle of a city. Arriving over Calcutta I circled the road and was not a little dismayed to see the minute hemmed-in little ribbon on which I had to land. My enthusiasm waned appreciably. There was no backing-out now, even if I had wanted to, because thousands of Indians and many dozens of Europeans had somehow heard of the proposed attempt and thronged the actual balustrade that ran down either side of the grass verges to the road. Also, at either end pressed tightly against the temporary road-blocks were similar seething masses. There is nothing like the possibility of a grandstand view of a "prang", unless it is the canteen wagon, for accumulating large quantities of RAF personnel!

'If those people had only known how easily an aircraft can

swing violently on landing even without the road camber which existed to accentuate the slightest deviation from a straight run, I'm certain they would not have been so keen to see the first landing at such close quarters. The wing tips of the Hurricane I was flying could not be much more than 20 feet from the balustrade even if I stayed in the centre of the road.

'I started my glide in to land from the north the latter part being between the houses of Old Courthouse Street, and such was the proximity of the high houses on one side and the Government House on the other that if I was to use all the runway the last part of the glide would be between the two. Later it was amply demonstrated that one could keep above the houses and still have plenty of room, but I was taking no chances of over-shooting into the crowd at the far end. It came off without mishap but the unique experience of virtually dropping down into the middle of a crowded street will always remain, and persisted even after we had all got quite blasé about it.'

Frank only flew three times in June, one air test and two 'sector recos and aeros' – in other words an excuse to get airborne and keep his hand in. He was always keen to get into the air and once there, aerobatics was a must. It became quite a feature over the places where Frank was based for people to come out and watch his unique routines.

July saw some of the first cannon-armed Hurricane IICs being used, Frank testing this armament firing into the sea on several occasions. Towards the end of the month Frank wrote in his log: 'Aeros for Chin Tribesmen!!', no doubt giving the natives of the Chin Hills in northern Burma something to wonder at. He followed this by beating up Dum Dum with aircraft of 67 and 607 Squadrons flying as top cover.

On his first flight in August – the 3rd – he gave a mock ground strafe on Dum Dum and had a nasty call by scraping past a tree, damaging BN468's tail, wing-tip and aerial. The rest of the month was routine with just a couple of scrambles to keep things interesting, plus a convoy patrol out over the Bay of Bengal.

September flying began with a solo flight to 25,000 feet on the 11th but his engine failed and he had to force land back on the aerodrome. Three days later came a scramble which ended in chasing one Japanese aircraft out to sea. By the end of the month Frank went down with another Far East favourite – dengue fever. More training followed, sometimes operating from Jessore, to the east of Calcutta. There was trouble with the 20 mm cannons on the IICs, Frank noting in his log that on 8 October 'all cannons fired for the first time!!' The problem must have been solved for on his next two flights he noted that all guns [four] had fired again. Frank was now operating more and more from Dum Dum, and finally he moved there in mid-October, and with this came a new command, wing commander flying to 165 Wing.

The Japanese were beginning to prepare for a march up the Arakan coast in an attempt to reach India by this route. The main RAF defence centre was at Chittagong and Hurricane and Blenheim squadrons were rapidly getting ready to meet that threat. Frank's regular Hurricane was now BN468.

He flew it to Chittagong for the first time on 24 October and two days later flew to Cox's Bazaar, again on the Arakan coast:

'The army was getting itself built-up to attack the Japs down the Arakan coast while we were preparing a number of jungle strips to use in their support. Before we began to make our actual advance against them, I flew to a recently repaired airfield at Cox's Bazaar to test its suitability for full operations. I had to refuel at Chittagong, which at the time had only emergency fuel supplies. The refuelling party were in the process of finishing their job and I was sitting in the cockpit waiting to start up. Suddenly I noticed a number of fighter aircraft appear from behind a cloud – about 27 in all. I knew they must be Japanese because we didn't have that many aircraft, not in one place at least.

'Being without radar cover or any other warning system was always a hazard and here it was in large lumps!! I started my engine, yelled to the ground crew to get under cover and then had to taxi quite a way to get to the end of the rather short runway. I opened up but long before I was airborne the bullets were flying and kicking up the dust around me. I got into the air and immediately began to jink and skid like mad to make myself an awkward target. I was helped by my own fury with myself for having been so stupid to take off into such a suicidal situation.

'However, luck was with me again and I led the Japs [they were Nakajima Ki-43 Oscars] on my tail up the river at absolutely nought feet between the river boats, over a bridge, then down into a slight valley, until gradually I worked my way up into the hills, all the while leading them away from their own base at Akyab. Eventually they had to break off, I suppose their fuel was getting low. I thought I saw one of them crash behind me, hitting some high ground, but that was never confirmed. I really lost some weight on that sortie.'

Bill Davis, of 136 Squadron, recalled this incident for me:

'Frank Carey was a supreme Hurricane pilot. In October 1942, he had flown to Chittagong to check the organisation. While he was there about 30 Oscars appeared. He waved the ground crews to the slit trenches, ran out, and started up. He was attacked by several Oscars who were firing at him while he was taking off. I talked to some of the ground crew who had observed these events a few days after it had happened. They said he disappeared below the level of the bund (a bank keeping the river away from the airfield), evading violently. It was said that one of the enemy aircraft flew into a tree or the ground trying to follow him.

'I seem to remember being at Dum Dum when he returned from this adventure. His aircraft had not been hit but he admitted he had been shaken and in the heat of the moment had failed to pull his boost override. It was typical of his modest approach not to make much of his escape. I can vouch that the ground crews at Chittagong had no doubt about what they had witnessed.'

In the book *Wings of the Phoenix*, the official story of the Air War in Burma, this passage found itself within its pages:

'Wing Commander Frank Carey DFC DFM, a Battle of Britain pilot who had also earned considerable fame in destroying Japanese fighters during the retreat from Rangoon, landed at an airfield immediately before a Japanese raid. All aircraft were away from base except an unservice-able Blenheim and Carey's Hurricane. As the enemy circled the field in line astern prior to bombing, Carey took off, while the Japanese bombers blasted installations, he led a chase with six enemy fighters on his tail, keeping only a few feet above ground level. Japanese fighters were fitted with telescopic sights which gave their pilots extremely accurate aim for their guns, but blinded them to anything not shown in their sights. In this instance items not shown in the Japanese sights included a small hill over which the Hurricane had gently lifted; Carey was accordingly able to claim one Japanese fighter destroyed, RAF losses nil.'

Chapter Nine

AFTU, Amarda Road

Another airfield now began to feature in Frank Carey's log book, Kanchrapara, but still close to Calcutta. The city was now becoming very well protected. At the end of October Frank ran into his brother Hugh, who was with the army, and had been for some years:

'He had been in Burma before and during the retreat and was having a rest period. He had walked out from mid-Burma during the retreat and brought out an Indian family for most of the way to India. Our meeting was a pleasant surprise as neither of us had any knowledge of the other's whereabouts. He had previously been on the North-West Frontier pre-war, having come from there when Japan entered the war.'

What Frank does not mention but his log book reveals is that he took Hugh on a flight to Jessore on the 31st, then back to Dum Dum on 1 November. The aircraft was a Fairey Tipsy trainer – MA930 – a two-seat, low wing monoplane, used by 221 Group Comms. Flight.

For the remainder of the year Frank carried out a variety of flying sorties, almost entirely in Hurricane IIC BN468. Formations, searches for lost aircraft, the odd scramble, none of which came to anything and of course, his favourite pastime – giving aerobatic displays. Any number of pilots I have spoken to over the years invariably mention Frank Carey's ability to thrill and enthral everyone with his flying ability. Work always seemed to stop whenever he was in the air. Gordon Conway was a pilot in 136 Squadron who once told me:

'Our wing leader at Chittagong was once again Frank Carey, under whose training we became increasingly more operational. To watch him fly was an education – he could make an aircraft talk. It was his practice to fly the last sortie of the day – a beautiful aerobatic display that brought out all the pilots to watch in disbelief and admiration.'

Another 136 Squadron – known as the Woodpeckers – pilot, was Viv Jacobs who wrote:

'...the show that would bring everyone to his feet was the performance put on most evenings by Wing Commander Chota Carey, the wing leader, as he demonstrated his utter unity with his aircraft and his ability to make it display both its talents and his own. It was always a superb demonstration of matchless skill which clearly affirmed his status as undoubtedly a master of his aircraft and a superlative pilot.'

R E 'Bob' Windle (135 Squadron) also has a view on Frank Carey as a pilot. Bob wrote to me once about him:

'Wing Commander Carey was our winco flying at Dum Dum and in my and many other pilots' opinions, the very best Hurricane pilot ever to fly in the Far East. While we talked of Rate 4 tight turns, he talked of Rate 7 – and meant it, and executed them at ground level.

'At Dum Dum normal flying would be finished by 4 pm. At about 4.30 every evening, an enormous flock of "Flying Fox" bats would fly slowly, low over the airfield. Always in the same direction and they never seemed in a hurry. Between 4 and Flying Fox time we would hear Wing Commander Carey's Hurricane start up. All pilots not on essential work would turn out and know that we were to be treated to the most immaculate display of Hurricane aerobatics we would ever witness. Everything he did was precise, and done with flair. It went on for eight or nine minutes and finished with the most incredible side-slipping approach we had ever seen, and then those three pointers! They never became just routine displays – but always something very special.'

Bill Davis, 136 Squadron:

'Carey gave immaculate displays in the evenings while we were at Dum Dum. His side-slipping approaches were, he claimed, to enable him to force land should his engine fail, but I thought it was really to demonstrate his superb control of his machine. So for me he was the greatest Hurricane pilot.'

Frank Carey had a unique end to his flying displays. Coming in to land he would be able to judge his final taxi in to dispersal faultlessly. As he neared his sandbagged enclosure he would give the Hurricane one last burst of throttle then switch off. The Hurricane would then continue to trundle forward, then he would kick the rudder and the aeroplane would skid round, roll backwards, and come to a halt right in the middle of its barricade. Frank would climb out nonchalantly, and why not. It wasn't difficult – not for him anyway.

Another Woodpecker, who recalled Frank's aircraft, was Flight Sergeant Frank Wilding, who once spoke to me about the day he borrowed Carey's personal Hurricane during a scramble:

'I was "spare pilot" when we got the scramble. Frank Carey was in the john! His Hurricane, with his initials FRC on its sides was just sitting there. It was a IIC with cannon.

'The squadron went off and I was told I could take FRC, and was quickly off after the others, like a rocket. As I caught up with them, they saw the FRC letters and so waved me through. So there was Flight Sergeant Wilding leading the squadron! I thought, fair enough, I'd as much experience as the rest.

'Unfortunately, some of the boys had to go back due to engine failure, glycol leaks, etc, so there were only about six of us when we got up to and saw a 17+ formation of bombers. They had fighter cover top and bottom, saw us coming and jumped us. They seemed to leave me above and I went sailing on up all by myself, with the large Vee formation of bombers in front of me, going away. I'd never fired cannon before and the recoil was terrific, almost stopped the aircraft, which seemed to "yaw" a bit. I was aiming at the lead bomber but the bits were coming off the second and third in the formation. Not that I was worried, I just kept on firing until I'd run out of ammunition, which didn't seem very long compared to our .303 aircraft.

'When the guns fell silent I dived under the formation and got well away and then hung around till I got to return to base, which I did. Some of the ground crew didn't know I was in FRC, and I received quite a reception until they realised who I was, but the best bit was we couldn't re-arm the cannon at Chittagong, so I had to fly it up to Feni to have the work done.

'When they saw FRC in the circuit there, everybody turned out and it gave me great pleasure to drape my arm over the edge of the cockpit as I taxied in, to show the assembly my crown and three stripes!'

At Feni Wilding was to discover that the Wingco's aircraft was still having gun trouble as an armourer told him that the two cannon on the starboard wing had jammed soon after the first burst, which is why he had yawed, and the remaining two jammed before he'd used all the shells. Even so, Wilding was credited with one Sally (Mitsubishi Ki-21) destroyed and another as a probable.

Eric Batchelor, who we met earlier while he was with Frank in 135 Squadron recalls:

> 'In December 1942 I was appointed flight commander on 17 Squadron operating from Red Road in Calcutta. FRC collected me in person to transfer me to the new post – a typical, generous gesture of great importance to me at the time.
> 'No.17 Squadron moved to "Acorn" in March 1943 for forward detachments to front-line bases, then later to Agartala, for long-range ground attack sorties. In March/April 1943 I attended the first course at AFTU, Amarda Road – commanded by FRC.'

Frank's time with 165 Wing came to an end in January 1943. Sadly he had been unable to meet any enemy aircraft in air combat over these recent months. He had gone on several scrambles and a couple of night shows, one being just before Christmas against raiders attacking Calcutta, but as he has said before, he never ever saw a thing at night.

Another Woodpecker pilot at this time was Australian D J Barnett. Barney Barnett wrote in his diary:

> 16 Dec 1942. Carey and P/O Fuge taking the long-range jobs (Hurricane IIs) to Akyab tonight in case the Japs raid Calcutta and have a crack at them as they put in for fuel.
> 7 Jan 1943. Chittagong. Readiness all day. Seems W/Com Carey has been given more or less the choice of flying as sqdn/ldr or retaining rank in ground job. He's lost to our wing. Jove we're having bad luck and the idea of stooge bastards being able to give a chap like Carey with his 24 a/c [victories], DFC and 2 Bars, DFM, such a choice.
> 11 Jan 1943. Chittagong. Carey back with us in some 'Bengal something' capacity. Damn glad he'll be flying.
> 31 Jan 1943. [Our acting CO] got a bollicking from W/Com Stevenson and S/Ldr Mowat, on 136 generally. Bloody

unjustified. God knows the squadrons need to pull together out here. Think it's Mowat's doing. As sqdn/ldr flying and with ourselves attached to 166 Wing and his former 607 Squadron, the latter are naturally his white-haired angels and we're all at fault. Wish Carey were here, he'd fix the petty swine.

In February FRC took his Hurricane BN468 from the forward base at Ramu, codename 'Reindeer', situated just south of Cox's Bazaar, and flew back to Alipore to pick up his kit. Heading south west he flew the 200 miles to his new command, the Air Fighting Development Unit at Amarda Road, Orissa, just inland from the coast. Such a unit was not a totally new idea, as the RAF in England had had an AFDU at RAF Northolt as early as July 1940, but this was the first in India. Frank relates:

'Finally in February 1943, after an active time in the Arakan giving ground support to the army, I was posted to the south west of Calcutta, in order to open up a School of Flying Tactics. Here all our experiences – successful or otherwise – were collected together to enable the best use of tactics against the Japanese.'

The main problem was that things had happened so rapidly in Malaya and Burma, and with the army and air force being in almost perpetual retreat since December 1941, not to mention out-numbered, and reinforcements stretched back over hundreds of miles, there had been no time to assimilate any sort of tactics against a resourceful foe.

Virtually all reinforcement fighter pilots from Britain were either experienced against the Germans, or new pilots without any operational background and anything the latter had gleaned by talking to UK veterans only applied to fighting the Luftwaffe. The Luftwaffe, of course, was very different from the Japanese air force, and the conditions over which fighting had taken place was equally different from that which had taken place over England or northern France.

Fighting Me109s was generally a turning battle, with RAF fighters – in the hands of skilled pilots – who could generally turn inside a 109, especially in a Spitfire. There were no Spitfires in Burma yet, but the Hurricane pilots would still have brought with them the knowledge that turning inside an opponent would usually give them an edge.

What the RAF pilots soon discovered in the early days, as well as the Americans in the Philippines and elsewhere, was that the Japanese fighters could easily turn *inside* them. Being so light in construction, and not having armour or radio, plus non-sealing fuel tanks, a

Japanese pilot – in a very nimble aeroplane – could turn on the proverbial sixpence. The problem the Japanese pilots had was that if an enemy pilot did get a good burst into their machine, it generally did one or more of three things. It either burst into flames, crumpled up or the unprotected pilot was killed or badly wounded.

While the RAF claimed victories in the usual fashion – ie: destroyed, probably destroyed or damaged – the Japanese were not so fixated. A 'victory' for them was to hit an opponent and force him out of the battle, to stop him doing his job of escorting, bombing or intercepting. The Japanese often claimed a number of these 'victories' but they were not necessarily Allied aircraft deemed 'destroyed'. There were no medals for a large victory score; indeed, most medals for Japanese pilots came after death.

Once the RAF and the USAAF had time to assess what was required to combat these nimble Japanese fighters, things began to change, and it was these sorts of changes and new rules of engagement that Frank Carey and his instructors were about to impart. The new rule was not to turn with the enemy but to employ dive and zoom tactics. Keeping the engine at full revs and ensuring height over an opponent was halfway to success. The other half was to be able to hit the enemy, either in a straightforward shot or by using the correct amount of deflection, and then climb away. Once height had been regained, a fresh opponent could be sought and another attack made. He who has the height controls the battle.

Frank, of course, was a master at attack. It was a rare fight in which he failed to hit an opponent. One only has to look at his log book and combat reports to see that on almost every occasion he was engaged, a German or Japanese aircraft suffered damage of some sort, mostly fatal. He was an experienced and able pilot, completely in control of his machine – in his case the Hawker Hurricane – and a fantastic shot. There were a good many excellent and experienced fighter pilots, but as many would admit, and some have said it to me, they were not the greatest of shots. I have also met others too who while admitting it, decided at an early stage to use their flying ability to get so close that their deficient skill at air-to-air firing mattered less. They were close enough not to miss.

Two of the early problems RAF fighter pilots had found in fighting the Me109, for instance, were that their own engines did not have fuel injection, and that both the Spitfire and Hurricane had a long nose – engine cowling – in front of them.

The German fighters had fuel injection so that their carburettors kept going if the aeroplane went into a negative-G position. The RAF fighters, on the other hand, if flown in negative-G, had their carburettors starved of fuel and the engine would splutter and lose power for a few moments, while the pilot sorted out his position. If chasing a 109, the German pilot could stick his nose down and head for the deck, knowing that if the RAF chap on his tail did the same, his 109 would be able to draw away from the Tommy as his engine lost power. Added to this problem was that as the 109 disappeared quickly beneath the RAF pilot's cowling, it took time to pick it up again – once he'd got his engine going properly once more. RAF pilots quickly discovered that to follow a diving 109 they had to roll over and down, staying clear of negative-G. While later RAF fighters sorted out the fuel injection system problem, the fighters used in the Far East were of the earlier – older – variety some of which did not have fuel injection. Therefore in the Far East, instructors at Frank's school had to ensure their pupils could handle negative-G as well as the nimbleness of the Japanese fighters.

During March and April Frank was flying Harvards, along with Barry Sutton who was attending the unit. Frank's log book notes rolling attacks and revision attacks. On 14 March the first course began. The press were taking an interest and Frank really impressed one reporter, a Mr Emeny, taking him up for an aerobatic display for the benefit of his companions. It must have been a trifle violent, as Frank noted in his log book that the hood caved in.

During April a number of former pilots who had flown with him from and around Rangoon were taken for rides in the back of his Harvard (F427). Jack Storey, Eric Batchelor, Barry Sutton, Guy Marsland, 'Watty' Watson, 'Kas' Mann, Maurice Cuthbert and Jimmy Whalen were some of them. On the 15th he air tested a Fleet Air Arm Fulmer (X8701) for fifteen minutes, an aircraft on the strength of 273 Squadron as a target tug. Frank's comment was: "first trip – and last!!!"

Frank had no sooner set up his establishment than he was posted back to England in order to gain experience on how he should run it, and at the same time be brought up to date on the latest aircraft and techniques. There seems a slight contradiction here in that techniques taught in England would not be of too much help to pilots fighting in Burma.

Nevertheless, it was also a chance to get home to his wife and daughter for a visit, however brief. So, on 13 June 1943, he began an eight-day trip back to England, which took 13 individual flights, in Empire flying boats to Cairo, then by Liberator to Hendon, finally landing at Hendon on the 24th, in a Flamingo. In all, 7,500 miles. The Liberator flights both to and back from Gibraltar had been with 511 Squadron, a unit formed specifically for flights between Gib and the UK. As a matter of interest, his flight out on 20 September and then back on 22 June, were both in a Liberator II – AL616.

After a couple of days with his family he attended the Central Gunnery School – No.30 Course – at RAF Sutton Bridge. This would take him till September to complete, but in Air Ministry Bulletin No.10939, dated 24 July 1943, publicity of Frank's new unit was given to the media:

INDIA FRONT FIGHTER ACE STARTS A SCHOOL

To perfect their gunnery technique and take a course which is rated as a high qualification to squadron gunnery leadership, fighter pilots from RAF home and overseas commands go to the fighter wing of the Central Gunnery School.

One of those taking the present course had travelled specially by air from India to study the school's methods so they can be applied to a similar unit which has been established there.

He is Wing Commander F R Carey DFC and two Bars, DFM, a Battle of Britain pilot who started his RAF career as an apprentice at Halton and began the war as a sergeant pilot.

He is one of "The Few" not only of the Battle of Britain but of the force which helped to stem the Japanese drive on India.

After a year's operational flying against the Japanese he founded an air fighting training unit in India, to perform similar functions to the Central Gunnery School here – "The university of air firing."

The idea is to give advanced gunnery instruction to operational fighter pilots and air gunners who can become gunnery leaders in their squadrons. The new unit will have the benefit of experience gained in the air battle against the Japanese, and will be able to apply the methods by which the Central Gunnery School maintains a high standard of marksmanship among British fighter pilots.

JAPANESE HUSBAND RESOURCES

Wing Commander Carey, who was also in the Battle of France, was among the first fighter pilots sent to Burma at the end of 1941. His hard-pressed squadron had to be very versatile, doing ground strafing, bomber escort, sweeps, ship reconnaissance and defensive fighting.

He has acquired an extensive knowledge of Japanese methods in a hard campaign over the jungle around Rangoon, and hopes that the Japs will soon feel the effects of the advanced gunnery training which RAF pilots and air gunners on the Assam front are to receive.

He has studied the Japanese tactics and the performance of such aircraft as Zeros and Oscar 1s and hopes to pass on his knowledge to other pilots on this front.

He has noticed signs that the enemy is having to husband his resources very carefully, for often he will remain quiescent in the air for two or three weeks, organising operations which last only a few days.

THE SUICIDE MENTALITY

Wing Commander Carey does not believe in under-estimating the enemy's ability in the air. Their fighters, he says, are very manoeuvrable, because of the sacrifice of armour, but this weakness in protective covering should make them vulnerable to accurate fire.

Japanese "suicide" methods have not diminished. They will try ramming in the air and some of their pilots have tommy guns, so that if shot down they can fight on the ground. It is quite common for Japanese pilots to commit suicide when captured.

The Wing Commander recalls one instance where a Japanese pilot who had to bale out, having one arm shattered, fired his tommy gun at random as he floated down by parachute.

(This last paragraph appears more like journalistic licence than something Frank Carey would have said. It doesn't say how a one-armed enemy pilot operated both his parachute and his tommy gun.)

While on 30 Course, Frank, a true-blue Hurricane pilot, had his first experience flying a Spitfire – P8444 – on 15 July. As the tail number suggests, this was an old machine, one of an order placed back in 1941. A Mark IIA, it had already seen operational service with 152 and 131 Squadrons in 1941, then 52 OTU the following year. It had arrived at the CGS on 28 June 1943. He made no comment other than – 'Experience on Type, 50 minutes'.

Over the following weeks he went through the various school curriculum: range estimation, deflection shooting, quarter attacks, drogue firing, various attacking approaches, being jumped by instructors in the air to test awareness and reactions, simulated air combat and evasive manoeuvres. One flight was in a Miles Master with Squadron Leader Archie Winskill DFC, making quarter attacks – avec patter! That is, talking through what one is doing, thereby showing the instructor his actual responses which would remove the possibility of him being just fortunate.

His air-firing drogue scores he recorded as follows:

25 July	2	7 Aug	27
„	11	„	8
27 July	31	8 Aug	177
28 July	31	9 Aug	29
„	63	10 Aug	145
„	35	„	212
31 July	130	„	34
„	230	15 Aug	114
„	198	16 Aug	291
„	124	17 Aug	285

Average 109 = 10.9%

Course Assessment:	Drogue – Above Average
As a Marksman in:	Fighter Combat – Exceptional
	Bomber Combat – Exceptional
As an instructor:	Exceptional
Degree of Pass:	"A"

Signed: W/Cdr P R Watkins
OC Fighter Wing
CGS Sutton Bridge

His total Spitfire time had risen to almost 43 hours, then in August he went to RAF Milfield, Northumberland, were the Specialised Low Attack Instructors School (SLAIS) was situated. Hurricane IV and Hawker Typhoon pilots were taught here, men who were destined for operations with 40 mm cannon or rockets and bombs. Then he had a brief time at Aston Down, flying a Typhoon and a Mustang.

On 20 September 1943, he began his journey back to India from RAF Lyneham, in Wiltshire, firstly in a Liberator to Cairo, via Gibraltar. Then by Empire flying boat across to Karachi then Calcutta – 12 flights in all. The last leg had to be aborted due to a monsoon storm, but he finally landed on the 26th. Next day he flew a Hurricane back to Amarda Road.

One positive result of his visit home came nine months later, with the birth of his second daughter Jane, born in Winchester on 13 June 1944.

Frank gradually built up his new unit. He was able to call on several experienced air fighters from nearby units, who had become tour expired, although this was an unreal term in the Far East. In Britain, or even the Middle East, a fighter pilot could generally expect to be rested after a certain amount of time on an operational squadron, determined also by the number of operations or operational flying hours he had flown. He could then look forward to a rest and a posting as an instructor at a flying school, although not everyone deemed that a 'rest'. In the Far East, being so far from home, an RAF pilot could expect one of two things. Firstly his 'tour' would be longer, and if rested, it probably meant no more than a few weeks in Calcutta say, plus a few days up in the cool hills of Darjeeling, and then a return to his squadron. In the UK a pilot might be on a squadron for a few months, in Burma, sometimes – on and off – a couple of years. Thus Frank, knowing most of the experienced bods, was able to have his pick of instructors, choosing, of course, those who he knew personally were exceptional, and certainly 'above the average'.

Pilots sometimes went on the courses as individuals, but most often as a squadron, especially when the Spitfires began to arrive in India in September 1943, going to just three former Hurricane squadrons, 136, 607 and 615. Although Frank had not flown a Spitfire operationally, his overall knowledge was no barrier to imparting to these squadrons the best way to handle them against the Japanese. Gordon Conway of 136 Squadron once related to me:

'We now flew as a squadron to Frank Carey's establishment at Amarda Road, where I had done my air fighting instructor's course the previous month. For three weeks the squadron concentrated on gunnery and combat practice under expert tuition and it was my task to analyse each camera-gun film. We flew several sorties against resident four-engined Liberator bombers and this was to pay dividends in the following weeks.

'On 18 November, several of us went over in our 15 cwt truck to meet the mail plane from base. The CO took the bundle of official mail, perused it, then turned smiling to me and handed over a pencilled note from the adjutant which was a copy of the signal from the AOC Bengal, congratulating Johnny Rudling on the award of the DFM and me, on the award of the DFC. They were the first awards to the squadron since it had been formed more than two years earlier.

'There was a very lively party in the mess that night and the next morning Frank Carey invited me to go to his bungalow where he gave me a piece of DFC ribbon. A typical jesture.'

Bill Davis also of 136 Squadron recalled for me this trip to AFTU in

November 1943:

> 'We flew down our new Spitfire Vs from Baigachi to Amarda
> Road for an Air Firing Course at AFTU. Carey did great
> work in improving the standards of visiting squadrons by his
> example and the facilities he had. We did air-to-ground and
> air-to-air firing and plenty of ciné-gun attacks including those
> on Liberators and B.25s. We used to watch the results of the
> ciné-gun attacks but what I remember most vividly were the
> ciné films produced by Carey – splendid range, line and
> deflection shots but quite amazingly, they included inverted
> attacks sharply pulling up to avoid defensive guns on the
> bombers. I later became a pilot attack instructor and saw a
> lot of ciné films but do not recall ever seeing any other
> inverted, accurate, attacks recorded. To dive alongside a large
> aircraft, such as a Liberator, pull up in a steep climb, roll
> inverted and get close to the target called for a very high
> standard of skill. Frank Carey was a great inspiration.'

Another familiar face now came to Amarda Road, Squadron Leader
Alan 'Kit' Kitley, bringing in his new command for instruction, 9
Squadron, Indian Air Force. Like most Indian squadrons, the pilots
were a mix of Muslims, Sikhs, Parsees, Christians, Hindus and Anglo-
Indians. In his book Alan records:

> 'We flew all the aircraft to Amarda Road. The training in the
> air-firing school was good; while mainly for the
> inexperienced pilots, we all took advantage of testing and
> improving our firing skills. Air-to-air firing involves a tricky
> technique and is very difficult to master. The target is moving
> at speed and likely to be manoeuvring; the attacking aircraft
> is a moving gun platform and the pilot has to aim ahead and
> along the line of flight to allow for target movement. It may
> sound obvious but the bullets have to hit the target and not
> where the target was when the guns were fired; the gun-sight
> has to track along the anticipated line of flight of the target
> and at the moment of firing the attacking aircraft has to be
> flown smoothly, with no jerkiness or side slip.
> 'So to sum up, the technique is to attack with an overtaking
> speed and to manoeuvre so as to move the aiming point along
> the projected line of flight of the target; when in range,
> normally 200 yards, to fire and break off the attack before
> flying into the target. That 200 yards is covered in no time
> when the attacking aircraft has, for example, a 100 mph

overtaking speed. Attacking static or slow moving ground targets is less tricky unless, having got sights on and firing, the pilot gets a bit mesmerised by the target, does not pull away in time, and flies into the ground, or flies into obstacles such as power cables, also with fatal results.'

A former Halton apprentice, Tony Carr (42nd Entry) recently wrote in to *The Haltonian Journal* about Frank at Amarda Road. The article recorded that:

'Amarda Road was commanded by Frank and its task was to instruct fighter and bomber pilots in the art of air attack and defence. They were equipped with Spitfire VIIIs and Liberator IIIs with both RAF and USAAF crews attending. The exercises were filmed with camera guns and then reviewed at the later exercise debriefs. At one of these, the film showed that a USAAF Liberator had, during a mock attack by Frank, carried out a complete roll. The pilot declared that this was impossible only to have Frank confess that during the attack he had rolled his Spitfire in the opposite sense whilst keeping the Liberator in his sights! An outstanding feat of airmanship and a demonstration of his sense of humour. What else would one expect from an ex-brat?'

Frank has another mention in *Wings of the Phoenix* in the chapter regarding the arrival of the Spitfire in the India/Burma theatre:

'Its arrival in the battle was not of course the result of sudden inspiration, but depended on months of foresight, planning and campaigning. In the vital battle for air supremacy the answer to successful aircraft must be immediate or it comes too late. In this case, had the RAF been unable to retain its temporary advantage, the results on the ground would without a doubt have been the loss of irreplaceable thousands of Allied lives and, as will be seen later in this story, the possible conquest of India by the Japanese.

'The reply to improved enemy tactics could similarly not be suddenly dreamt of in an operations room. Here the man chiefly responsible was that experienced pilot Frank Carey. He was the "backroom boy" of the Burma victory in air supremacy, the man whose refresher courses in gunnery and tactics at his school near Calcutta produced some of the most ingenious fighter pilots of the war. In Burma it was said that a remarkable proportion of enemy fighters brought down were destroyed by pilots listening to the echo of Carey's voice and obeying his teachings.'

Several people have told me how good Frank was as a commander and leader of men. Coming up through the ranks no doubt helped to mould him and temper the way he acted, especially if faced with a disciplinary problem. One arose in November 1943 involving the 'Woodpecker' squadron and in particular, Dudley Barnett. Barney Barnett, the Australian who had been in Frank's wing at Chittagong, wrote in his diary:

7 Nov 1943. Amarda Road, Orissa. Few lectures, some very good. Flying in afternoon, one Spit trip, range estimation astern with camera. *Very bad evening* [author's italics].

9 Nov 1943. Amarda Road. Lectures and further ciné [gun practice]. Seems Bevan[11], Garvan[12] and self may be in trouble over the 7th doings. We certainly put up some blacks. After a few drinks went to No.1 Camp with Bev, he to arrange drogue towing. Bags of drinks, and started home. Acting the fool at 50 mph in 3-tonner, lights, steering, etc. Further bottle of gin.... Tangled in guard-room gate (gave false names), also tangled with sundry outlying camps – contractors – bogged down twice. Don't know how we preserved our necks. Dennis [Garvan] and I fighting like billy-oh beside Bev at 50 mph. Blacks!! Contractor put stinker in today. W/Comm Carey roped in station for line-up identification – poor results. Finally rounded to us. We are to see him in the morning. [He] was pretty wild. Does not seem to mind our escapades so much, but naturally very brassed off at wasting most of the day getting to the bottom of things. Oh well, he's a good scout and bloody sorry to have troubled him.

10 Nov 1943. Three of us at HQ. Torn off pretty big strip by Winco Carey. [He has] half a mind to let matters go to AOC, which would mean a court martial. Looks grim on paper; conduct to the prejudice etc., stealing petrol, use of service vehicles, no licences, false names, under the influence, going outside camp area, etc. Means being torn to pieces. [Wingco] advised us to come to his room at 11.30, he wanted time to

[11] Flying Officer D Bevan, 136 Squadron. Badly injured in another motoring incident on New Year's Day 1944, in which another officer was killed. Bevan was not driving.
[12] Flying Officer D E W Garvan, 136 Squadron. An Australian, he later won the DFC having scored 4 confirmed, 2 probables and 4 damaged combat victories.

think things over. There had to be a punishment. Much relieved. Tore off an unholy strip when we presented ourselves. [He] said only the fact that Garvan and I were going forward [operations soon] and the CO had spoken so well of us, he was letting us away. Bevan took a beating too. Carey 'threatened' to do his best until we left the station. He made a fist of it; he [was] very quiet, very at ease, very much to the point. I've got such faith in him that I've bet Bev his posting is not stopped. [Carey impressed on us that the] case needs to be kept very quiet. Carey reckons any talk may bring him the completest rocket for not putting it all up further. What hell to have slipped up just for a night like that!

About his new job, Frank wrote:

'At Orissa I was asked to gather together a few experienced pilots, who had operated against the Japanese and form a small specialist team. The team and I worked out a suitable training syllabus to get things going. Very quickly, after starting with a few chaps from each squadron, they went back to pass on the details to their other pilots. In a month or two we began to collect quite a few squadrons who were then well provided with their own instructors. All this rapidly expanded, and we then began covering some USAAF fighter squadrons as well as all the bomber squadrons. The latter used the flying training to help in evading enemy attacks while giving their air gunners training too.

'We were living in a very quiet area well away from the chance of enemy attack. The evenings became quite lively with all these short-stay visitors attending courses. Thus it became essential to arrange some "services" to control these evenings. The *Screecher Club* was formed to control drinking to an acceptable level – allowing drink as long as you remained amusing. The club also had its ranks.

'The bottom grade was "Hiccough", then "Roars", followed by "Screams", with "Screech" at the top. Everyone but me had to start with "Hiccough". I permitted myself one grade up at the beginning, since I was running the blooming thing. Everyone else started at the bottom.

'You had to behave yourself because if you went over the top you were downgraded. The only way to move up a grade was to hang around at the bar and buy drinks for one of the higher grades. When we had graduation nights (about one a week), if a chap had bought me a few drinks, he was certainly worth a higher grade. Chaps would hang inverted from the ceiling Punkahs [fans] and things like that, which would also gain them a higher ranking, as long as they weren't stupid and injured themselves.

'Someone gave us a grand piano. We used to have sing-songs and I started to "compose" two pieces of "music". One was called the *Prang Concerto* and the other was the *Symphonic Alcoholique*. I could play the symphony all ways, i.e., you didn't necessarily have to use your hands. The *Prang Concerto* was very physical and had three movements. The last movement demanded the complete demolition of the piano.

'I had to go through and play the third movement on my last day there, before being posted to the Middle East. It cost me quite a lot to replace that darned piano. Actually, I never did really complete the third movement, because it is almost impossible to break the heavier range wires of a piano, even using a broken-off piano leg.'

Frank continued running AFTU into 1944. By this time the Second Arakan Campaign was in full swing, the Japanese trying once again to move north into India by this route but with the arrival of the Spitfire in the India/Burma theatre, the RAF fighter pilots were getting the upper hand. On the ground too the army had learnt to dig in and fight it out with the Japanese army. The new commander in the Far East was Lord Louis Mountbatten, and his strategy was that if the ground troops did not retreat, he promised they would be supplied by air. The Japanese had no air supply organisation, their doctrine having always been, take what you need from the defeated and retreating enemy. With nothing to capture and the British and Indian forces refusing to retreat, their meagre supplies of rice and bullets soon began to run low.

Frank also had his own Spitfire VIII, which he often flew, which had a red spinner and a red lightning flash on the fuselage as a personal identification. Students in the air were always on the look-out for this Spitfire. This machine was also flown by Tim Elkington, one of Frank's instructors. Elkington, it will be recalled, was in hospital with Frank in August 1940.

Another new type in Frank's log in April 1944 was the American P47 Thunderbolt which would soon replace Hurricane fighter-bombers in the Far East. In June he was flying tactical trials with the new Spitfire VIII against the P.47 – at 25,000 feet. By this date the Japanese had now been defeated in their third attempt to get into India. This time they had tried to go via the Imphal Valley and Kohima. Again air supply and the well-trained fighter pilot of the RAF defeated the

Japanese both in the air and on the ground. Virtually all the fighter pilots involved had gone through Frank's AFTU. He once told me, with his usual modesty:

'The pilots already possessed all the necessary enthusiasm and ability required, and I was merely put into a position of being able to pass on the results of my own experience to a very capable and willing audience. Much of what was passed on had already been pushed into me during a course at the Central Gunnery School, Sutton Bridge. It was there that I first encountered the technique of flying not looking on the horizon or with instruments, but solely on the gun-sight and the rear of one's pants, which is the ultimate achievement of a pilot in a front-gun fighter aircraft in action. Of course, I was only one of a number of instructors at Amarda Road, all of whom had been through recent combat experience against the Japanese.'

Frank and his instructors were now teaching their pupils the 'rolling attack', in order to combat the agile Japanese fighters. To quote from an RAF paper on tactics distributed at the time:

'The attacking aircraft passes over the target from the beam position approximately 1,500 feet above. As the target disappears under the wing, the attacking aircraft swings the nose back in the opposite direction to that of the target and goes over into a barrel roll, which is controlled so as to bring the guns to bear as soon as the manoeuvre is completed. The value of the momentary point turn in the opposite direction at the commencement of the roll and the quick breakaway made possible by the fast overtaking speed, thereby permits a series of attacks to be delivered.'

Frank was a keen advocate of this form of attack because:

You have a good plan view of your target.
It is easy to assess the line of flight as the ground helps you.
Your aircraft is a comfortable platform for shooting.
You always come out of the sun round mid-day
and achieve surprise.
To get away, let your stick go forward and duck under.
You are a difficult deflection shot for anyone else.

Frank always liked to keep the enemy in sight, especially with such a large nose on the Spitfire and Hurricane, so by ignoring the horizon and concentrating solely on the target, wherever it may be and in whatever attitude, by rolling over and looking 'up' he could always keep it in sight. He would also tell his pupils:

> 'The average tour is 300 operational hours or one year whichever is the shorter. In this time you may be in contact with the enemy for 30 hours. Approach and attack probably occupy three minutes of this time. Consequently, as it takes one year's tour to do three minutes firing, you must do your best to make that three minutes as effective as possible.'

Putting it to them in this down-to-earth fashion undoubtedly had a sobering effect on all the would-be fighter 'aces' who passed through Amarda Road. There is no doubt that the instruction and tuition these pilots received by attending Frank's courses, paid handsome dividends in the Burma, Arakan and Imphal battles.

Mention was made earlier that the USAAF also took advantage of AFTU. Early in January 1944 Frank received a letter from Air Vice-Marshal Tom Williams OBE MC DFC, a successful ace in WW1, now at HQ Eastern Air Command, South East Asia, which read (in part):

> 'My dear Frank,   27 January 1944
> 'You will probably know that I am now here as Deputy Air Commander to General [G E] Stratemeyer, who commands the Eastern Air Command, which embraces all what used to be Bengal Command plus the tenth USAAF units, the Troop Carrier Command and the Photographic Reconnaissance Force. As such, I come into very close contact with a very large number of American COs and their units. I wanted you to know I have heard nothing but universal praise for the very great value the American airmen say they get out of their courses at Amarda Road.
> 'This state of affairs is, as I well know, to a very large extent due to your own personal efforts and the high state of efficiency which you have developed in your unit.
> 'In addition to the above I have had most excellent reports of the high standard you yourself achieved in courses during the visit we sent you on to England last year.
> 'I hope very soon to be able to visit your unit with General Stratemeyer. In the meantime we are proposing to make increasing use of your unit by USAAF crews, and I know they

can count on getting all help possible.

Yours sincerely,

T M Williams

PS. I have just shown this letter to General Stratemeyer who asks me to add his appreciation.'

Not long after this, one unit in particular were rewarded for their time under Frank Carey's tuition. This was the 459th Fighter Squadron which flew P38 Lightnings, which had twin engines and twin tail-booms. Although under the 80th US Fighter Group, this squadron mainly acted independently of Group HQ, and were named the 'Twin-Tailed Dragons'.

They had particular success against the Japanese over Burma in March and April 1944 and again at the end of May. They received a Distinguished Unit Citation for this period, whilst operating from Chittagong. General H C Davidson of the US Strategic Air Force sent a signal to Frank dated 12 March 1944, with a copy to the RAF's 3rd Tactical Air Force's commander, Air Marshal Sir John Baldwin KBE CB DSO. It read:

> Carey from Davidson.
> Recent exploits of 459 Fighter Squadron have proven definitely the value of your training course. This Squadron for its first all out attack against enemy aircraft destroyed 15, repeat 15, and 11, repeat 11 probables and damaged. We are indebted to you for the fine training you have given them. Accept our sincere thanks.

This in turn caused Sir John Baldwin to respond and to send another signal to Frank:

> You will be glad to know that during the morning of 3rd March, 459 Squadron brought great credit to themselves and to your AFTU. In action over the aerodromes at Heho and Aungban by destroying 9 aircraft in the air and 6 on the ground and damaged a further 8 in the air and 3 on the ground with only one loss to themselves. Positive rules in combat are what we are striving for and I am satisfied your course is accomplishing this. My hearty congratulations to you and your staff for your continued excellent training work and the best wishes for continued success of all Squadrons

passing through your hands.

Frank, despite all this adulation, remained his usual modest self. Another reason for being so was his general demeanour as, having just injured his ankle in a football match he was hobbling about ingloriously on a couple of crutches. (Frank had a sport medal, inscribed with the words 'SHQ FC, India 1943, Winners. F Carey', so must have been some sort of footballer.)

Then came a personal letter from Sir John Baldwin dated 5 May:

'My dear Carey,
'I am very glad to send you the enclosed copy of a letter which I have received from General Slim, GOC-in-C, 14th Army, in connection with a job of work recently carried out by personnel from Amarda Road.

'You will see that the General wishes his "grateful thanks and congratulations" to be conveyed to all who took part in this work – and particularly to Flight Lieutenant N Sims and Sergeant Day. Will you see that this is done and also add my congratulations for a useful piece of work well done?'

Lieutenant-General Sir William Slim's letter, dated 23 April 1944, read:

'I have received from my Staff certain reports of the arrangements which were made at Amarda Road for flying in the 4th Brigade.

'The RAF Station Commander and his Staff gave us the very greatest assistance and did not hesitate to put themselves out to ease the task of my Staff and to help the troops. I should be most grateful if you could convey to them my appreciation of all that they did. I am informed that the work of F/Lieut N Sims, the Engineering Officer at the Station, in repairing and maintaining the aircraft was of an extremely high order and much appreciated by the American Squadron Commander. The work of Sergeant Day, who was in charge of refuelling, has also been brought strongly to my notice. On one occasion he refuelled seven C.46s, each with 1,400 gallons, and thirty C.47s at 800 gallons each, within an hour. The American Air Officers on the Station considered this the best they had ever seen under such conditions.'

All this was happening at a time when Imphal and Kohima were under siege and the Chindits were being flown in and supplied by air in central Burma during 'Operation Thursday'.

One final story from Frank's period at Orissa concerns him in the role of 'the big white hunter'. It was recalled for Max Arthur in his book *There Shall be Wings*, by Lucien Ercolani[13], who, in mid-1944 was commanding a B24 Liberator Squadron at Salbani. His squadron often acted as 'targets' for AFTU's Spitfires, training for air-to-air combat against bombers.

Wing Commander Ercolani related that in June 1944 he had called in to have lunch with Frank and had only just started when a distraught villager arrived asking for help to deal with a leopard which had attacked a child and was in danger of attacking again. Rushing off to help, armed with .303 rifles, they found the villagers in a high state of agitation, running around with spears, bows and arrows, plus an assortment of machetes. In the midst of this village of tiny huts stood a large mango tree, in which the offending leopard lay draped over a branch.

Frank and Ercolani both took careful aim, fired, and while they succeeded in wounding the beast, did not kill it, whereupon it came leaping down from the tree, scattered all the on-lookers, including the two RAF men, and ran off. They obviously had to finish it off but they had no idea how to track it until a headman ran up and told them that the leopard had not fled any distance and in fact was taking refuge in the eves of a nearby hut.

Pushed unceremoniously forward by the villagers and when they were just about ten yards from the hut in question, there was a roar and the leopard leapt down and headed towards them. The two pilots were so hemmed in they could not raise their rifles, but luckily the cat was more intent on escape than ripping bodies, bounding harmlessly between them, then taking refuge again up a tree.

With a modicum of calm restored, Frank and Ercolani fired again, this time killing the animal. The dead leopard was decorously draped over the front of Frank's jeep with photos of Frank standing and then kneeling in front of the trophy, Lee-Enfield in hand, looking every inch a cross between a great-white hunter and a hero. He must have had hopeful intentions of having the head and skin preserved as a souvenir of his moment of glory(!), as he sent the carcass off to a firm of curers in Calcutta. Unfortunately when it was returned, the skull had not been properly cleaned out and the wingco's new fireside rug soon began to rot around the skull area. Gradually the rotting and then hairless, wrinkled grey mass prompted a story that far from shooting the beast himself, Frank had actually paid some local boys to club it to death.

---

[13] Wing Commander L B Ercolani DSO & Bar, DFC (99, 355 and 159 Squadrons.)

Chapter Ten

Fayid and Peace

Finally Frank's time at AFTU came to an end, and he was assigned another job in the RAF's training schemes, Officer Commanding 73 Operational Training Unit at Fayid, Egypt. With it came promotion to group captain. Not bad for someone who had started out as a Halton Brat, then later a sergeant pilot. Frank related:

> 'In November 1944 I arrived to command Fayid in Egypt as a group captain. Fayid was a big airfield adjacent to the Great Bitter Lake. This was a very pleasant variation from the rather jungly Amarda Road. Being a major flying training station it had lashings of aerial activity from many different two-seater trainers and fighter types. These included Spitfires, Harvards, Thunderbolts, Hurricanes, Fairchilds and Masters.
>
> 'The war in Europe was beginning to show signs of an imminent conclusion, while in the Far East there was every indication that it was developing into a long-drawn-out battle. Accordingly the Air Ministry instructed that this operational training unit was to change its role from supporting the European war to the new requirements of the Far East, and I was sent there temporarily to oversee these changes.'

There must have been some earlier consultation on this matter, for Frank records in his log book several legs of a flight to Cairo in early July 1944, a visit to Fayid in the middle of that month, and a return to India as the month ended. When he finally made the move to Egypt, he flew out in a Liberator from Amarda Road to Delhi on 26 October, then by BOAC Ensign aircraft to Heliopolis (11 flights in all) before flying the last leg in a Fairchild on 2 November.

Eric Batchelor, one of his instructors, told me that when that first Liberator took off and headed west, his pilots: '...gave him a farewell fighter escort from Amarda Road – a very fitting tribute indeed.'

The aircraft he flew mostly at Fayid were Spitfire Vbs – particularly ER566 – and also Thunderbolts, again particularly JL348; also North American Harvard trainers. The Thunderbolt was an all-black affair with a red stripe painted down the fuselage on both sides, and just like at Amarda Road, was undoubtedly a marking to make him instantly recognisable in the air.

Air Marshal Sir Keith Park KBE CB MC DFC, was, in December 1944, in the Middle East. Park, of course, had been AOC 11 Group of Fighter Command in the Battle of Britain, and therefore, Frank's 'big boss'. Frank immediately took the opportunity to ask Sir Keith if he would attend a mess party on 15 December. Unfortunately, Sir Keith wrote back saying he had to attend an official 'do' in Cairo, so could not come. Frank kept the letter, most probably for the typing error it contained. At the bottom, where the addressee's name was placed in RAF communications, it had read, Group Captain F R Carey DSO DFC, RAF Station, Fayid. Frank had circled the DSO and placed a question mark under it. Did he think, perhaps, a DSO was on the way and the AVM had made a Freudian slip? No, I don't think so either. Higher authority had already been given the chance to give him one – and muffed it.

However, it was no error when it was announced that in the New Year's Honours List, Frank was rewarded for his fine work at Amarda Road, with the award of the AFC. Air Marshal Sir Guy Garrod, the Allied Air Commander-in-Chief, South-East Asia, wrote to him on 1 January 1945 – 'My warmest congratulations on the award of your Air Force Cross.' This was Frank Carey's fifth decoration.

One of Frank's instructors at Fayid, was none other than Bill Davis, formally of No.136 'Woodpecker' Squadron, who told me:

'I was posted to Fayid in February 1945. On reaching Cairo from Ceylon at the Postings Department the officer arranging postings, rather than sending me to Italy, as I requested, rang up FRC, who promptly said that I should be sent to him as an instructor. Frank, of course, had a good knowledge of all the aviators from the Far East, and was always on the lookout.

'At Fayid, Carey was highly regarded by everyone. We had a lively, experienced, bunch of instructors from both the Desert Air Force and from the Far East.

'Carey had a smart Thunderbolt II [JL348] painted black with a red stripe down the sides (of which I have a plastic model) on which he occasionally demonstrated his skill despite the Thunderbolt weighing in at seven tons. We all had a friendly relationship with him – the CO. I have photographs of him enjoying a party in the mess including one of him having his trousers removed. I am not sure many station commanders would join in such frolics.

'I did meet a sterner side of him. On 5 March 1945, I was leading a formation of Spitfires to practice battle formation and to demonstrate spinning. It was a rather daft idea where the leader would spin and then get the rest to do the same in turn. The Spitfire could be tricky to recover from the prolonged spin but as briefed and lectured, new pilots were instructed that if they got into difficulty, they had to trim the aircraft nose down and let go of the controls. The Spitfire would then pull out on its own.

'As we were starting at 20,000 feet this was quite practical. We did a couple of "turn abouts" over the Bitter Lake and maybe because of the tension, the formation broke up. In my exasperation I foolishly called on the radio for them to "spin down and return to base" as a way to sort out the muddle. On rejoining the circuit at Fayid I was aghast to see a Spitfire spinning quite flat, and crash onto the airfield. To my regret, which I still feel, the pilot was killed.

'Afterwards I was hauled up in front of the group captain and was admonished, and as a punishment, made the officer in charge of the service funeral. As I have often said before, the RAF took much too casual an attitude to fatal aircraft accidents, which gradually improved over the post-war years.'

Frank's CFI (Chief Flying Instructor) at 73 OTU was Squadron Leader D H Clarke DFC, known to everyone, inevitably, as Nobby. Nobby Clarke had had a long war in both Europe and the Desert, firstly on Spitfires and later on Kittyhawks. By his own admission he had something of a rebellious nature and on occasion liked to be on his own. He recalls one story which eventually involved Frank. With desert all around them, it was easy to slip off on your own and indulge in whatever activity gave one a break from instructing, routine, and a chance to be away from fellow aviators:

'I used to enjoy myself alone some afternoons naked out in some wadi or other, 5-10 miles from the aerodrome. Certainly it was known that the CFI "pissed off" alone in his jeep on some afternoons, but it remained as a minor eccentricity until one day Frank actually asked me where I went. I told him that I just enjoyed being free in the nude, jumping off sand-dunes, rolling about, etc. Frank quickly suggested we made a party of it, with a brigadier chum of his joining us.

'So in due course, Frank, the brigadier, the acting CFI and myself, went off to a quiet spot, disported ourselves and began jumping off the biggest sand-dunes we could find (believe me it is fun!!) and generally forgetting what we were – a flight lieutenant (the acting CFI), me a squadron leader, Frank a group captain, and the brig! There was nothing untoward about all this. It was no different from what nowadays is called "skinny dipping" – except we enjoyed it in sand rather than water.

'I forget whether Frank or I discovered the 18-foot sail boat [the *Irma*] at the Officer's Club on the Bitter Lake, but I do remember Frank solved the difficulty of a missing mast (it had boom and sails) by locating a spar from a crashed Wellington bomber. I rigged the boat in due course and Frank and I (with one or two others) had many a sail across the lake, with a luncheon basket filled with good food, and plenty of Stella – Egyptian beer. As far as I remember Frank, like me, preferred beer to spirits.

'When I had been with 450 Squadron in the desert in late 1942, the boys managed to kid me into "weightlifting". I was told that so-and-so could lift three heavy people to shoulder height with one hand. Having got suckered in, I was told to sit down. Someone sat behind me and I was told the secret was in the careful locking of arms. Having carefully locked my arms, the "strong-man" then straddled my legs and began to slowly undo my flies. In due course everyone emptied their drinks into the gap! It was a ritual which several newcomers fell for including medium senior officers – all Aussies as far as I can remember.

'Now I was quite impressed by this rotten trick, so I invented another scam, but went one better – I would. I called it "hypnotism", and used it in my next Kittyhawk squadron – 250. "Hypnotism" began with a casual remark at the bar that Nobby was a hypnotist. After due discussion over several pints about whether hypnotism was rubbish or fact, someone would ask the "sucker" if he thought I could hypnotise him. The "sucker" would inevitably say no – and bet on it!

'I would then take him to one side and explain hypnotism, telling the man to close his eyes and imagine he was on the front buffers of a train in a dark tunnel, pitch black, and he could see nothing until a tiny spot of light appeared that only increased very slowly. By this time I had eased the man onto the floor, so I could be sure – I told him – he would not fall and hurt himself if in fact I succeeded in hypnotising him. Telling him to keep concentrating on the light in the tunnel, while lying flat on his back, I asked him to lift his left arm to show he knew what I was saying. The arm would come up and then I told him to put it down and raise the other arm. I followed this in turn by getting him to raise his left leg, keeping it up, then raise his right leg too. It was at this stage that we grabbed his feet and everyone poured their drinks down his trouser legs! It worked every time.

'Now Frank had seen me perform this gag many times since arriving at Fayid, and on one occasion when he was entertaining the brigadier he asked me to do it on our army friend. Now I wasn't particularly bothered about the brig's trousers, but I was dubious about discipline, especially with the army. Frank told me "Don't worry about that, I'll take care of him." And this was how the brigadier's trousers were soaked. However, it didn't quite work out in the usual fashion.

'Generally, the moment the victim felt liquid being poured down his legs, he generally erupted into frenzied action. But on this occasion, the brigadier stayed put – his legs remaining in the air. Somewhat baffled, the "jokesters" went suddenly quiet. Eventually Frank gave him a hand to get him on his feet, took him into a quiet corner of the mess, and had a chat. It transpired I had actually hypnotised him! Frank assured me he was OK and remembered nothing about the event. I never saw the brigadier again – and it was the last time I performed that trick.

'One of the ground officers who watched this performance subsequently became a professional hypnotist as a direct result and I later met him in Doncaster in the mid-1950s. In his professional booklet in which he describes the above event, he mentions Frank and myself in his introduction.

'Another event took place during Christmas 1944. I decreed – backed by Frank – that all officers should dress in Arab garb, and for two days most did. Result – near chaos. But great fun, and it passed the time.

'Frank and I shared the black Thunderbolt, and we often discussed the merits of air-to-air firing against air-to-ground firing. I knew his air-to-air scoring was exceptional but I reckoned his air-to-ground was not as good as mine. So we challenged each other. On a towed target, beam attacks (the most difficult), Frank scored easily; I scored absolutely nothing. On the air-to-ground, Frank missed the target drums completely, whereas I scored pretty well. Honours were even.

'With Frank at Fayid was just one of those weird occasions when two very different characters gelled. Apart from the all-Aussi 450 Squadron, which was the best squadron (and CO) I ever flew in, Frank Carey was easily the best-ever CO for me – and there is no doubt I was difficult to deal with in those days. I'm afraid that age and rank prevented any closer friendship, but Frank certainly helped me by making me accompany him on official duties, including HQ get-togethers, dances, and the like, which I hated. He never ordered me to do anything, he simply "invited" me, and I was a little surprised that I went. Thanks to Frank, I was awarded my AFC.

'As far as I am aware everyone liked Frank Carey.'

Another small snippet of information concerning Frank at Fayid was that he had had a church built under his instructions. It was a solid brick affair and with a stone-built altar. Rows of four folding chairs each side of the central aisle gave room for a fair-sized congregation. In a photograph of the interior I have, there are at least 80 chairs. There are also two pulpits. Frank did have some religious beliefs, occasionally took communion, but was certainly not devout, however.

In May 1945 the war finally came to an end in Europe, although the war with Japan dragged on until August. Two atomic bombs quickly ended Japanese defiance to the 'writing on the wall' and undoubtedly saved the lives of many Allied soldiers, sailors and airmen. Before that occurred, Frank was posted back to England, in June, flying by Dakota to Northolt. For some days he was reunited with his family, although it appears that the relationship between him and his wife was under strain. However, it was great to see his two girls; Anne was now eight, and Jane close to a year. Of his new appointment, Frank wrote:

'I was posted to the UK to become head of the tactics branch of a recently formed Central Fighter Establishment at RAF Tangmere. This newly formed CFE was in fact a fighter university, busy collecting all the information available connected with the world-wide fighter experience and recording it for future use. It had an extremely high-powered staff. Regular courses were run for experienced fliers from various countries. It meant world tours, and discussing with my small team of experts from the CFE, the events of the European war. Lessons had to be learnt. In Indonesia a "small war" was still rumbling on between the RAF, the Indonesians and the Dutch, many elements of which were far from accepting that the "big war" was over.

'It was a most attractive post and I enjoyed every minute of it and would have stayed there forever. However, to continue my career in the RAF, meant I had to look ahead, so I grabbed the chance of applying to attend staff college. In fact, although granted, I was sent to the Army Staff College at Camberley rather than the RAF one.'

There was a bevy of brilliant former fighter pilots at CFE, which was run by Air Commodore R L R Atcherley. Douglas Bader was there, Bobbie Oxspring, Dutch Hugo, Bob Tuck, Hawkeye Wells, Johnny Checketts; even some top German aces, brought in for interview/interrogation – Adolf Galland being the most famous. Bob Tuck wrote in his log book: 'Posted to the Central Fighter Establishment at Tangmere for duties with the tactics branch in the capacity of Wing Commander Air Combat. G/C F Carey, OC tactics branch. W/C G R A McG Johnston, dive bombing. W/C C D North-Lewis, R.P. Lt.Col. Stanford, close support, FSOS, Commander. M Newman, FAA tactics.'

'Robin' Johnston DSO DFC and Bar, had been a fighter pilot with 73 Squadron in the desert between 1941-42 and in 1944 led 122 Mustang Wing. Kit North-Lewis DSO DFC and Bar had been associated with Typhoons for much of the latter half of the war. He had flown with 175, 182 and 181 Squadrons, before leading 124 Wing. The 'R.P.' noted by Tuck referred of course to rocket projectiles, and North-Lewis was well versed in their use.

It was while Frank was at CFE Tangmere, that he learnt of award number six, the American Silver Star. Although these 'foreign' decorations often came up with the rations, to be handed out almost at the whim of the latest incumbents in the headquarters concerned, there is no doubt that Frank's achievements with the Americans and their fighter tactics training at Amarda Road, would have been a good enough reason for him to receive the award.

Nobody would deny Frank had a good sense of humour. In July 1945 there appeared in a newspaper, a small article together with a photograph of Batchy Atcherley with Mr Anthony Eden, then Britain's Foreign Secretary. Atcherley was seeing to it that Mr Eden got safely away to a big conference at Potsdam. Frank cut out the article and picture and sent it to Atcherley with a memo:

From: Officer Commanding, Tactics Branch,
    Central Fighter Establishment.
To: Commandant, Central Fighter Establishment
Date: 18 July 1945

The Skymaster as a Ground Attack Aircraft
 1. Please see attached for your 'edification and delight'.
 2. In view of this latest information may Tactics Branch, in conjunction with F.S.D.S., commence trials of P.F.F. technique for Skymaster?

Atcherley returned the memo to Frank, with some annotations on the bottom:-

Just because the Foreign Secretary called in for 'briefing' before the Berlin Conference – I see no reason for 'tittle tattle'.
 You may commence trials on the Skymaster at your convenience. I'm too busy personally with this Berlin business. Anyway, Eden and I don't think much of such remarks and we're not people to run up against!! Richard. 25/7/45

During August, with the Japanese war ending, there was talk of a party from CFE going out to Japan in order to do similar work to that it had been doing in England. Frank was not slow in asking Air Ministry if he could go, writing to his old boss, AVM Tom Williams who was now in Whitehall. Williams wrote back on the 29th:

My dear Frank,
'In confirmation of what I told you during your unofficial visit here the other day, we cannot arrange for a specific C.F.E. party to go to Japan but we are asking the Americans if we can send an Intelligence party from A.D.I.(K) and I have asked A.C.A.S.(I) to include two or three C.F.E. representatives in the party specifically to study past and present Japanese fighter tactics, training, development, etc.
 'This will be coming through to C.F.E. officially in due course. In the meantime I should prefer that you did not disclose this information.
 'I have made enquiries about your permanent commission and find that the recommendation has been received and is under consideration. I am told the recommendation is a strong one and there is every chance of it being favourably

considered. I hope, therefore, to see your name in the next list and if by chance it does not come out I shall take a hand myself and see that it gets further consideration.

'This information is also, of course, strictly confidential!'

It appears however that Frank did not immediately get his permanent commission. (Nor did he swing the Japan trip.) True to his word, Tom Williams wrote personally to those in charge of such decisions on 29 October:

'I should be grateful if you could give me some information regarding the application of the above named officer [Carey] for a Permanent Commission.

'He served for a long time under me whilst I was A.O.C. Bengal and as a result I formed a very high opinion of his capabilities and am very anxious that he should receive consideration for appointment to the Permanent list.

'I questioned him on this matter today and he informed me that he had apparently omitted to send in some important form with the result that his application had not been considered. If this is the case perhaps I can assist.'

Whilst he was waiting for those on high to make up their minds about his future, the Central Flying Establishment moved to RAF West Raynham, Norfolk, during October where Frank continued working. This same month Frank had a couple of rides in gliders, also flew a Spitfire IX (BS116) to Celle in Germany, and flew around to other destinations in Germany before returning to West Raynham on the 25th. Frank got his hands on a Meteor III jet on 3 November, his first jet aircraft and within a fortnight was performing aerobatics in one – of course. The following month he was a passenger to Group Captain C H Hartley DFC AFC, head of CFE's night-fighter wing, on a trip to Germany in a Mosquito VI, bad weather delaying their return by a couple of days.

Just before this, however, Frank became part of another significant moment of history. In mid-September 1945, he received an Immediate signal from HQ 11 Group concerning a planned RAF flypast to celebrate the fifth anniversary of the Battle of Britain. Most people interested in RAF history will have seen the newsreel clips of Group Captain Douglas Bader swinging his tin legs into the cockpit of a Spitfire on this occasion – as well as many still photographic shots. In *Reach for the Sky* (Bader's life story) the film ended with this scene and the reconstruction of the flypast over London. Frank kept a copy of the signal which (in part) reads:

A0809 13 Sep unclassified. Commemoration of the Battle of Britain air display.

Ref this Hqrs A0780 12 Sep the following officers with aircraft required to report to Group Captain Bader at North Weald by 10.00 hrs 14 Sep for final practices 14/15 Sep

Group Captain Carey	CFE Tangmere
Wing Commander Tuck	CFE Tangmere
Wing Commander Brothers	CFE Tangmere
Wing Commander Deere	Andrews Field
Squadron Leader Bush	Andrews Field
Group Captain Turner	Aldermaston
Wing Commander Vigors	Castle Camps
Wing Commander Crowley-Milling	Air Ministry
Wing Commander Lofts	No.11 Group
Group Captain Thompson	RAF Staff College
Wing Commander Drake	[FLS, Milfield]
Wing Commander Ellis	Fighter Command

Para 2. Aircraft for Group Captain Thompson and Wing Commanders Drake and Ellis are available at North Weald. Group Captain Thompson requested to contact Group Captain Bader direct for further instructions.

Frank flew up from Tangmere on the 14th in a Spitfire coded ST-T. On the 15th he flew this same machine in the flypast (one hour, 15 minutes), then flew back to Tangmere later that day. It will not surprise the reader that among the photographs taken of the pilots this day, especially those gathered around their old C-in-C, Lord Hugh Dowding, Frank is missing. No doubt he was nearby, but had yet again managed to slide-slip away from the spotlight.

The weather on the 15th was marginal, so much so that Bader was given the final word on whether to fly or not. Bader was already aware that other aircraft were even then forming up over East Anglia, their pilots getting themselves into position for the flight across London. He made the decision and shortly afterwards this band of fighter pilot brothers were taking off. It must have been the most decorated bunch of pilots to be in one formation, for between them (and joined by Wing Commander E P 'Hawkeye' Wells), they had won nine DSOs, one Bar to DSO, 14 DFCs, 12 Bars to DFCs, two second Bars to DFC, one AFC, one DFM and three American DFCs. Also between them they had accounted for over 200 enemy aircraft – confirmed.

In due course Frank received his Permanent Commission and was thus free to continue his service within the ranks of the Royal Air Force. Then he left the Central Fighter Establishment, his request to go to staff college having been approved. He recalled:

> 'My session at the Army Staff College proved very interesting and enjoyable as well as instructive, and it seemed to me to be very generous in the report that I received on completion. Whilst there I noticed that the small RAF contingent with me (about five I think) all had to lose their acting ranks, whereas the army (and navy as well I think), were able to keep their acting rank. I might have had second thoughts about being so keen to attend, as it took me seven years before I regained by group captaincy. Once again! By which time the consequent delay prevented me going on any higher in the RAF.'

Meantime, from Frank's log book it seems as though he spent much of 1946 in the air. One trip began on 27 February, when Flight Lieutenant Roberts, in an Avro York (MW117) took him from Lyneham to the island of Malta and then on to Cairo. Further York aircraft took him to Colombo, then by Sunderland (RN289) to Singapore. Various Dakota aircraft then hauled him to Batavia, Samarang, Sourabaya, Kemjoran and back to Kallang by 15 March. For the rest of that month and into April Frank was flown all round Burma, Malaya, etc, before heading back to RAF Lyneham – via Castel Benito – on 4 April.

The purpose of the February trip was for Frank to lead a team from CFE to the Far East. It consisted of five or six people, including Kit North-Lewis and 'Hawkeye' Wells DSO DFC. North-Lewis, who was with CFE from July 1945 to August 1946, recalls:

> 'In 1946 I was a member of a team led by Frank going to Malaya [and then] we flew to Jakarta to report on the civil war between the Indonesians and the Dutch. We flew out to Jakarta via Colombo and Singapore, visiting Sourabaya while we were there. I do not think we gathered much information as it was clear that the Dutch hold on Indonesia was virtually over. We returned via Malaya, Burma and India. Other than this I did not have much dealings with Frank, except socially, but I remember him as an extremely likeable man.'

Still keeping his hand in, June and July saw him flying VIPs about in an Oxford, including Lieutenant-Commander Bigg-Wither, his old 52 OTU CO, Group Captain John Grandy DSO, and Group Captain Chaplin. Frank went on:

'My next posting, in December 1946, was to Germany, and to the RAF's 84 Group HQ, situated at Celle. My first impressions of Germany were very mixed. Celle was a very attractive, even picturesque place, with deep snow just like one sees on Christmas cards. However, with the town being only a few miles from the Russian-held sector of Germany and things being quite edgy at that time I was very aware that we had no fixed position and we could easily be over-run at any time within a few minutes.

'There was no central heating and little fuel for fires, and what supplies did move about were often stolen en-route long before we saw them. We occupied some brand new German army quarters with triple glazing, but even shaving was an ordeal. All in all it was quite wearisome. One of the few advantages was the fact that labour was unlimited as the populace had nothing else to do until businesses began to get re-started. Living with German staff took a little getting used to. In many cases all the civilian staff were the same as those that had run it earlier for the German air force. Furthermore, normal German currency was almost valueless. I remember my predecessor handing me several large suitcases full of marks – practically useless! The distinct advantage however, was this. Devaluation of German notes and coinage had been catastrophic to the local populace as apart from being in free-fall it was changed several times during my time there. However, we were able to afford cigarettes, chocolate, etc., from the NAAFI canteens. The Germans who worked for us, male or female, such at cleaners, would work all week for a bar of chocolate or small packet of cigarettes.

'I was able to get our lovely Officer's Mess – I was also the PMC [President of the Mess Committee] – completely re-decorated and set up to depict Piccadilly Circus tube station, and its environs, at the mess entrance, including a little shop. This was accomplished by hanging a huge lined cloth painted to resemble this tube station entrance, complete with flower ladies for guests. The various corridors were fitted with more canvas and painted to show well-known stores. Main rooms were made to look like familiar London restaurants. All this was achieved without one single piece of wartime damage showing, all for cigarettes, chocolate, etc, plus some very minor cash outlays for certain expenses. We were also able to obtain first-class wines and spirits, while we took over, complete with staff, one of Hermann Göring's very well established hunting lodges, where we could move to for weekend breaks.

'My position at headquarters was that of wing commander training, and therefore, not a full flying post. However, there were usually many opportunities for borrowing some fighter aircraft to keep my hand in. There were many light aircraft such as Austers lying around for moving about from one place to another. Fortunately one of the "plums" of my post gave me more or less control of a "Hitler Youth" gliding and ski-ing club in the Hertz Mountains, just south of Hannover. I spent many happy weekends at that establishment.

'It was a happy time. I had a personal light aircraft, continued enjoying the gliding and ski-ing, plus the wines. So life was pretty good even after winding up our ex-army headquarters at the end of 1947, at which time I was moved to Gütersloh.'

Auster aircraft always seemed available as Frank testified, but there were also trips in Mosquitos, Spitfire XIs, Spitfire XIXs and then a Tempest II on 19 July 1947. The following month his marriage to Kay was annulled. It had been under pressure for a long time. While Frank was overseas, his eldest daughter had been put into boarding school, while the youngest was more or less brought up by her grand-parents. Kay was living with another man, having even changed her name to his. These two were finally married in January 1948, a daughter being born to them just over two months later.

Frank did not let the grass grow under his feet either. He met Bertha Kathleen Walters Jones, known to everyone as Kate. She had been an army nurse. Kate and Frank were married at Stockton-on-Tees Registry Office, on 18 December 1947. He gave his address as 18 Chalfont Road, Weston-Super-Mare, where his father was living. Kate took on Frank's two daughters and she proved a good mother to them both. She was 30, while Frank was now 34. The marriage came just as Frank was on the move once more, but still in Germany.

'After about a year, 84 Group Headquarters was disbanded, in December 1947. I had the good fortune of being posted to a full flying job as wing commander flying at RAF Gütersloh.

'Gütersloh was a very pleasant station, still being serviced by the original staff who ran it for the Luftwaffe. During the Berlin Airlift all the fighter aircraft in Germany were moved to Gütersloh and this kept us all going full speed. The wing was boosted to five squadrons during the airlift.

'So my life was full as, in addition, the wing had an operational responsibility for keeping an element permanently at Berlin's Gatow airfield. We also had to fly right down to the Austrian Alps in order to "show the flag" as well as to give the appearance of being a much bigger force than we really were. Heaven knows who fell for that one. However, it did give us a bit of long distance experience especially getting in to Zeltveg, our base some 500 miles away, near Graz. We even went as far as Trieste as we had some vague duty of providing emergency cover for that Italian city. Meantime we were able to relax in both Holland and Belgium, as well as being able to fly back to the UK for a weekend at regular intervals.

'Late in 1948 the wing re-equipped with Vampire jets, which required our careful attention, as the earlier versions only had about 30 minutes flying duration. They were beautifully light and responsive in the air which was a tremendous difference from our heavy, powerful but tricky, big radial air-cooled engine of the Hawker Tempest II. Five months after the arrival of the first Vampires I was posted back to the UK and Fighter Command.'

At Gütersloh, Frank's flying hours reached the 2,000 mark. His usual Tempest II was PR674, assigned officially to 26 Squadron of his 135 Wing. It was later destroyed in a crash on 5 January 1949, the pilot being killed.

'I spent four months hanging about at the pleasant location of RAF Thorney Island, near Chichester. This delay was caused by the new Commander-in-Chief of Fighter Command [Air Marshal Sir Basil Embry KBE CB DSO DFC AFC], and resulted in a number of re-arrangements of senior staff. In my case my destination was changed to HQ 12 Group, near Nottingham. Although my post was mainly connected with buildings, etc, thanks to the generosity of the AOC, I was given a great deal of freedom to fly his personal Vampire jet fighter.'

At Thorney Island, Frank's title was wing commander admin (supernumerary), and what flying he could get was mostly in Meteor IVs. While 'hanging about' he got himself on No.40 OATS Senior Course in August (Officers Advanced Training School). At this time his family was living in Seaford.

At 12 Group he not only flew Vampires but also Meteor VIIs. On 17 September 1949 he entered the Newton Air Race, flying a Vampire, coming in third. His time at 12 Group came to an end in July 1951, with a posting as wing commander operations in the newly organised

Fighter Defence, Scottish Sector, where, fortunately, he was able to get a good deal of flying. This was mainly on Vampire Vs but other types crop up in his log book: Austers, Oxfords, Harvards and Meteor IIIs. On 15 September 1951 – Battle of Britain Day – he again entered an air race, this time at RAF Leuchars, improving his positioning by coming in second, in a Vampire.

Just before his next posting, Frank was flown in an Oxford by his old CO, George Lott (by now an air commodore) who it will be remembered lost an eye in the early stages of the Battle of Britain. Lott was now chief instructor at the RAF Flying College at Manby. The trip was from Turnhouse, Scotland, down to RAF Raynham on 30 June 1952, then back to Scotland on 4 July.

In October 1952 Frank was posted to RAF Honiley, where he had been with his 135 Squadron back in 1941. Now, 11 years later, he got the job of forming a wing of several auxiliary squadrons and effectively became OC at Honiley. These squadrons were based not only at Honiley, but also used Manchester airport, and Aldergrove in Northern Ireland. He had his own personal aeroplane, an Oxford, which was stationed at RAF Squires Gate, Blackpool. The three squadrons were 603 at Turnhouse, 605 at Honiley and 502 at Aldergrove. Also at Squires Gate he met up with Alan Kitley – former 136 Squadron Woodpecker – who used the airfield to fly Meteors, 'to keep his hand in'.

After what Frank described as a very pleasant six months at Honiley he was finally promoted back to his former rank of group captain, following a period – which still grated – of seven years. He was appointed Officer Commanding Western Sector of Fighter Command. For the first time in his career he was not stationed on an RAF airfield base but in a hole in the ground – an underground defence headquarters. He and his family lived in a civilian house that was administered by the nearby RAF unit at Blackpool.

All his work here embraced air defence planning, for this was the period of the cold war, with everyone looking for any hostile signs or intentions by Soviet Russia. It was all a necessary evil, and Frank, like most pilots, had to come to terms with being more on the ground – or in his case, under the ground – than in the cockpit, where most self-respecting aviators wished to be. But he was now nearing his 41st birthday and accepted that flying modern jets was a younger man's game. Not that it stopped him grabbing every opportunity to get himself into that blue and white environment.

Indeed, Frank Carey managed some useful 'rides' during his tenure. He logged his first flight across the Atlantic on 5 July 1953, in the Stratocruiser 'Cabot'. The pilot was a famous name not only in civil aviation but in the wartime RAF. Captain T M Bulloch DSO & Bar,

DFC & Bar, had been a pre-war airman like Frank but his training and wartime experience was with Coastal Command. Ranging over the Bay of Biscay and out into the wilds of the Atlantic, Terry Bulloch became the most successful Coastal pilot in terms of U-boats attacked and sunk during the war. Now with BOAC the Atlantic was something merely to cross, not to search. Frank was flown from London Airport to Keflavick, and after refuelling, continued on to Dorval, Montreal, Canada, a total flying time of just over 14 hours.

He was on a fact-finding tour and went to St Hubert, the Canadian airbase just to the east of Montreal. Here he met another highly decorated former RAF fighter pilot, Wing Commander J R D Braham DSO & 2 Bars, DFC & 2 Bars, AFC, CD, Belgian Order of the Crown and Croix de Guerre, who was with the RCAF Defence Headquarters. Bob Braham had been in the RAF during the war but left the service in 1952 and moved to Canada. Joining the RCAF as a wing commander he had been working-up the Canadian Air Force's all-weather defence capabilities.

At St Hubert Frank managed to wangle a ride in a T33, with Bob Braham in the pilot's seat. They flew to Bagotville and back on 9 July, a nice entry for his log book – indeed for both their log books.

Heading back to London in mid-July, Frank continued flying a desk at his underground workplace, but still managed to add flying time in his log, with trips in Oxfords, Vampires and Meteor VIIIs, plus a few Anson rides.

Then in the early summer of 1956 he became Group Captain Operations 2 at Headquarters Fighter Command, RAF Bentley Priory. Frank noted this move as in November, but a letter dated 27 June 1956 seems to indicate the job was certainly made official earlier:

> From: Air Chief Marshal Sir Francis J Fogarty KCB KBE DFC AFC ADC
> Air Ministry, Adastral House, Theobalds Road, London, WC1.
>
> To: Group Captain F R Carey DFC AFC DFM
> Headquarters, Fighter Command, RAF Bentley Priory, Stanmore, Middx.
>
> Dear Carey,
> Just a line to send you my warmest congratulations on your promotion.
> I am delighted that your sterling services to the Royal Air Force have been recognised by this well-merited advancement.

To confirm it was earlier than November 1956, there is an entry in his log book for 31 July 1956, his first ride in a helicopter. He was taken from Bentley Priory to Wartling in a Westland Whirlwind, a trip of 45 minutes. Frank's final job in the Royal Air Force came in 1958 as he recalled:

> 'I was then posted as group captain for two years as Air Advisor to the UK High Commissioner in Australia, as part of the UK Joint Services Liaison Staff in Melbourne.'

A new life was opening up.

Chapter Eleven

Australia and *Finals*

The job in Australia meant quite an upheaval for the Carey family but finally everything was in place and they set sail for their journey half-way across the globe. His new position would be as part of the UKJSLS – UK Joint Services Liaison Staff. He would be working under an Admiral, who was then chief of the UKJSLS, whilst reporting to the High Commissioner, at the British Embassy in Canberra.

Frank loved cars and loved driving, but in Australia his rank and position afforded him his own chauffeur. At this period, virtually all British embassies employed RAF drivers, and in this particular case, Frank had one too.

Corporal Ted Evans had already been to Australia in the early 1950s during the time of the A-bomb experiments. Having, therefore, been given a higher grade of clearance, he had become part of the RAF's special duties unit. Once again in England, he was told of a driving job in America and along with around 200 other hopefuls, applied. He was whittled down to the last two, going along for the final interview that was being held at the RAF Records Office. In the event he came second, the other driver having already had experience in the US, but before he left the office, a flight sergeant asked if he would like a consolation prize. Ted asked what that might be and the flight sergeant said that he would like Ted to go to Australia for two-and-a-half years. Not a bad result, but the only drawback was that he would be going in two weeks.

Ted said yes, was immediately given his travel warrants and other documentation, and told to get back to his camp where his bags – already packed – would be waiting for him. After a quick party and family goodbyes, Ted reported to RAF Lyneham for his flight out. The orders were for him to be sent out on the first available aeroplane, and the transport officer, getting over that initial shock, said how about a Comet that was leaving shortly? It was full of civilian scientists and climbing aboard a flight sergeant in charge of cabin services took one look at Ted and said: 'If you think I'm going to wait on you all the way to Australia, you've got another think coming. Get your jacket off, you're going to work your way there!'

After dispensing food and drink to the bevy of scientists, the Comet airliner duly arrived in Darwin, then another flight took Ted down to Adelaide, then finally on to Melbourne. He was met by the driver he was going to replace, who told him he had a week to 'learn' Melbourne. He also met the group captain that Frank was replacing and Ted had to drive him around for some days until Frank's boat docked.

On the due date Ted drove to the docks and had his first glimpse of his new boss. Ted was a lean six foot, three inches, and the scene can be imagined as he came to attention in front of Group Captain Carey's five foot, three inches. Frank returned Ted's salute, looked up and said exasperatingly: 'They've done it to me again, haven't they? The long and the short of it!' It was a remark which set the tone of their future relationship. Ted remembers:

> 'We stayed in Melbourne for several months until they set up a new office in Canberra where we then moved. The family moved into 4 Somers Crescent, on the deluxe side of the city, the Capitol Hill side. Canberra was like a city of offices, there appeared to be no "civilians" – everyone worked for the government, or something. Frank, at that time would have been 46-47 years old – still a very young man. Yet nobody really knew who or what he was. He was just another group captain to most of us. There were no books around in those days where you could read about such men. His medals indicated a story but I for one had no real idea what that story might be.'

The High Commissioner at this time (1955-59) was The Right Honourable Peter Carrington MC – about to become Lord Carrington – who had previously been with the Ministry of Defence. A major in the Grenadier Guards during the war (his Military Cross was gazetted in 1945), Frank would have acknowledged that this man at least had some 'time in'. When I recently asked Lord Carrington about Frank, he replied: '...he was a splendid man I very much admired and relied on.' Ted continues:

> 'Carrington and Frank got on like the proverbial house on fire and became fantastic friends. I also used to drive him around too. Frank was always keen to lend me to anybody, for if he could get rid of me, it meant he could drive the car himself. He always wanted to drive. I used to pick him up each morning and drive him to the office. If he had some

work to do, papers to check over, or wanted to read his daily paper, he'd sit in the back.

'One particular morning early on, I duly arrived at his house, and Frank said that he would drive. As I moved to get into the passenger seat, he told me to get in the back, as he was taking his daughter Anne into the city, and being a bad traveller, she would want to sit next to him in the front. The three of us went off and after arriving at the barracks he said he wanted to see me in his office. This was normal, for he would then give me the day's itinerary and my duties. Entering his office with my pad and pencil, I went to sit down, but he stopped me.

'"Stand there," he said. This was new. Looking intently at me, he continued: "I don't mind driving you to work. I don't mind you sitting in the back. I don't even mind you acknowledging the salute as we drive through the gates, but I do object to you reading my newspaper!"

'Frank went berserk. Much later I mentioned this story to Jane, his other daughter, and she smiled and confirmed that nobody in the family ever touched Dad's newspaper before he did.'

Jane also recalled that as children they were acutely aware that Dad always had the cream off the top of the milk with his breakfast. When they asked why, they were told that he was the man in the family. That, to him, appeared to be enough said.

Jane also related that her father was something of a disciplinarian, no doubt a throw-back from his old Halton days. They were not allowed to have untidy bedrooms and beds had to be made properly before they came down to breakfast. When Jane later went into the nursing profession, one thing she did not have to learn was how to make beds. Ted again:

'The duties Frank had in Canberra were completely different to what he'd been used to in the air force. I would think he came to work much of the time in civilian clothes, for we seldom saw him in uniform. He had to entertain a lot too, in fact almost every night there was some kind of function either at home, at the Embassy or some other embassy or ambassador's residence. At least we always had the week-ends free. Australians don't work at weekends, not even socialising work. In Canberra, I remember, on Friday nights it used to close, and nothing opened on a Saturday morning.

'Officially I was just a driver but once Frank got to know

me, I became part of the family. I would even baby-sit the girls. His wife Kate taught me how to wait table and help at cocktail parties, which were always brilliant. If one was held in Frank's house, his first drink would always be a modest gin and tonic, plus ice and lemon. Nobody was allowed to serve him drinks except me, for I knew that for the rest of the evening I had to serve him just tonic, ice and lemon. He wanted to ensure his brain was never addled enough to give anything away about his air attaché work. Once the evening was over and everyone had departed, Frank would have a large G & T, and be finally able to relax.

'I have seen him happy on some nights, coming home from a function but he never drove at all if he had had a drink. He was a very good host and was always on the top of any guest list. Everyone wanted Frank at dinner parties. I recall one night going to a dinner party held by Robert Menzies, the Australian Prime Minister. As I dropped him off at the door, he, as he always did, looked at his watch and said, right – 10.30. I knew that I had to be back at 10.30, in fact 10.25, as he was always five minutes early; he was generally early for everything.

'So, I got there at 10.25, and inside Frank told the PM that he'd have to leave now as his chauffeur would be waiting. As I sat in the car outside, this gentleman came out of the front door, walked to my window and said that he wanted to keep my boss a bit longer. He was enjoying his conversation with Frank and wanted a bit more time with him. Did I mind, he asked, waiting a bit longer? I replied, no I didn't mind a bit. The man then gave me a big fat cigar and said that if I could smoke it, by the time I had finished, my boss would be out. The man was Robert Menzies himself!

'Punctuality with Frank was of paramount importance. If he gave a time nobody could be late. If he said to meet him at 11 o'clock, he would invariably be ready himself at 10 and pacing up and down until my arrival.

'Whilst in Canberra, the Admiral who had been in charge of our UKJSLS was replaced by Air Vice-Marshal F S Stapleton DSO DFC BA, which was some relief for Frank as he now had a fellow RAF man above him which took some of the pressure off. They in turn became good friends.[13]

---

13 Frederick Stapleton was just three months older than Frank and had joined the RAF in 1934. In WW2 he became a fighter pilot, leading the Hornchurch Wing with distinction in 1941. Before retiring from the RAF in 1966 he had added a CB to his list of honours.

'I got caught speeding one day, and Frank was not pleased. He then taught me the number one survival technique. Just like his old wartime flying, Frank said that one must assume everything in the rear-view mirror was the enemy until it proved otherwise. That had been his main rule in combat and was a big factor in his survival for so long. It was a lesson I have never forgotten.

'Then one day Frank called me into his office and said that I was going to be the AVM's driver. I said I didn't want to be his new driver, I wanted to stay with him. Sorry, said Frank, but we've made the decision. I was not at all happy and said I was going to speak to the AVM direct. So Frank was forced to tell me that he had arranged a job with Rolls-Royce and would be leaving the RAF, but staying on in Australia. I still wanted to wait until he'd finished but he was keen for me to get on and hopefully, with an AVM, I would get my third stripe. So I did move, but still ended up doing more work for Frank and his family, than with the AVM, who already had a cook and a batman to help look after him.

'Another thing was that Frank was to get a Bentley (company car) with his new job and he certainly did not want a driver – not even me. He always loved his cars. He had a few Hondas, the first was a Prelude 4ws, the one before his last was a Civic CRX a sporty two-seater. He took Jane to Wales in it once, during one of her visits to England. It turned out to be a white-knuckle ride and she vowed not to do it again. Not many people would get in it with him as he behaved as if it was a road-going Hurricane! He said it was good at high-speed tight turns.'

Ted got married during his time in Australia, to Jeanne, an English girl who had gone out to Australia to work. He had lived in a hostel called Reid House, which also housed people from England who'd come out on the £10 scheme, as Jeanne had done. Ted had to ask permission from Frank to get married, and to wear a white shirt whilst wearing his uniform. Group Captain Frank Carey not only attended the wedding, but had also to sign the marriage certificate. Not bad for a corporal driver.

Frank apparently bought the champagne for the wedding although he later claimed he could never have been that generous.

Frank's replacement at UKJSLS was another former Battle of Britain pilot, Group Captain J B Coward AFC. James Coward had been in 19 Squadron – Spitfires – but on 31 August 1940 had been badly wounded attacking a Dornier 17, and as a result had lost his left leg. He remembers Frank:

'I had met Frank after the war at Battle of Britain reunions and we knew each other by sight. I only got to know him better when I took over from him as Air Advisor to the High Commissioner in Canberra, in February 1960. I must say he gave me an excellent hand over. He had clearly been very popular with the Australians.

'He returned to Canberra very soon as the Rolls-Royce representative but both being very busy we only met at parties. The next time I met Frank was in 1990, at the 50th Anniversary of the Battle of Britain. There was an amusing incident at the Lord Mayor's party for us all at the Guildhall. Before she left, the Queen Mother asked to meet us all, so we were lined up by squadrons. While talking to Frank he said, "I do hope you will be here for our 60th Anniversary Ma'am." She replied. "I shall certainly be there if there are enough of you left."'

James' wife Cynthia also recalled:

'Frank was an extremely modest man, never mentioning his exploits during the war, always cheerful and kindly. He told me once that he had offered a young woman a lift on an unpleasant rainy evening. She was standing by the side of the road trying to wave down a car. He had two daughters of his own so stopped to give her a lift. When their routes diverged he stopped to allow her to alight. She told him, "If you don't drive me right to my door I will say you tried to interfere with me," so Frank didn't stop but drove right on. When he reached the local police station he said, "Well, here we are. Go in and tell them your story."'

Frank was awarded, or became, a CBE in the 1960 New Year's Honours List; a Commander to the Order of the British Empire. It was a fitting end to a long career in the Royal Air Force, spanning 33 years. He returned to England in April 1960 and left the service on 2 June.

Once retired he went back to Australia to take up his appointment with Rolls-Royce Aero Engine Division, as sales representative for them in Australia, New Zealand and Fiji. Setting up home once again, things went along nicely. He had a good and interesting job, a loving wife, two daughters who would marry Australians and set up home there too, and was still only 48. On a sad note his father Jack died in

1962, aged 75. We might mention here too, that his brother Roy died in 1976 (60) and brother Hugh in 1983 (69), so Frank outlived both by some years.

In 1963 Frank was in contact with his old CFI when he was OC at Fayid, Nobby Clarke. Nobby was writing about another matter at this time, but Frank spoke to him about his life in Australia:

> 'Well, here I am very happily doing this job – with the two plus years that I was here in the RAF I have just about had five years altogether in Australia. I find myself singularly unsuccessful as a salesman and frequently wonder how long the company will put up with me. My two daughters, 25 and 18, are with us and the elder got married a few weeks ago, while the younger has just left school to take up a career. So my roots are already beginning to spread in Australia and I find, what with occasional trips back to the UK for Farnborough, etc., that the whole thing is amazingly painless.
>
> 'I occasionally see ex-RAAF and ex-RAF chaps that I knew which calls for more drink than is good for me and I am told by people who may be just wanting to be kind that I am unchanged except for a little extra weight and an ever higher hair-line. I have twice looked at Fayid through binoculars going through the Suez Canal, and although it looks, at that distance, quite clean and tidy, the lack of activity bears a striking resemblance to the odd occasion when the station was closed and we were sailing on the Irma. I even have one photograph of you, sitting up in the sharp end completely bereft of any clothing, although in a modest posture which does not preclude the picture being shown in anyone's drawing-room.'

Frank retired from Rolls-Royce in 1972 when he reached 60. He had decided he would remain in Australia but a sudden devaluation of sterling – by some 17.5% – from which source all his income would be received, meant that his standard of living would have been reduced considerably. This compelled him to return to England, rather than be, in his words, 'a poor white in Australia'.

Frank decided to leave as soon as possible, and took the opportunity to sail rather than fly, travelling via the Panama Canal. On the journey Kate suffered a slight stroke, but thankfully she recovered well.

Just before we leave the Australian part of Frank's story, one amusing incident that his daughter Jane remembered was on the occasion he went to be measured for a new suit. Having had the tape measure treatment by the tailor, the man, almost to himself, stated: 'Short, portly and forty.' Obviously with his guard down (nor was he looking in his rear-view mirror), he related this to his family when he arrived home, and to his regret, these four words were often repeated.

Once back in England, Frank and Kate set up homes in the Midlands, then in Sketty Green, Swansea, South Wales before they eventually settled in Bognor Regis on the West Sussex coast in 1980, above which he had fought several air battles during the Battle of Britain. He still remained in relative obscurity as far as many RAF historians were concerned, this author among them, for it soon became apparent that getting him to talk freely about his wartime experiences was not an easy task. Not that too many tried but every now and again someone got lucky and he would jot down a few career notes for them.

He kept in touch with a few former RAF colleagues and occasionally was persuaded to attend the odd reunion. The nearby Tangmere Museum would have been an obvious centre of attention but he rarely visited it and when he did, it was unobtrusively as a 'civilian'. He could have easily become an honorary member, which would have meant less cost when he did visit with family and friends, but he was never one to push himself forward.

In 1990 Frank was again in the news, this time because his nephew had taken him up in a helicopter. Squadron Leader David Carey was the son of Frank's brother Hugh. At this time he was a SAR (search and rescue) pilot, flying Sea King helicopters with 202 Squadron RAF. David flew his uncle round his old haunts, including Tangmere. As luck would have it an emergency call came though during the flight and David had to land to off-load his uncle.

Frank had three nephews and a niece. Brother Hugh, as well as David, had a daughter, Elizabeth. Roy's son by his first wife was Michael, who later became a brigadier in the REME. Son Stephen came from a second marriage but tragically he and his wife were killed in a sport car accident, leaving a small daughter.

Kate's death in November 1991 hit Frank very hard. Friends rallied round and he was often invited round to drinks and dinner parties in his local area. In 1992 he met Marigold Crewe-Read, who was on a visit to friends in Bognor Regis from her home in Berriew, near Welshpool, Wales. Frank and Marigold – a widow for some years – got on famously and they were married at Chichester Registry Office on 5 April 1993.

Frank's hearing had become difficult, a common occurrence with former RAF pilots who had lived with the roar of aero engines in their ears for many years. Because of his age the RAF decided to give him a lump sum for compensation rather than increase his pension. The money came in handy, using it to finance a honeymoon with Marigold in Australia, where he could also visit his daughters and introduce the girls to his new wife.

By this time a familiar face had returned to Frank's life, his former RAF driver in Australia, Ted Evans. Having left the service himself, he was now a sales rep, covering an area in southern England, and living in nearby New Milton. One day Ted was watching television when up popped the face of his old group captain talking on some TV programme about the Battle of Britain. Ted set out to find where Frank was living and to his delight discovered it was only a few miles away along the coast. He immediately contacted Frank and he soon became a regular visitor for tea, biscuits and a chat, whenever his job took him to Bognor.

To Ted's mind Frank used Bognor as some sort of extension to the RAF Club. Every Friday he played snooker with the boys, then drinks in one or other of their homes. Then came drinks at 'The Ship' pub on Wednesday lunchtimes. Frank seemed very content with life. Ted Evans:

'In 1998 Frank bought a sedate Honda Accord which I now drive. He managed to dent both wings, the marks are still there, so we decided it was time for him to stop driving. The following year the optician diagnosed bad eyesight forcing him to give up his licence. I bought his car and said that if ever he wanted to go anywhere, I would drive him. I had done it before.'

In April 2000 Frank was invited to the RAF Museum at Hendon by the *Daily Mail* to commemorate the 60th Anniversary of the Battle of Britain. Ted took him and stood in awe to see and meet so many great men. Although often shuffling to the back Frank met many old friends and enjoyed the day. He laughed a lot.

News that his daughter Anne had died in May 2002 gave him a jolt. Diabetes and heart problems lead to a stroke. She was 65 and she and her husband David had provided Frank with two grandchildren (one by adoption) and two great-grandchildren.

In June Ted took him to see the Brooklands' rebuilt Hurricane. It had been 40 years since Frank had sat in a Hurricane and invited to do so, his hand went straight out to the footstep as he hauled himself up, as if those 40 years had not existed. Frank commented that the visibility seemed better than he remembered, then he was told that there was no gun-sight in the way. He also laughed when it was explained that aircraft now had satellite navigation systems. In his day, he told them, they had to find their own way home.

On one of these occasions, Ted had driven him to a reunion, and in due time Frank indicated that it was time to leave, even though the 'do' was far from over. Ted went off to get the car and when Frank estimated that Ted would be about ready and waiting, he said to a high-ranking former Battle of Britain pilot he was chatting to, that he had to go as his RAF driver was waiting. The man was visibly taken aback, thinking, how on earth did a retired group captain still merit a driver? Frank more than likely saw the questioning expression on the man's face but did not think it appropriate to enlighten him. His sense of fun never deserted him.

Tangmere now came back into his life again, albeit briefly, as Ted remembers:

'The first time I took Frank to the museum, all he wanted was to view the aeroplanes outside. However, once there he needed to use the loo so I said there must be one he could use just inside, and in he went. Moments later he emerged and asked if he could borrow two pounds. I gave it to him but then wondered why on earth he should need it. I went in too and asked a chap at a counter if he had seen an old gentleman come in, which he said he had, and I then asked if he had been charged an entrance fee merely to use the toilet? The man said yes.

'I then asked if he had any idea who the man was, and of course he hadn't a clue, but when I said that I could see three photographs of him from where we were both standing, his eyes opened wide. I gave the man Frank's name and rank. There was a very red face, especially when the man said he was unable to give a refund as a ticket had been issued. However, it was quickly agreed, once Frank emerged from the WC, that if he filled in some forms he would be made an honorary member of the museum. Frank was not fussed, but it got everyone out of a difficult situation.

'Probably his last visit was on his 90th birthday. After a good lunch at *The Olde Cottage Inn*, Frank's favourite eating place, I asked him what he would like to do and Frank said he wished to visit the museum. This time I went in first and warned them he was coming. There were few visitors in there, but three chaps on the counter quickly began to remove empty cups and polish the counter top. When I returned with Frank, the three were standing to attention.

'We mooched about for an hour looking at various photos and other things Frank wanted us to see, and I gradually became aware that the museum was filling up. Someone must have made a few telephone calls, for suddenly people were taking pictures and coming up to shake his hand, all of which totally bemused Frank. My wife was standing at his side and said to him that a lady was trying to take his picture. My picture? No, no, she doesn't want my picture. But Frank, my wife insisted, they've come here to see you. Who's come to see me? He could just not imagine why anyone would want to come and see him. He was simply Frank Carey.'

Frank Carey died on Monday 6 December 2004, 63 years to the day he had sailed from Greenock taking his squadron overseas and ending up in Rangoon. His health had deteriorated during the previous five years and his last three and a half years were spent in a rest home where better care could be maintained. His funeral and cremation took place on 17 December, at St. Stephen's Church, North Mundham, followed by a Service of Thanksgiving. His daughter Jane journeyed from Australia to attend.

The first tribute was given by Air Commodore Terry Carlton, followed by another, by Ted Evans – to 'his Group Captain'. The lesson was read by Air Commodore Harry Davidson OBE, who had commanded 43 Squadron between 1965-67.

Then on 7 May 2005 his ashes were interred in the graveyard at Tangmere, to rest with others who had flown from this famous RAF fighter station, although in contrast to Frank's 92 years, most were just young men – boys. But it is fitting that he should be laid to rest there alongside them. Home is the hunter ....

O Ruler of the earth and sky
Be with our airmen when they fly;
And keep them in thy loving care
Amid the perils of the air.
O let our cry come unto thee
For those who fly o'er land and sea.

In July 2005 Marigold presented, on loan, Frank's impressive row of medals to the Tangmere Museum. Despite his close association with this fighter airfield none of his decorations were earned whilst operating from the station, but there can be no more fitting place for them to reside and be on display. He was truly one of Tangmere's gallant sons.

Afterword

The Score

When I was young and starting to read about fighter pilots, my youth's brain took hold of the notion that the higher a fighter pilot's victory score, the better one should hold him in one's esteem. As I grew older – and hopefully wiser – I quickly realised that this was not the way to look at things. Yet still today, some people will regard a victory tally in a distinct way and fail to realise the difficulties involved with this sort of reasoning.

During World War One for instance, if we look at three German aces, Manfred von Richthofen, Oswald Boelcke and Max Immelmann, whose scores were 80, 40 and 17 respectively, some would say that von Richthofen was the greatest fighter pilot due to his high score, in fact the highest of any pilot in WW1. However, he scored his victories between 1916 and 1918, whereas Boelcke scored his 40 between 1915-16, a time when air fighting was in its infancy and aircraft and conditions in the skies over France were very different to 1917-18. Then again, Immelmann was as famous as Boelcke in those earlier years and his score was then on a par with Boelcke's, but his death in June 1916 ended his victory run. The point being in his case is that had he not been killed who knows what sort of score he would eventually have achieved?

In World War Two, we might look at three British fighter pilots, Johnnie Johnson, Thomas 'Pat' Pattle and 'Sailor' Malan – 38, 52, 35. Johnnie Johnson's rise to fame was due to him being the RAF's top scorer over northern Europe, his tally made during the years 1941-44. Pattle gained all his victories in nine months between August 1940 and April 1941, although, fighting in the Middle East and Greece, his score was not fully appreciated till long after the war had ended. Malan's 35 victories were all scored in roughly the same time, but over England and northern France, between May 1940 and July 1941. Three different scores, three very different men, and fighting in three very different climates of the air war.

I merely make these points to emphasise that there is more to a man's victory score than mere numbers if you're seeking to find the best. His equipment, the war front, the conditions, the opportunities, the opposition – all have to be taken into consideration. Boelcke and Immelmann were fighting together in a machine called a Fokker Eindecker, which was not a particularly good aeroplane but it did have the advantage – which its pilots took – of having the first machine gun specifically fitted to fire through the whirling blades of a propeller. Boelcke went on to fly the early biplanes but his death came before better fighters became available in late 1916. Von Richthofen had the advantage of using only these newer biplanes – the Albatros Scouts – and later the Fokker DrI Triplane – but had died before the best German fighter even reached the Western Front, the Fokker DVII.

Johnnie Johnson flew the Spitfire Marks II, V, IX and IXb – each in their day the best RAF fighter available. There were periods when some Me109s or FW190s were better, and better still if flown by an experienced German pilot, but generally these Spitfires could hold their own. He could also boast that he was never hit by enemy fire in combat. Pattle flew the antiquated Gloster Gladiator biplane, before finally getting hold of a Hurricane. Yet he held his own against all opposition, although one might argue that this Italian opposition was far different from that found by the RAF operating over and from England. Malan also flew the Spitfire I, II and V but in a very different climate than Johnson. Malan was flying during the desperate times of Dunkirk, the Battle of Britain and in the early fighter sweeps over northern France. At this period the German Luftwaffe pilots were on the crest of their particular wave – 'gung ho' the Americans might call it.

Over Europe, for the RAF, the air war had two distinct phases, defensive then offensive. RAF fighter pilots came into their own and into their country's history and folklore, during 1940. They had been on the defensive once the French campaign began on 10 May, had been on the defensive over the beaches of Dunkirk as the British army evacuated the continent, then defending Britain during the Battle of Britain – both day and night. Even in North Africa, Greece and Malta, it had been all defensive actions, trying to stem Italian and German aggression.

By the time Johnnie Johnson and pilots like him were gaining victories over northern Europe between 1941-44, the RAF, along with the American air forces, were taking the war to the Germans. Their equipment was better, their training was better, their awareness was better and their strength in numbers was better.

All this leads me to Frank Carey's score of victories. All fighter pilots are different. They have different ideas, different make-ups, different experiences, are on a scale of pilot quality of their own making. Frank was different too, he had to be. His early life affected his later life, most people's do.

When the war began Frank was an NCO pilot and undoubtedly aware of his origins. He did not come from a wealthy family, the death of his mother had given him a knock. His step-mother and he didn't get on, so at the first opportunity he left home, entering the world of harder-knocks within the RAF apprenticeship scheme. Yet he survived and came through his training well enough to join an RAF fighter squadron as ground crew.

He 'kept his nose clean', learnt more about his trade while always looking and waiting for that opportunity he craved, the chance of becoming a pilot. When that chance came he grabbed it with both hands, succeeded, and, with unprecedented luck, returned to the very same fighter squadron, but this time as a pilot – a sergeant pilot.

Frank Carey would still have been painfully aware that he was an NCO however accepted he would be by the squadron's officers. Then his skill as a pilot got him noticed by these officers, especially when he became part of the unit's aerobatic team. You had to be good to compete at this level. He had a winning smile too, and was no doubt something of a champion to all the NCOs and men of the squadron. He was doing things some of the officers could not do, or certainly not do as well.

In the squadron's first actions he was fortunate enough to be on hand – be in the right place at the right time – and his success brought him the squadron's first decoration in WW2. From now on he knew he could use his skill and experience against his country's enemies, so long as they did not get him.

Frank Carey was always reluctant to elaborate on his personal victory score. That in itself is not unusual. Most fighter pilots would say it was their job. If some were more successful than others, that had been in the lap of the gods. One can imagine too that after a while, continually being asked about his score would easily turn a man like Frank Carey off.

More likely, however, is that over the years his score has been talked of, written about, guessed at, pooh-poohed, etc, and being a modest man not given to the elaborations or embarrassment of 'line-shooting', he would remain decidedly silent on the matter. One could imagine too, that having come up through the ranks, where in the beginning he would have been only too aware of his position in the service, he, like many other self-respecting senior NCO pilots, would not dream of putting himself on a par with officers. Once he became an officer, that stance would not only remain but be reinforced.

When dealing with victory scores it is well known that errors are easily made and claims, while generally made in good faith, can be over-stated. Fighting in the third dimension and at high speed, with adrenalin running high, plus youthful exuberance, the heart can often see what the eye does not. Clouds, glaring sun, the ever-swivelling head watching out for other enemy aircraft, make most glances at any object fleeting. There were also a few fighter pilots who over-cooked their claims, in a, 'what does it matter?' attitude, or 'who will know?' Of course, there are enough historians and sufficient surviving records for people *to* know.

Fighter Command issued a list of their successful air aces with 12 or more confirmed victories in mid-1941, with scores up to and including 30 June. The names on that list are as follows:

Name	Day	Night	Total
W/C A G Malan DSO* DFC*	27	2	29
S/L R R S Tuck DSO DFC**	24	2	26
P/O J H Lacey DFM*	23	–	23
S/L M N Crossley DSO DFC	22	–	22
P/O E S Lock DSO DFC*	22	–	22
F/L H M Stephen DSO DFC*	21	–	21
F/L G Allard DFC DFM*	19	–	19
S/L R G Dutton DFC*	19	–	19
P/O H J L Hallowes DFM*	17	1	18
F/L F R Carey DFC* DFM	17	1	18
F/L A C Deere DFC*	17½	–	17½
S/L M H Brown DFC*	17½	–	17½
S/L R F Boyd DFC*	17	–	17
S/L W D David DFC*	17	–	17
F/L D A P McMullen DFC*	13½	3	16½
F/L C F Gray DFC	16	–	16
F/L J G Sanders DFC	11	5	16
W/C D R S Bader DSO* DFC*	15½	–	15½
S/L N Orton DFC*	15	–	15
F/L J W Villa DFC*	15	–	15
S/L A H Boyd DFC*	13½	1	14½
F/L R F T Doe DFC*	14½	–	14½
S/L J Ellis DFC*	13	1	14
S/L J I Kilmartin DFC	14	–	14
F/L A McDowell DFC*	13	1	14
Sgt D A S McKay DFM*	14	–	14
S/L T F Dalton Morgan DFC*	10	4	14
S/L J Cunningham DSO DFC	–	13	13
S/L C F Currant DFC*	13	–	13

Name	Day	Night	Total
S/L G R Edge DFC	13	–	13
F/L J J O'Meara DFC*	13	–	13
S/L J W C Simpson DFC*	13	–	13
F/S E R Thorn DFM* F/S F J Barker DFM* (AG)	12	1	13
F/L J C Freeborn DFC	12¹/₂	–	12¹/₂
F/L F W Higginson DFM	12¹/₂	–	12¹/₂

Despite the assumed assurance that this list is correct as it came from official sources, this does not preclude it from errors. With Frank Carey for instance, while it does show his score as 18, it includes one night victory, and Frank never had a success at night. Also absent from the list are some high scorers from the Middle East, but this is because they were not under the operational control of Fighter Command in Britain. From this list we can see that Frank is 10th.

The list of top scoring fighter pilots from all theatres according to present day historians, including shared victories, reads as follows:

S/L T StJ M Pattle DFC*	52
W/C J E Johnson DSO** DFC*	41
G/C A G Malan DSO* DFC*	34
S/L W Vale DFC*	33
W/C B E F Finucane DSO DFC**	32
F/L G F Beurling DSO DFC DFM*	32
W/C C R Caldwell DSO DFC*	30
W/C J R D Braham DSO** DFC**	29
W/C C F Gray DSO DFC**	29
W/C R R S Tuck DSO DFC**	29
S/L N F Duke DSO DFC**	28
G/C F R Carey DFC** AFC DFM	28
S/L J H Lacey DFM*	28
W/C B Drake DSO DFC*	26
F/L E S Lock DFC*	26
G/C G K Gilroy DSO DFC*	25
W/C L C Wade DSO DFC**	25

Frank's name is now joint 11th (with two others) on this list of 17 pilots credited with 25 or more victories. Had Pattle and Vale been included in the 1941 list, Frank would have been joint 12th (with one other) on it. (Also interesting is that of the top 14, only Caldwell, Vale and Frank have either not written their autobiographies or had their biographies written by others.)

Most of these pilots did not run into complications about their scores caused by either speculation, misinterpretation or journalistic 'guesstimates'. Much of Frank's problem was that this went on while he was away in the Far East, and he probably did not see some of the more fanciful stories about him until he returned home in 1945, or began reading stories of his war long afterwards. By this time, even if he had been moved to refute some of the more outlandish tales, Frank was not the sort of man who would have done so, as we have seen. One of the more extreme came with a poor-ish photograph of Frank – taken at the time of the Bengal Tiger incident – and produced in an aviation magazine. It read:

Wing Commander Carey

Wing Cmdr. F R Carey DFC and two bars, DFM, fought in the Battle of Britain, went to the Middle East, and then in 1944 to Burma. Early in 1945 he was credited in the Service with some eighty aircraft destroyed in three theatres of war – a record for both the First and Second Great Wars.

The only things correct in this piece was his name, rank and decorations. It omits the Battle of France, adds the Middle East, by which one would understand North Africa, gets him to Burma in 1944 when he had already been there for two years, and mentions a magical and fanciful score of 80 – that equal to Baron Manfred von Richthofen in WW1 – by 1945, although his last claims had been in 1942. How could Frank even start to refute this load of rubbish even if he had a mind to?

While I am extremely grateful to Nobby Clark for his recollections of Frank at Fayid, in an article by Geoffrey Norris in *RAF Flying Review* in 1963, Nobby did not help to clarify Frank's score. When Norris posed the question about Frank's score, this was the reply:

'His final score of enemy aircraft destroyed? "Forty or more," say some sources, but evidence cannot be provided to support this. 28 is the conservative estimate of the Air Ministry.'

Norris continued: 'Nobby Clarke is among those who support the higher claims. "Frank Carey was almost certainly the highest-scoring fighter pilot among the Allies," he says. "Once at a party at his house in Fayid, I picked up his log book. I was flicking through the pages when he saw what I was doing and snatched it back – but not before I had seen his total score: 51. As far as I can remember these consisted of 25 Germans and 26 Japs."

'What does Carey himself say? Referring to Clarke's statement he [Frank] says: "I can only think that Nobby must have opened my log book late in the party when units of anything are liable to suffer multiplication! I think he must have added up 'destroyed on the ground' – in spite of his earlier statement I even hit stationary targets sometimes – 'probables' and 'badly damaged', in which case the number he quotes would be about right.'"

Later in this same article, Frank says:

> 'I can only recall 28 certainties, and 18 of these were Germans.' Then explained '...I know that much larger numbers have been credited to me, and this can be explained as follows. Very often one fired some shots at a Jap and he did not crash immediately and confirmation over the wild country was difficult. Reports often came in later that the remains of a Japanese aircraft had been found. The Press heard of this and, I think, in an endeavour to make a hero out of some one, picked on me as the most likely person to have destroyed them.'

That sounds typically like Frank. If you can't explain it, make something up like it was the Press guessing. I have gone through his log book and the results are to be found in Appendix C. That list shows 28 destroyed, perhaps one more, two destroyed on the ground, eight probably destroyed and ten damaged. The log book actually makes mention of 42 aircraft 'hit', plus the three victories in early 1940 noted in the log book which he lost in France, plus two other possible victories. The damaged bomber in early 1941 and that Oscar which may or may not have crashed into a hill when chasing Frank away from Chittagong in October 1942. These together with mentions of aircraft that could be mistakenly taken for claims when they were not, brings the figure closer to Nobby's count of 51.

Nobby had written to Frank in January 1963, when Frank was still with Rolls-Royce in Canberra, and had asked him about his score. Frank had replied:

> 'Perhaps the first point to tackle is to emphasise that any mystery which exists about the number of aircraft I have shot down is simply because:-
> (a) I lost my log book with all my kit in France in 1940. By the time I could settle down to think when I got back to England about a month later, it wasn't easy to recall all that had happened. For similar reasons of disorganisation and chaos, the squadron records (No.3) proved equally unreliable as an aide memoir when that squadron returned to England.
>
> (b) In Burma, I deliberately put my log book in a safe place and kept a rough log which also suffered loss in the mad

scramble of being chased out by the Japs. Once again, the Squadron records were not too reliable, especially as most of them went laboriously by road up to China and did not get out for many months to India.

In addition, it wasn't easy to pin-point crashes over the jungle or, in fact, to know of them with certainty from the ground until the passage of time, and by then no-one knew for certain whose they were.

'With that background, plus the fact that the Press seemed determined to try and produce a hero in the Burma fiasco, you have all the necessary ingredients for a never-ending argument.

'Now as far as I can remember, I have shot down 28 aircraft of which about 18 were Jerries[14], but of course, as far as the Japs are concerned, they carried practically no armour at all and it was very frequently found that they fell into the jungle (miles from anywhere) on their way home. There was always a feeling among us that our Jap claims were underestimated but there was nothing one could do about it – probably many of their crashes will never be traced. So there you are – and as far as the 51 is concerned you must have added all the destroyed on ground, probables, etc., together when you saw my log book.'

It is pretty much established now that 28 is Frank's accepted score in air combat. What I have also determined is that once in action with enemy aircraft he rarely failed to hit anything. All his victories were claimed whilst flying the Hawker Hurricane, and in consequence he is the second highest scoring pilot on this type. Only Pattle with his total of 52 victories scored more – 36 – with the rest on Gladiators.

Amongst Frank's papers I found that at some stage he had jotted down on a small piece of paper, his victories as he saw them:

Northern England 1940
3 shared He111s

---

[14] It is possible Frank confused himself by only counting the seven victories in the Battle of Britain rather than five, and omitting to count the three shared victories before the Battle. The total therefore is 3+13+5+7 = 28.

France 1940
13 destroyed
3 probables
1 damaged

Battle of Britain 1940
7 destroyed
3 probables
6 damaged

North Sea, Scotland, 1941
1 damaged

Burma 1942
7 destroyed
1 damaged
3 destroyed on ground
1 possible crashed behind me

Total: 27 destroyed + 3 shared
                6 probably destroyed
                9 damaged
                1 possible crashed behind me
                3 destroyed on ground

Concerning his operational sorties during the Battle of Britain, no doubt taken from his log book, Frank noted the following:

> From 1 July to 18 August 1940, 112 sorties. 97 of these between the dates of 10 July (the official start of the Battle of Britain) and 18 August – 37 of which were flown in the last nine days [before his final wound. During the Battle of Britain period he was operational on 49 days, with just seven days off – four in July and three in August.]

Purely out of interest and to show what Frank thought of noting records, there is another piece of paper on which he listed his motor car accidents and convictions!

> Fine £2 – Aldwych, London.
> Accident, icy hill, Barrowby. Claim on insurance.
> Hit from behind by ambulance when stationery. No Claim.
> Canberra; Jane hit by car from behind. (FRC was passenger.)
> Claim on insurance.

Side-swiped by car from minor road. No Claim.

Frank liked the Hurricane. Although he did not fly Spitfires in combat, and may have done well on the type anyway, his love was always the Hurry. Of it he said:

> 'Almost without exception my entire operational flying was undertaken in Hurricanes. Although other aircraft may have attracted more glamour and boasted higher speeds, the Hurricane ploughed into every task that it was given and still came back for more.
>
> 'Built like the Forth Bridge, it could take enormous punishment and yet get you home. On one occasion in the Battle of Britain, I had my entire rudder and all but a tiny portion of one elevator blown off together with a hole in the port wing that a man could have fallen through. Although its unusual silhouette attracted local AA fire in the circuit, the Hurricane landed quite normally even though it needed a long rest.'

So, was Frank Carey the best? I don't really think in those terms. Each fighter pilot was individual, did the job given to them to the best of their ability, and sometimes did not survive their last air battle. Many aces did not think too keenly about a 'score' while others did. There are probably football stars today who have no exact idea of how many goals they have scored, while others can give you an exact total. In air combat Frank Carey was good, and, as I said earlier, rarely missed once that right thumb jabbed the firing button. He was a superb shot, wonderful aerobatic pilot, liked by those who flew with him and was always in the forefront of any action. If these epithets put him among the best, he would be happy to let it rest there.

Appendix A

Record of Service

September 1927	Aircraft Apprentice at Halton
September 1930	A Flight, No.43 Squadron as AC1 Metal Rigger
January 1934	Halton for Fitter I Course, as LAC
January 1935	No.7 Squadron as Fitter
August 1935	No. 6 FTS, pilot's course
August 1936	A Flight, No.43 Squadron as Sergeant Pilot
April 1940	No.3 Squadron as Pilot Officer
May 1940	France with No.3 Squadron
June 24, 1940	A Flight, No.43 Squadron
July 1940	A Flight Commander 43 Squadron
August 18, 1940	Hospital – wounded
September 23, 1940	A Flight Commander 43 Squadron
February 20, 1941	To No.52 Operational Training Unit
July 25, 1941	No.245 Squadron as Flight Commander
August 25, 1941	No.135 Squadron as Officer Commanding
November 28, 1941	Posted overseas with 135 Squadron
December 6, 1941	Sailed for Middle East
December 13, 1941	Arrived at Freetown, Sierra Leone
January 19, 1942	Arrived Rangoon, Burma
February 6, 1942	Promoted OC 267 Wing, Burma Acting Wg Cdr
March 21, 1942	Sick leave, India
April 2, 1942	OC Wing, Alipore, India
October 12, 1942	OC 165 Wing at Dum Dum, India
December 24, 1942	OC 165 Wing at Chittagong, Arakan
February 1943	OC Air Fighting Training Unit, Amarda Road, Orissa
June 13, 1943	Left India for UK
June 27, 1943	Central Gunnery Course, UK
September 20, 1943	Returned to India
September 26, 1943	OC AFTU, Amarda Road
November 2, 1944	OC No.73 Operational Training Unit, Fayid, Egypt, G/Capt
June 10, 1945	Central Fighter Establishment, Tangmere, OC Tactics
May 1946	Army Staff College, as Wing Commander
November 27, 1946	Wing Commander Training, 84 Group, Celle, Germany

January 9, 1948	Wing Leader, 135 Wing, Gütersloh, Germany
February 1949	Wg Cdr Admin. (supernumerary) RAF Thorney Island
July 1949	Senior Course at Officers Advanced Training School
August 18, 1949	Wing Commander Org, 12 Group HQ, Fighter Command
July 2, 1951	Wing Commander Ops, Scottish Fighter Sector
October 1952	Station Commander RAF Honiley & Wing Leader
April 1953	Acting Group Captain, OC Western Sector
January 1956	Group Captain Ops 2, HQ Fighter Command
January 1958	UKJSL Staff, Senior RAF Liaison Officer, Australia
April 1960	Returned to UK
June 1, 1960	Retired from the Royal Air Force

Appendix B

Awards, Citations and Medals

Commander to the Order of the British Empire

Birthday Honours List, *London Gazette*, 3 June 1960.

> *To be Ordinary Commander of the Military Division of the*
> *Most Excellent Order of the British Empire.*

Distinguished Flying Cross

Pilot Officer Frank Reginald Carey DFM (43132) RAF. 3 Squadron.
London Gazette, 31 May 1940.

This officer destroyed five enemy aircraft early in the operations in May, 1940, and by his dash and courage set the highest example of gallantry to the squadron.

Bar to the Distinguished Flying Cross

Pilot Officer Frank Reginald Carey DFC DFM (43132) RAF. 3 Squadron.
London Gazette, 31 May 1940.

This officer has shot down four more enemy aircraft bringing his total to nine. Throughout the operations he was continuously on the search for enemy aircraft and was an inspiration to all who flew with him. His morale was always of the highest order.

2nd Bar to the Distinguished Flying Cross

Acting Wing Commander Frank Reginald Carey DFC* DFM (43132) RAF. 267 (Wing) Burma.
London Gazette, 24 March 1943.

When leading the squadron or wing, this officer has displayed high qualities of leadership and has set a high example by his courage and devotion to duty. Wing Commander Carey has destroyed at least five enemy aircraft.

Air Force Cross

New Years Honour's List, 1 January 1945.

Distinguished Flying Medal

561516 Sergeant Frank Reginald Carey, No.43 Squadron (Immediate)
London Gazette, 1 March 1940.

On 30th January 1940, with his section leader, he successfully engaged an enemy aircraft over the North Sea whilst it was attacking shipping. Again, on 3rd February 1940, Sergeant Carey, this time acting as section leader of a section of two aircraft, engaged an enemy aircraft over the North Sea and shot it down. The weather conditions during these engagements were such that low cloud provided almost immediate cover for the enemy and it was mainly due to Sergeant Carey's initiative, determination and skill that this cover was denied the enemy and the engagements brought to a successful conclusion. It is recommended that he be decorated by the award of the Distinguished Flying Medal.

Czechoslovakian Flying Badge

Czechoslovakian Inspectorate,
19-29 Woburn Place,
London, WC1   20 September 1941

It gives me great pleasure to award you the Czechoslovak Air Force Pilot's Badge, as a mark of gratitude and appreciation of all the help and co-operation you have given to the members of the Czechoslovakian Air Force serving in the RAFVR.

Air Vice-Marshal K Janousek
Inspector General of the CAF

American Silver Star

June 1945

Coronation Medal

Wing Commander F R Carey DFC AFC DFM, 2 June 1953.

Farrington Kennett Trophy
RAF Halton

1930 Shooting – Winners, No.4 Wing. Aircraft Appentice – F R Carey.

The RAF Rifle Association
For Marksmanship

Apprentices Match Winners 1930 – F R Carey.

Station Headquarters India 1943

Football – Winners. W/C F Carey.

Note: In the original *Supplement* to the *London Gazette* of 31st May 1940, an error occurred with the two entries of Frank Carey's awards for the DFC and Bar. Instead of his correct name and number, the entries show the name Pilot Officer Frederick Carey, service number 70116, although the actual wording of the citations was correct. Once the error became known the entries were amended in the *London Gazette* dated 14 June 1940:

ERRATUM

The following amendments should be made to the *Supplement* to the *London Gazette* of 31st May, 1940, page 3254. First Column, for Pilot Officer Frederick Carey (70116), read Pilot Officer Frank Reginald Carey DFM (43132). Second Column, for Pilot Officer Frederick Carey DFC, read Pilot Officer Frank Reginald Carey DFC DFM.

Frank Carey's Combat Success

43 Squadron

Date	Aircraft	Result	Time	Serial	Unit	Location
1940						
30 Jan	He111	Destroyed	1230	L1728	KG26	Shared with F/L C B Hull
3 Feb	He111	Destroyed	1120	L1726	KG26	Shared with Sgt Ottewill
28 Mar	He111	Destroyed	1230	L1726	F/KpsX	Shared with F/L Hull & Sgt Gough

3 Squadron

Date	Aircraft	Result	Time	Serial	Unit	Location
10 May	He111P	Destroyed	1935	L1932	KG54	nr Lille
,,	He111P	Destroyed	1940	L1932	KG54	nr Lille
,,	He111P	Destroyed	1940	L1932	KG54	nr Merville
,,	He111P	Damaged	1942	L1932	KG54	nr Merville
,,	He111P	Damaged	1943	L1932	KG54	nr Merville
,,	He111P	Destroyed	2110	L1932	KG27	Shared with FLCarter & F/O Ball, nr Merville
11 May	He111P	Destroyed	1730	L1932	KG54	nr Lille
12 May	He111P	Destroyed		L1932		S of Brussels
,,	He111P	Probable		L1932		S of Brussels
13 May	Ju87	Destroyed	0800	L1932	StG2	nr Louvain
,,	Ju87	Destroyed	0810	L1932	StG2	nr Louvain
,,	Ju87	Probable	,,	L1932	StG2	nr Louvain
,,	Ju87	Probable	,,	L1932	StG2	nr Louvain
,,	He111			L1932		
,,	Do17	Destroyed	0820	L1932	KG77	nr Louvain
,,	Hs123	Destroyed	0910	L1932	LG2	SE Brussels

Date	Type	Result	Time	Serial	Unit	Location
"	He111P	Destroyed	1130	L1932	KG54	nr Namur. Shared with S/L Churchill & Sgt Allen
14 May	Do17P	Destroyed	0450	L1932	3(F)/11	nr Wavre
43 Squadron						
9 Jul	Me110C-2	Damaged	1145	P3786	V/LG1	off Isle of Wight
19 Jul	Me109E	Destroyed	1715	P3527	JG27	off Selsey Bill
"	Me109E	Damaged	"	P3527	JG27	"
"	Me109E	Damaged	"	P3527	JG27	"
8 Aug	Me109E	Damaged	1630	P3202	JG27	Channel/IoW
12 Aug	Ju88	Probable	1215	R4109	KG51	Channel
13 Aug	Ju88A	Destroyed	0700	R4109	KG54	Claim uncertain
"	Ju88A	Probable	"	R4109	"	Littlehampton-Petworth
"	Ju88A	Damaged	"	R4109	"	"
"	Ju88A	Damaged	"	R4109	"	"
15 Aug	Ju88A	Destroyed	1800	R4109	LG1	" Southbourne, with S/L Badger and P/O Upton
16 Aug	Ju87B	Destroyed	1300	R4109	StG2	Selsey Bill
"	Ju87B	Destroyed	"	R4109	StG2	Selsey Bill
"	Ju87B	Probable	"	R4109	StG2	"
"	Ju87B	Probable	"	R4109	StG2	"
18 Aug	Ju87B	Destroyed	1430	R4109	StG77	Thorney Island
1941						
20 Jan	Ju88	Damaged		V7206		North Sea
135 Squadron						
1942						
29 Jan	Ki-27	Destroyed		BE181	77th S	Mingaladon

Date	Aircraft	Result	Serial	Squadron	Location
"	Ki-27	Damaged	BE181	77th S	Mingaladon
267 Wing					
23 Feb	Ki-51	Destroyed	BM914	70th Ind	Sittang Bridge
24 Feb	Transport	Destroyed	BM842		Moulmein
"	Ki-27	Destroyed	BM842		Moulmein
26 Feb	Ki-27	Destroyed	BM914	50th	Moulmein
"	Ki-27	Destroyed	BM914	and	Moulmein
"	Ki-27	Destroyed	BM914	77th	Moulmein
"	2 Ki-27s	Destroyed on ground	BM914		Moulmein
25 Oct	Ki-43	Crashed into hill	BN468		nr Chittagong

Total:

Destroyed in the air 28
Destroyed on ground 2
Probably destroyed 8
Possible – crashed 1
Damaged 10

Index